英语演讲与辩论

主 编 王 倩
副主编 屈江丽
编 者 王晓丹 邹甜甜 赵红霞 王博佳

U0360046

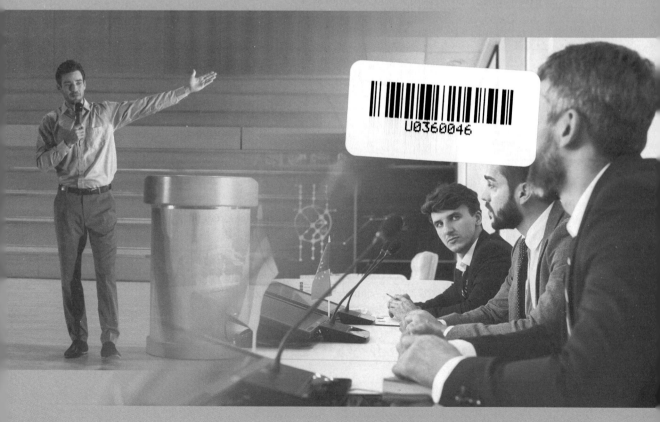

清華大学出版社
北 京

内 容 简 介

本书围绕英语演讲与辩论的核心基础知识，借助案例分析，系统讲解如何选择演讲主题、分析听众、构拟演讲稿提纲、组织演讲逻辑、巧妙开头结尾、有效呈现演说、进行辩题解读、立论与驳论、提供论据支撑、甄别逻辑谬误等。本书服务于培养国际传播人才的国家战略，能够帮助学习者提升以信息整合、判断、质疑为特点的思辨能力、跨文化交际能力与用外语阐释问题、捍卫自身立场的国际化公民素养。

本书适合各类专业的大学本科生、研究生和有意提高自身英语沟通能力的社会学习者。

图书在版编目（CIP）数据

英语演讲与辩论 / 王倩主编. —北京：清华大学出版社，2022.4（2025.1 重印）
国家精品在线开放课程配套教材
ISBN 978-7-302-57319-7

Ⅰ.①英… Ⅱ.①王… Ⅲ.①英语—演讲—高等学校—教材②英语—辩论—高等学校—教材
Ⅳ.①H311.9

中国版本图书馆 CIP 数据核字（2021）第 012331 号

责任编辑：钱屹芝　徐博文
封面设计：子　一
责任校对：王凤芝
责任印制：杨　艳

出版发行：清华大学出版社
　　　　　网　　址：https://www.tup.com.cn, https://www.wqxuetang.com
　　　　　地　　址：北京清华大学学研大厦 A 座　　　　邮　编：100084
　　　　　社 总 机：010-83470000　　　　　　　　　　邮　购：010-62786544
　　　　　投稿与读者服务：010-62776969，c-service@tup.tsinghua.edu.cn
　　　　　质量反馈：010-62772015，zhiliang@tup.tsinghua.edu.cn
印 装 者：涿州市般润文化传播有限公司
经　　销：全国新华书店
开　　本：185mm×260mm　　　印　张：18.5　　　字　数：349 千字
版　　次：2022 年 4 月第 1 版　　　　　　　　印　次：2025 年 1 月第 4 次印刷
定　　价：78.00 元

产品编号：090892-01

前　言

　　古往今来，演讲与辩论的魅力在中外舞台上都熠熠生辉。在中国历史上，从先周的运象以思到春秋战国的百家争鸣，无不体现演讲与辩论的重大意义。当前，中国正站在"两个一百年"历史交汇点上，传播能力更是成为衡量我国国家软实力的重要指标。2021 年 5 月 31 日，中共中央政治局就加强我国国际传播能力建设进行第三十次集体学习，习近平总书记发表重要讲话，提出"讲好中国故事，传播好中国声音，展示真实、立体、全面的中国，是加强我国国际传播能力建设的重要任务"。在我国日益接近世界舞台的中央、参与全球治理能力不断提高的新时代，语言表达及沟通能力成为提升我国国际传播力、讲好中国故事的关键因素。特别是英语作为国际通用语的背景下，外语教育作为加强国际传播力建设的重要一环，承载着培养国际化人才的重任。无疑，良好的英语口头沟通能力是加强国际交流和合作、增强国际理解和提升中国国际话语权的重要因素。

　　如今，国内各高校广泛开设的《英语演讲与辩论》课程是培养国际化人才的重要抓手之一。该课程旨在帮助学习者掌握英语语言的使用艺术，提升其跨文化交际思辨能力，使其能用清晰、生动、有力的语言传播中国文化，推动中国与世界深度对话，推进国际理解与文明互鉴，提升中华文化的国际影响力。

　　本教材致力于服务高校培养高素质拔尖创新人才，以"理念革新""内容更新""形式创新"为编写出发点，聚焦英语演讲和辩论两大语言技能，围绕英语演讲及辩论的相关基础知识（如巧妙选题、听众分析、提纲撰写、逻辑组织、语言修辞、开头结尾、演说呈现、辩题解读、立论与驳论、论据支撑、逻辑谬误甄别等）展开讲解。全书共分十个章节，每个章节包含两个部分。第一部分"知识讲解"用浅显易懂的语言介绍演说和辩论相关知识点，搭建学习者知识框架；第二部分"习题检测"形式多样，促进学习者知识内化。每章末尾增加 Key Takeaways of This Chapter，用于梳理本章节重要内容，帮助学习者进行知识自检。

　　通过扫描书中二维码，学生可以获取案例评析、名篇导读、习题答案以及线上慕课视频。"案例评析"提供演说和辩论相关案例分析，夯实学习者知识基础。"名篇导读"结合时代主题，拓展学习者知识广度。

本教材在讲解专业知识的基础上充分挖掘了演讲与辩论中的育人元素，将"思政"素材贯穿全书的开篇名言、教学示例、名篇导读和教材习题当中，凸显外语教育的育人价值。开篇部分体现"中国智慧"，每章以国学经典，如《论语》《老子》《战国策》等中与主题内容相关的名言警句引入教学内容，以文载道、以文传声，推介更多体现中国精神、蕴藏中国思想的优秀文化。教学辅助示例侧重"中国特色"，适当加入了展现中国故事及其背后思想力量的范例。名篇导读强化"中国声音"，如选取首位在哈佛大学毕业典礼上演讲的中国学生何江讲述中国故事的经历及习近平主席2019年国庆演讲节选等，围绕中国精神、中国力量，从政治、经济、文化等多个视角进行选材，激发学习者在新时代提升国际传播的意识。

本教材的编写坚持守正创新原则，选材与时俱进，语言难度适当，适合意在提高英语沟通交际能力的在校学生和社会学习者。由于编者水平及获取的资料有限，书中错误之处在所难免，恳请专家、同仁及读者朋友们批评指正。

编者

2022 年 3 月

Contents

Chapter **1**

Understanding Public Speaking

Part I

Introducing Public Speaking

1. A single remark makes a country prosper. (一言可以兴邦。)

    —*Confucius*

2. Words have magical power. They can bring either the greatest happiness or deepest despair; they can transfer knowledge from teacher to student; words enable the orator to sway his audience and dictate the decisions.

    —*Sigmund Freud*

Communications in their multiple forms pervade today's international context. With numerous job interviews, conference calls, meetings, product presentations, workshops, and public events, more and more leaders realize the importance of developing good interpersonal communication skills. Whether our goal is to enhance professional growth, or inspire, persuade and motivate other people to follow our lead, we will have to learn how to convey our ideas in front of a group of people in a clear, structured and captivating manner.

Arguably, improving the ability to speak in front of others and learning to talk about who we are and what we do with natural grace and authenticity can go a long way in expanding our social circles, building strong relationships with successful, like-minded people and making new friends.

Developing communication skills and learning to speak in the public can:

- increase our self-confidence;
- improve our communication skills;

- enhance our persuasion ability;
- open up new opportunities for career advancement;
- help us to easily assume leadership and train others;
- prepare us for spontaneous speaking challenges (e.g., delivering a speech at short notice);
- make us a desirable guest on regional, national and international conferences, seminars and public speaking events;

   ...

1.1   What Is Public Speaking?

Public speaking, as a language communication behavior by which people express their views of a particular topic or event, plays an essential role in people's daily life. Public speaking is not only a simple oral conversation skill; instead it is a comprehensive quality involving language knowledge and skills, appropriate expression and adaptation ability.

1.1.1   Defining the Term

Public speaking is a social activity in which a speaker announces oneself, states one's opinions, or persuades people to do things, etc, using verbal and nonverbal language in front of an audience, in a set time or space. Simply put, public speaking is a way of making our ideas public—a way of sharing them with other people and of influencing other people.

1.1.2   Key Elements of Public Speaking

The speech communication process can be broken down into several basic elements, usually expressed as "**Who** is saying **What** to **Whom** in **What Context** using **What Medium** with **What Effects?**"

1) Who—the speaker

The speech communication process starts with the speaker—the person who is delivering, or presenting the speech. The success of the talk will be based on the credibility, preparation, and knowledge of the speaker about the topic. Thus, these qualities and strategies do matter for a successful speaker: positive moral character; exhausted research and analysis of the topic; strong self-confidence and self-control; appropriate physical appearance and use of verbal and non-verbal languages;

effective delivery skills, etc. When we are able to successfully communicate our message, that is, when the audience can decode what we are conveying, then we have become a successful communicator.

When preparing the speech, the speaker is supposed to consider these questions:

Am I interested in the topic?

Do I have enough knowledge on the topic?

Have I chosen the most effective language to express what I intend to convey?

Do I look confident when rehearsing?

2) What—the message

Another crucial element in the speech process is the message. The message is what the speaker is discussing or the ideas that he/she is presenting to the audience as he/she covers a particular topic. The word "message" comes from the Latin *mittere*, "to send". The message is fundamental to communication. With regard to public speaking and speech communication, our speech is our message. However, we may have other intentions for the speech as well: the message behind the message. Perhaps we have a singular goal, point or emotion we want the audience to feel and understand. Every single word that we use to craft our speech then works to achieve that singular goal, point or emotion.

Messages can be sent both verbally and nonverbally. The actual words that we say certainly influence our speech. Do remember that the non-verbal communication is equally as important as the words we have to say. The body stance, posture and eye contact can also be crucial in building up bonds with the audience as well. For example, we are supposed to keep an assertive body posture—stand up straight and maintain eye contact when we can. In addition, be mindful of gestures—don't overdo it, but don't stand there rigidly, either. Gesture and movement build visual interest for the audience. In other words, it's important to consider all aspects of our overall message, from verbal to non-verbal to the meaning and message behind the message when crafting your speech.

When preparing the speech, the speaker is supposed to consider these questions:

Is the subject or theme an appropriate one for me?

How does the message relate to the audience?

How does the message relate to the situation?

Is the message written effectively?

3) Whom—the audience

The audience refers to people who receive the message. There will be no public speaking without the audience. The audience receives the information a speaker transmits such as his/her knowledge, experience, goals, values and attitudes. The audience generally forms an opinion as to the effectiveness of the speaker and the validity of the speaker's message is based on what they see and hear during the speech. The audience may be represented by a variety of distinguishing characteristics and commonalities, often referred to as demographics. It is important to remember that we should not stereotype or make assumptions about the audience based on their demographics; however, we can use these elements to inform the language, context, and delivery of the speech.

Whatever the occasion is, the speech must always be targeted at our audience. If we are familiar with our audience, for example, if the occasion is a large family gathering, then the speech should acknowledge and build upon our existing intimacy with the audience. The use of names and personal details of members of our audience can help engage our listeners. If the speech is delivered to an unfamiliar audience, then an early goal of our speech must serve to build a degree of trust with the listeners. We must know who our audience is in order to best decide how to get our message across. In public speaking, what is suitable for one group of the audience may not be appropriate for another. Analyzing the audience before composing the speech will enable us to give a more acceptable speech, and enable the audience to follow our message more easily.

When crafting the speech, the speaker is supposed to consider these questions:

Who will be the audience? What are their age, gender, occupation, educational or cultural background?

What does the audience have in common?

What will be the audience's attitude towards the topic?

Is the audience there voluntarily?

When listening to the speech, the audience is supposed to think about these questions:

Who is the speaker?

What are the speaker's qualifications and background?

Why is the speaker addressing the audience?

Do you know anything about the speaker before the speech? If yes, what?

What do you know about the speaker by the end of the speech?

4) Context

(1) Physical context

Physical context refers to the physical space in which the speech is delivered.

For example, we may find ourselves speaking in a classroom, a corporate board room, or a large amphitheater. Each of these real environments will influence our ability to interact with our audience. Larger physical spaces may require us to use a microphone and speaker system to make ourselves heard or to use projected presentation aids to convey visual materials.

How the room is physically decorated or designed can also impact our interaction with the audience. If the room is dimly lit or is decorated with interesting posters, audience members' minds may start wandering. If the room is too hot, we'll find people becoming sleepy. As speakers, we often have little or no control over our physical environment, but we always need to take it into account when planning and delivering our messages.

(2) Temporal context

The temporal context has to do not only with the time of day and moment in history but also with where a particular message fits into the sequence of communication events. The time of day can have a dramatic effect on how alert one's audience is. Don't believe that? Try giving a speech in front of a class around 12:30 p.m. when no one has had lunch. It's not surprising how impatient audience members get once hunger sets in.

In addition to the time of day, we often face temporal dimensions related to how our speech will be viewed in light of societal events. Imagine how a speech on the importance of campus security would be interpreted on the day after a safety incident occurred on campus.

Another element of the temporal dimension is how a message fits with what happens immediately before it. For example, if another speaker has just given an intense speech on death and dying and you stand up to speak about something more trivial, people may downplay your message because it doesn't fit with the serious tone established by the earlier speech. You never want to be the funny speaker who has to follow an emotional speech where people cried. Most of the time in a speech class, we probably will have no advance notice as to what the speaker before us will be talking about. Therefore, it is wise to plan to be sensitive to previous topics and be prepared to ease our way subtly into the message if the situation dictates.

(3) Cultural and gender context

When considering both gender and cultural contexts, we often encounter bias, both intentional and unintentional, and implicit or explicit. We may have presumptive judgments or opinions about those cultures and races that differ from our own, which are often the result of our own upbringing. In addition as much as we might be biased toward or against certain gender and cultural groups, our audience will have just as much bias as us, in different ways. As such, it is radically important to know exactly to whom we are speaking when giving our speech. It's helpful for us to anticipate not only the biases we might bring to the podium but also those biases of our audience towards us as well.

Before giving the speech, the speaker is supposed to consider these questions:

What is the occasion for the speech?

Where will the speech take place?

When will the speech take place?

Do I speak to a domestic or international audience?

Do I use some kind of language that may offend some audience?

5) Medium—the channel

The channel is the means by which the message is sent or transmitted. Different channels are used to deliver the message, depending on the communication type or context. For instance, in mass communication, the channel utilized might be a television or radio broadcast. A cell phone is an example of a channel that we might use to text a friend in interpersonal communication. However, the channel typically used in public speaking is the speaker's voice, or more specifically, the sound waves to carry the voice to those listening. We could watch a prerecorded speech or one accessible on the internet, and we might say the channel is the television or our computer. This is partially true. However, the speech would still have no value if the speaker's voice was not present. Therefore, in reality, the channel is now a combination of the two, i.e., the speaker's voice broadcast through an electronic source.

6) Effects—the feedback

The final component of the speech process is feedback. While some might assume that the speaker is the only one who sends a message during a speech, the reality is that the listeners in the audience are sending a message of their own, called feedback. Often this is how the speaker knows if he/she is sending an effective message. Occasionally the feedback from listeners comes in verbal form—questions from the audience or an response of agreement/disagreement from a listener about a key point presented. However, in general, feedback during a speech is typically non-verbal: an audience nodding his/her head in agreement or a confused look from an audience member. An observant speaker will scan the audience for these forms of feedback. For example, As we look around, are people returning our gaze? If so, we have an engaged audience, attentively listening to our speech. If we see half-closed or closed eyes, we have to try adjusting our tone and volume, or add some interesting points to lift them up.

1.2 **Traditions of Public Speaking**

1.2.1 Public Speaking in the West

The roots of the tradition of public speaking can be traced back to the ancient Greek period when scholars elaborated and developed novel techniques of public speaking. About 2,500 years ago, four ancient Greek scholars developed and mastered the art of rhetoric in public speaking. These scholars are also known as the "fantastic four"—Aspasia, Socrates, Plato, and Aristotle. Aspasia is often regarded as the "mother of rhetoric" and believed to have taught rhetoric to Socrates. Socrates greatly influenced the thought during the Classical Period (500BC–400BC). Later, the writings of his student—Plato are the main source of Socrates' teachings. Plato wrote about rhetoric in the form of dialogues with Socrates as the main character. In that period, the emphasis was on the best ways to write and deliver speeches, with a great amount of focus on the importance of truth and ethics in public speaking. Afterwards, the tradition was taken to new heights by Aristotle, Plato's student and whose contribution to the field of public speaking and rhetoric is unparalleled. Aristotle defined "rhetoric" as "the art of identifying and using the best available means in a given situation to ethically persuade an audience". Aristotle divided the "means of persuasion" into three parts, or three artistic proofs necessary to persuade others: logical reason (logos), human character (ethos), and emotional appeal (pathos). Logos is the presentation of logical consistency in reasons or arguments that support a speaker's talk. Ethos refers to the speaker's credibility or trustworthiness. Pathos occurs when a speaker evokes particular emotion in the audience.

After the Greeks, Romans scholars such as Quintilian and Cicero made a momentous contribution to the study of rhetoric and oratory. Quintilian's masterpiece Speakers' School is called the "syllabus for cultivating public speech talents". Like Aristotle, Cicero saw the relationship between rhetoric and persuasion and its applicability to the political sphere. Cicero is well known for creating the five canons of rhetoric, a five-step process for developing a persuasive speech. This five-step process is comprised of **invention** which contains collecting and making the analysis of facts and evidence; **arrangement**, which is also called organization; **style**, which is the eloquent and effective language use; **memory**, which is the recollection of the public speaking to deliver; and **delivery.**

The above orators such as Aristotle, Cicero and Quintilian promoted classic rhetoric throughout periods of Renaissance, reforms in England and revolutionaries in colonial America, during which a number of eloquent politicians, such as

Abraham Lincoln, Theodore Roosevelt, Franklin D. Roosevelt, John F. Kennedy and Martin Luther King, applied ancient speaking principles to a more ethical and political course of action for their nations. The spirit of rhetoric is fitting into the political system and social cultural values, especially in the United States where democracy and individual voice are valued.

1.2.2　Public Speaking in China

Although the term "public speaking", known for rhetoric as a Latin word, is generally considered to be born in Western civilization, the Chinese roots of rhetoric could go back the same further. As early as more than two thousand years ago, numerous philosophical schools had emerged in ancient China, bringing up rhetorical significance. Public speaking was greatly valued during the ancient times. The school of logicians in the late Han Dynasty, founded by Deng Xi (546BC–501BC) was recognized to share Aristotelian logic in speech production and created the notion of "argumentation". At that time, the speech was highly valued and encouraged. Argumentation and debates were common among philosophers and disputers (called *bian shi* 辩士). There have been periods in Chinese history when oral persuasion has been prevalent, most notably during the period of the Warring States (475BC–221 BC). This was a time when central control collapsed and China comprised several competing fiefdoms when kings and lords recruited learned individuals (*you shi* 游士) to form advisory boards.

An important figure in the history of rhetoric and persuasion who lived sometime during this period (481BC–221BC), and was thus more or less contemporaneous with Aristotle, was the philosopher Gui Guzi, whose name means "The Ghost of the Valleys". As a philosopher of the Warring States period, Gui Guzi clearly understood the importance of the relative power of the speaker and listener in such persua-sion. As the founder of the Zong Heng (纵横) school, Gui Guzi understood that the persuader needed to know how he related to the audience. He held that the ideal persuader requires several further key qualities: he is quick and perceptive; he is in control of himself and the situation; he is resourceful; he can assess people well; he can look after himself, and he can shepherd people.

Perhaps the most famous essay on the persuasion of the Warring States period was written by the legalist philosopher Han Feizi (280BC–233BC), who was born towards the end of the Warring States period. He has a privileged background, that is, he was a royal prince of the State of Han (one of the Warring States) and was a student of the Confucian philosopher, Xunzi. His book on political strategy, *the Han Feizi*, was read by the Prince of Qin over whom it exerted a significant influence. He was remembered for applying persuasion to suit political ends.

In addition, another outstanding rhetoric school in ancient China is represented by Confucius (551BC-479 BC) who is very influential in the Chinese communication style. Within the framework of Confucian ethics, public speaking is defined as Confucian argumentation which provides ethical disciplines for people's speech.

During Tang Dynasty, several new persuasive genres were introduced by Chinese Buddhists like sermons. Even in the last century, public speaking seemed to be a beneficial and powerful weapon to fight against imperialism and feudalism during the "May Fourth Movement". Nowadays, as one outcome of the information era and socialist democratic process, public speaking is more frequently used in cross-cultural exchanges and international corporations. Society attaches great importance to the proper and efficient use of language in public speech.

 # 1.3 Classification of Public Speaking

1) By styles of delivery

The three most common styles of speeches that we encounter in today's business and social world are **impromptu**, **manuscript** and **extemporaneous**.

Impromptu speech is prompted by the occasion rather than being planned in advance. Some examples of impromptu speech could be our employer asking us to bring the rest of the team up to date, or a group of friends urging us to say a few words on a special occasion.

Manuscript speech is a type of speech written like a manuscript and is meant to be delivered word for word. Manuscript speeches are used on many political and social occasions when every word carries a lot of weight and should not be misquoted. One of the most common examples of a manuscript speech is a political figure delivering a speech that has been written in advance.

Extemporaneous speech is the most commonly used type of speech that helps to establish an emotional connection with the audience. It is built around key points, but the material can be presented freely, allowing the speaker to make changes in their speech based on the listeners' reactions.

2) By goals intended to achieve

As far as goals or functions are concerned, public speaking can be divided into **speaking to inform**, **speaking to persuade**, and **speaking on special occasions**.

Informative speech provides the listener with a particular state of affairs. The information helps the audience to acquire awareness, understanding, and preparation for effective actions.

Persuasive speech persuades the audience to accept a specific opinion relevant to a particular state of affairs. Persuasion can make the audience attain one of the followings: belief in the speaker's description of a specific topic; acceptance or rejection of a specific event or policy; or motivation to participate in a particular course of action.

Special occasion speech, also referred as ceremonial speeches, is designed to captivate an audience's attention or amuse them while delivering a message. Like more traditional informative or persuasive speeches, special occasion speeches should communicate a clear message, but the manner of speaking used is typically different. These speeches are often delivered on special occasions (e.g., a toast at a wedding, an acceptance speech at an awards banquet, a motivational speech at a conference). Other examples of this type of speech include the message delivered by President Xi Jinping at a grand rally at Tian'anmen Square in Beijing to celebrate the 70th anniversary of the founding of the People's Republic of China, Tom Hank's Academy Award acceptance speech, the Queen's annual Christmas address and US President Reagan's eulogy for the victims of the Challenger explosion.

1.4 What Makes a Better Speaker and a Listener?

1) Becoming a qualified speaker

Good speakers are not born. Why are some speakers better in getting their messages across while others are not that effective in their oral communication? Do good speakers share some essential qualities?

How to become a better speaker?

(1) Tailor the speech content to the audience: choose a topic that meets the needs or interests of the audience.

(2) Communicate with the audience through clarity: use proper words, phrases, sentences, voice and gestures to convey information clearly.

(3) Be logical and organized: organize the speech content clearly to make sure the main points and supporting details of the speech can be easily identified.

(4) Apply effective delivery skills: vary the pace, tone, volume to be expressive and emphatic; maintain eye contact and use appropriate gestures to convey the idea.

(5) Exhibit poise and confidence: be confident and calm while giving speeches; never rush to a start and haste to an end.

2) Becoming a qualified listener

Listening has been called "a lost art" because most people are shockingly poor listeners. Most of us take our listening skills for granted. We don't regard it as a skill to be fine-tuned; rather, listening is an act we assume we're good at. Being able to listen well is just as important for communication as an eloquent speaking manner.

We fake paying attention. We can hear "sounds" instead of listening to "ideas". Hearing is a physiological process, involving the vibration of sound waves on our eardrums and the firing of electrochemical impulses from the inner ear to the central auditory system of the brain. But listening involves paying close attention to and making sense of what we hear.

Four levels of listening

- Level 1—Active listening: listening for pleasure or enjoyment, as when we listen to music, to a comedy routine, or an entertaining speech.

- Level 2—Empathic listening: listening to provide emotional support for the speaker, as when a psychiatrist listens to a patient or when we lend a sympathetic ear to a friend in distress.

- Level 3—Comprehensive listening: listening to understand the message of a speaker, as when we attend a classroom lecture or listen to directions for finding a place we want to visit.

- Level 4—Critical listening: listening to evaluate a massage for the purpose of accepting or rejecting it, as when we listen to the campaign speech of a political candidate or the closing arguments of an attorney in a jury trial.

How to become a better listener?

(1) Be an active listener: give our undivided attention to the speaker in a genuine effort to understand his/her point of view. In conversations, don't interrupt the other person or finish his/her sentences.

(2) Resist distractions: make a conscious effort to pull our minds back to what the speaker is saying. Don't be diverted by appearance or delivery.

(3) Recognize the difference between facts, opinions and assumptions: learn to separate opinions from facts, and be aware of whether a speaker is delivering a factual message or a message based on opinions, as well as the interplay between opinions and facts. Pay special attention to assumptions which are gaps in a logical sequence that listeners passively fill with their own ideas and opinions and may or may not be accurate. For example, suppose we're listening to a speech on weight loss. The speaker talks about how people who are overweight are simply not motivated or lack the self-discipline to lose weight. The speaker has built the speech

on the assumption that motivation and self-discipline are the only reasons why people can't lose weight. Then, we may think: what about genetics? Isn't it also one of the reasons? By listening critically, we will be more likely to notice unwarranted assumptions in a speech, which may prompt us to do further research to examine the validity of the speaker's assumptions. If, however, we sit passively by and let the speaker's assumptions go unchallenged, we may find ourselves persuaded by information that is not factual.

(4) Listen ethically: extend to speakers the same respect we want to receive when it's our turn to speak. We should avoid any behavior that belittles the speaker or the message. Respect, or unconditional positive regard for others, means that we treat others with consideration and decency whether we agree with them or not. We should treat the speaker with respect even when we disagree, don't understand the message, or find the speech boring.

Like so many of us, I used to take listening for granted, glossing over this step as I rushed into the more active, visible ways of being helpful. Now, I am convinced that listening is the single most important element of any helping relationship.

Listening has great power. It draws thoughts and feelings out of people as nothing else can. When someone listens to you well, you become aware of feelings you may not have realized that you felt. You have ideas you may have never thought of before. You become more eloquent, more insightful...

As a helpful listener, I do not interrupt you. I do not give advice. I do not do something else while listening to you. I do not convey distraction through nervous mannerisms. I do not finish your sentences for you. In spite of all my attempts to understand you, I do not assume I know what you mean.

I do not convey disapproval, impatience, or condescension. If I am confused, I show a desire for clarification, not dislike for your obtuseness. I do not act vindicated when you misspeak or correct yourself.

I do not sit impassively, withholding participation.

Instead, I project affection, approval, interest, and enthusiasm. I am your partner in communication. I am eager for your imminent success, fascinated by your struggles, forgiving of your mistakes, always expecting the best. I am your delighted listener.

—Taken from Lippman, D. (1998). *The storytelling coach: How to listen, praise, and bring out people's best*. Little Rock, AR: August House.

Note: This excerpt expresses the decency with which people should treat each other. It doesn't mean we must accept everything we hear, but ethically, we should refrain from trivializing each other's concerns. We all have had the painful experience of being ignored or misunderstood. This is how we know that one of the greatest gifts human beings can give to each other is listening.

1.5 Cultivating Critical Thinking in Public Speaking

One of the distinguishing factors separating humans from other species is our ability to think, visualize, and act on factors in our daily lives. Critical thinking is the process by which people qualitatively and quantitatively assess the information they have accumulated, and how they in turn use that information to solve problems and forge new patterns of understanding. Critical thinking clarifies goals, examines assumptions, discerns hidden values, evaluates evidence, accomplishes actions, and assesses conclusions. At its most basic, we can think of critical thinking as active thinking in which we evaluate and analyze information in order to determine the best course of our action.

When we address, theorize, examine, explain, and review our work (whether written or verbal), we are thinking critically. Critical thinking helps us to grow over time through preparation outlines, speaking notes, audience analysis, topic research and support, delivery, and review. Not being afraid to ask questions such as "How can I make this better? Stronger? What do I need to do?" and "How can I make the greatest impact?" is the application of critical thinking skills. As we go through the entire speech-making process, we are involved in critical thinking.

Critical Thinking Process Adapted for Public Speaking

Based on the work of Richard Paul and Linda Elder in *The Miniature Guide to Critical Thinking: Concepts and Tools*, we have developed these steps for critical thinking in the speech-making process.

Purpose—What is the purpose/goal/intent/outcome I am trying to accomplish in my speech? What do I want the audience to know, think, feel, or do when I am done with my speech?

Question—What question am I addressing? What are the needs of my listeners?

Information—What information am I providing to support my goal and purpose? What experience do I bring to the topic, method, and goal?

Concepts—What are the concepts I want my listeners to understand? Are they clear? Are they relevant? Do they make sense?

Assumptions—What assumptions have I made about my listeners, their knowledge level, their interests, their needs? Are my assumptions valid? Am I taking my listeners for granted? How can I answer the listeners' questions or assumptions?

Inferences—Have I reasoned out all aspects and lines of thinking in presenting my evidence? What is my support for the inferences and suggestions I am making in my speech? Have I evaluated the sources I will use for support?

Points of View—Do I acknowledge, allow, and respect other points of view from my listeners? In the speech-building stages, how do I incorporate these opposing views? How do I respond to other points of view?

Implications—Do I understand the ramifications and results of the position and the goal I am presenting in my speech? How can I incorporate the pieces of information as I progress as a speech writer and presenter for critical thinking for public speaking?

Another analysis tool is referred to as "**the five Ws** and **one H.**" Use the **who, what, where, when, why,** and **how** questions to examine our work and the work of others. These are universal questions and tools that directly ask us to seek more in-depth information. They are similar to the Paul-Elder model but prove to be useful in their own right.

Who—Who is affected by my message? Who is my intended audience?

What—What do I want to accomplish in my speech? What information will I use to support my ideas? What should I wear to present?

Where—Where am I presenting? A large/small room, etc.?

When—When will I be speaking? Before or after others? As a lone presenter? Morning or evening?

Why—Why was I chosen to speak? Why does this topic matter?

How—How can I organize my message for the greatest effect? How can I vocally make an impression on my audience?

For each question asked, it should lead to more questions, and those answers lead to more questions, and the cycle repeats! It is a never-ending cycle of questions. It is up to us to decide when the cycle will end. It is based on:

- when we have enough information for our speech;
- when time doesn't permit us to keep seeking;
- when we must put thoughts to paper for our preparation outline.

1.6 Dealing with Stage Fright— "Nothing to Fear but Fear Itself"

1.6.1 Common Fears of Public Speaking

Did you know that public speaking tops the list of phobias for most people? Not spiders or heights—public speaking—speech in public!

Now, think about these questions. Do you feel nervous when you are asked to give a public speech? Do you feel your heart beating fast before you are going to talk in front of an audience? Will your hands sweat and your mouth go dry? Will your knees shake and a quaver affects your voice?

When all that happens, most people don't think of getting their message across in a compelling and interesting way; they just think of getting off the "stage" as quickly as possible! If so, you suffer from stage fright, a kind of anxious feeling, or a kind of psychological weakness.

Stage fright, also termed as "platform panic" or "podium panic", may display various symptoms like sweaty palms, feeling hot or blush, dry mouth or throat, trembling limbs, etc. The heart may race and those well-known butterflies invade our stomach. Apparently, this excessive anxiety or fear does harm to the speech, or even prevents us from speaking at all.

Stage fright, however, is not uncommon. It happens, actually, to most people, including experienced speakers. It's quite normal to be nervous and have a lot of anxiety when speaking in public. Nevertheless, enough has shown that stage fright can be conquered or controlled. In fact, stage fright or the nervousness can turn into a constructive motive.

1.6.2 Two Biggest Myths about the Fear of Public Speaking

Myth 1:

Great public speaking skills are an inborn talent. Of course, some people find it easier to speak in public than others, but the majority of successful speakers have trained themselves to perform through persistence, preparation and practice. The bottom line is that if we can speak in front of two friends, we can deliver a presentation before an audience.

Myth 2:

Fear of public speaking is negative and undesirable. This is another common misconception that holds many new speakers back. We believe that stage fright is a sign of our inadequacy and lack of public speaking skills. No one escapes the rush of adrenaline that accompanies a public speech in front of an audience. The difference between successful speakers and "rookies" is that they have learned to transform and use fear to their advantage.

Fear is not only a normal reaction to a public speaking event, but actually boosts our performance. Psychologists agree that some amount of fear heightens our awareness, improves our concentration, sharpens our thinking and gives us an energy boost. It is fear that allows most speakers to perform better during the actual presentation than during practice.

1.6.3 Ways to Transform the Public Speaking Fear into Excitement

1) Think positively

Believe that most of the audiences we face are friendly and willing to accept our talk. They understand us if we are somewhat nervous. Even though we make some errors, they tend to forgive us since they are not fastidious or faultfinding in general.

Negative self-talk

- I'm afraid I'll stumble over my words and look foolish.
- I'm afraid everyone will be able to tell that I'm nervous.
- I'm afraid my voice will crack.
- I'm afraid I'll sound boring.

Positive self-talk

- Even if I stumble, I will succeed as long as I get my message across.
- They probably won't be able to tell I'm nervous, but as long as I focus on getting my message across, that's what matters.
- Even if my voice cracks, as long as I keep going and focus on getting my message across, I'll succeed at what matters most.
- I won't sound bored if I focus on how important this message is to me and to my audience. I don't have to worry about keeping their attention because my topic is relevant to them.

---

2) Maintain eye contact with the audience

Look at them while talking to them as if we are talking to some individuals. Use the 3-second method: look straight into the eyes of a person in the audience for 3 seconds at a time; have direct eye contact with a number of people in the audience; and every now and then glance at the whole audience while speaking. Do remember to use eye contact to make everyone feel involved.

3) Prepare our speech attentively and in detail

When preparing, try to refer to all relevant factors and predict all possible difficulties. Enough preparation always leads to more confidence and less fear. Practice and rehearse our speech at home or where we can be at ease and comfortable, in front of a mirror, our family, friends or colleagues, videotape our speech and analyze it. Know what our strong and weak points are and emphasize our strong points during the presentation.

4) Concentrate on nothing but what we intend to get across to the audience when delivering

If we really focus on something we are prepared for, we can gradually overcome the nervousness. Do not read from notes for any extended length of time although it is quite acceptable to glance at our notes infrequently. Speak loudly and clearly. Sound confident. Do not mumble. If we made an error, correct it, and continue. There is no need to make excuses or apologize profusely.

5) Build our speech on clarity, not complexity

Organizing the speech or presentation around two or three main points allows us to relax and not worry so much about running out of time or forgetting to mention something important to the listeners.

6) Add humor whenever appropriate and possible

Keep audience interested throughout our entire presentation. Remember that an interesting speech makes time fly. Tell jokes if you are good at telling joke. If you aren't good at doing so, best to leave the jokes behind. There's nothing worse than a punch line that has no punch. Self-deprecation is good, but do not overuse it.

7) Use visual aids if possible

Visual aids such as PowerPoint slides can draw the audience's interest, but remember to speak to the audience, not the slides. The slides are there to support us, not the other way around. Ideally, slides should be graphics and not words (people read faster than they hear and will be impatient for the speaker to get to the next point). When using audio-visual aids to enhance the speech, be sure all necessary equipment is set up and in good working order prior to the speech. If possible, have an emergency backup system readily available. Check out the location ahead of time to ensure seating arrangements for audience, whiteboard, blackboard, lighting, location of projection screen, sound system, etc. are suitable for the speech.

8) Try not to get stuck in one place

Use all the available space. One way to do this is to leave the notes in one place and move to another. If the space is confined (say a meeting room or even presenting at a table), use stronger body language to convey the message.

9) Visualize the success

Visualization or mental rehearsal has been routinely used by many top athletes as a part of the training for a competition. In addition to athletics, research has shown that visualization helps to improve performance in such areas as communication, public speaking and education. To ensure that the presentation goes smoothly, aside from actual preparation and the rehearsal of the speech, take 10-15 minutes a day to relax, close the eyes and visualize the room in which we are speaking, the people in the auditorium and ourselves confidently delivering the speech, smiling, and moving across the stage.

10) Learn how to breathe

Breathe in and out deeply several times, which can relax us especially when our breath is subconsciously quick and shallow because of nervousness.

By overcoming the stage fear, we can enjoy public speaking and become far more effective speakers when standing in front of a group of people and delivering a potent message. When it comes to improving public speaking skills, we have three words: practice, practice, practice!

1.7 Ethics in Public Speaking

The study of ethics in human communication is hardly a recent endeavor. One of the earliest discussions of ethics in communication (and particularly in public speaking) was conducted by the ancient Greek philosopher Plato in his dialogue *Phaedrus*[1]. In the centuries since Plato's time, an entire subfield within the discipline of human communication has developed to explain and understand communication ethics.

Communication Code of Ethics

When you think of ethics, what comes to your mind? Perhaps we think of words and phrases such as ethical behavior, professional ethics, ethics boards, or code of

---

1   *Phaedrus*, written by Plato, is a dialogue between Plato's protagonist, Socrates, and Phaedrus, an interlocutor in several dialogues. *Phaedrus* was presumably composed around 370 BC. Although ostensibly revolving around the topic of love, the discussion in the dialogue focuses on the art of rhetoric and how it should be practiced, and dwells on subjects as diverse as metempsychosis (the Greek tradition of reincarnation) and erotic love.

ethics. At its heart, ethics refers to the concept of having morally acceptable values and behaviors. When we align our behaviors and actions with these values, we engage in ethical behavior.

Why would we need to even consider ethics in public speaking? First and foremost, our audience not only needs to believe in our words and message, but also needs to trust us as the message giver. Engeging in unethical behavior when speaking erodes that trust.

As public speakers, one of the first ethical areas we should be concerned with is information honesty. While there are cases where speakers have blatantly lied to an audience, it is more common for speakers to prove a point by exaggerating, omitting facts that weigh against their message, or distorting information. We believe that speakers build a relationship with their audiences, and that lying, exaggerating, or distorting information violates this relationship. Ultimately, a speaker will be more persuasive by using reason and logical arguments supported by facts rather than relying on emotional appeals designed to manipulate the audience.

It is also important to be honest about where all our information comes from in a speech. As speakers, examine the information sources and determine whether they are biased or have hidden agendas. While we may not know all the sources of information firsthand, we should attempt to find objective sources that do not have an overt or covert agenda that skews the argument we are making.

The second part of information honesty is to fully disclose where we obtain the information in our speeches. As ethical speakers, it is important to always cite the sources of information within the body of a speech. Whether we conduct an interview or read a newspaper article, we must tell our listeners where the information comes from. Using someone else's words or ideas without giving credit is called plagiarism. The word "plagiarism" stems from the Latin word *plagiaries,* or kidnapper. The consequences for failing to cite sources during public speeches can be substantial. When Senator Joseph Biden was running for president of the United States in 1988, reporters found that he had plagiarized portions of his political speech from British politician Neil Kinnock. Biden was forced to drop out of the race as a result.

Thus, knowing about ethics is essential, but even more important to being an ethical public speaker is putting that knowledge into practice by thinking through possible ethical pitfalls prior to standing up and speaking out. The following table is a checklist to help you think through some of these issues.

Public Speaking Ethics Checklist

Instructions: For each of the following ethical issues, check either "true" or "false".	True	False
1. I have knowingly added information within my speech that is false.		
2. I have attempted to persuade people by unnecessarily tapping into emotion rather than logic.		
3. I have not clearly cited all the information within my speech.		
4. I'm using the information in my speech that a source gave me even though it was technically "off the record".		
5. I wrote my speech based on my own interests and really haven't thought much about my audience's needs and desires.		
6. I have altered some of the facts in my speech to help me be more persuasive.		
7. My goal is to manipulate my audience to my point of view.		
8. My personal opinions are just as good as facts, so I don't bother to distinguish between the two during my speech.		

Key Takeaways of This Chapter

★ People have many reasons for engaging in public speaking, but the skills necessary for public speaking are applicable whether someone is speaking for informative, persuasive, or entertainment reasons.

★ Taking a public speaking class will improve your speaking skills, help you be a more critical thinker, fine-tune your verbal and nonverbal communication skills.

★ Getting your message across to others effectively requires attention to message content, skill in communicating content, and your passion for the information presented.

★ Hearing is the physiological process of attending to sound within one's environment; listening, however, is a focused, concentrated approach to understanding the message a source is sending.

★ There are many steps you can take during the speech preparation process to manage your speech anxiety, including thinking positively, analyzing your audience, clearly organizing your ideas, and practicing.

★ When preparing a speech, it is important to think about the ethics of public speaking from the beginning. When a speaker sets out to be ethical in his/her speech from the beginning, arriving at ethical speech is much easier.

Part II

Exercises

I. Discuss the following questions.

1. Could you name some use of public speaking in your real life? In what kind of situation are you a public speaker?
2. You are advised to talk to people who are currently working in the career you hope to pursue. Of the three types of public speaking discussed in the text, which do they use most commonly in their work?
3. What are the features of a successful speech? What makes a good speaker?
4. Can you think of some reasons for the possible failure of public speakers? Name some of them and illustrate your points.
5. What are the possible ways that may work for you to deal with stage fright? Share some of your public speaking experience with your classmates.
6. What do you mean when you say that public speaking is both an interactive and a dynamic process? Please illustrate with examples.
7. What kind of possible impact does human diversity have on public speakers?
8. What interesting benefits do you receive from a public speaking class? Why?

II. Complete a survey.

A Survey for Public Speaking Class

1. What makes a good speech? List three things that you think can contribute to a successful speech.

   a. _____

   b. _____

   c. _____

2. What are your strengths as a speaker? List three of them (e.g. ideas, good pronunciation, confidence, humor, etc.)

    a. _____

    b. _____

    c. _____

3. How would you like to improve as a speaker? What kind of speaking skills would you like to work on (e.g. eye contact, body language, speaking rate, etc). List three of them.

    a. _____

    b. _____

    c. _____

4. Do you have fears in speaking publicly? What are your major concerns for public speaking? (e.g. I may forget what I have prepared / I will probably make a fool of myself / My speech will not impress the audience). List them below:

    _____

5. Which of these types of presentations do you like to make? (Check all that apply)

    a. impromptu speech

    b. speaking to inform

    c. speaking to persuade

    d. speaking on special occasions

    e. memorized speech

    f. speaking with the help of notes

6. What exactly do you want to learn from a public speaking class?

    _____

Ⅲ. Practice your speaking skills with the given scenarios.

1. Please prepare a 2-minute speech of self-introduction. Present yourself in such a way that will help your teacher and your fellow students remember who you are. You can speak casually and informally, with notes if you like, but certainly without a manuscript. You could include the information such as the meaning of your name, your major, your hometown or anything that you think the class will be interested in.

2. Suppose one of your classmates thinks it useless to learn public speaking and is not willing to take the public speaking course. By taking your college life into consideration, you should determine at least three occasions/reasons when/why he/she needs to make public speaking on campus. Then tell him/her your ideas, try to convince him/her of the importance of learning public speaking. You may divide your ideas into three parts: in the first part, introduce the concept of

public speaking; in the second part, list at least three occasions/reasons when/why you need to make public speaking; in the last part, restate the key points and bring what you have said to a natural conclusion.

Ⅳ. Never neglect speaking ethical issues. Discuss the situation with your partner and provide your thoughts on the questions given.

The ethical rule in public speaking dates back thousands of years as the word "ethics" is derived from the Greek word "ethos". In line with what has been discussed in this chapter, generally, the responsibilities of an ethical speaker are as follows:

(1) Say something meaningful to offer the audience take-away messages.

(2) Choose topics that promote positive ethical values.

(3) Use truthful, accurate supporting materials and valid reasoning.

(4) Let the audience know your true motives for speaking.

(5) Consider the possible consequences of your words.

The Scenario

> As Marna and Gloria were eating lunch together, Marna happened to ask Gloria, "How are you doing in Woodward's speech class?"
>
> "Not bad," Gloria replied. "I'm working on this speech about product development. I think it will be really informative, but I'm having a little trouble with the opening. I just can't seem to get a good idea for getting started."
>
> "Why not start with a story—that always worked for me in class."
>
> "Thanks, Marna. I'll think on it."
>
> The next day when Marna ran into Gloria again, she asked, "How's that introduction going?"
>
> "Great. I've prepared a great story about Mary Kay—you know, the cosmetics woman? I'm going to tell about how she was terrible in school and no one thought she'd amount to anything. But she loved dabbling with cosmetics so much that she decided to start her own business..."

Questions:

(1) What are the ethical issues in the scenario?

(2) Will anyone be possibly hurt by Gloria's opening in the speech with this story?

(3) As a public speaker, what kind of ethical issues should be kept in mind?

(4) What is the most ethical choice in the following situation?

Imagine that you're in the audience when the main speaker proposes an action that you feel is unacceptable. As a result, you earnestly want to stand up and walk right out of the room. You are sitting near the end of a row, so it would be possible to do so. You notice that other people are listening intently. What will you do? Discuss your choice with your classmates.

- Continue listening to be sure your understanding is accurate and to see whether the speaker explains the point of view in a way that makes it more acceptable.
- Interrupt the speaker so other listeners will not be "taken in" by the message.
- Walk out as a symbolic gesture of disagreement.

Chapter **2**

Speech Preparation: Getting Started

Part I

Speech Preparatory Work

1. Preparedness ensures success and unpreparedness spells failure. (凡事预则立，不预则废。)

   —the Doctrine of the Mean (《中庸》)

2. Talk in terms of the other person's interests.

   —Dale Carnegie

2.1 Choosing a Topic

It's commonly known that many people fear public speaking more than they fear death. The feeling of butterflies-in-the-stomach is all too familiar for many, even for the most experienced speakers. The hardest part might be getting started. Choosing the topic for our speech is a very complex and personal decision. It's complex because there are so many possibilities. It's personal because there are some subjects that possibly interest us a great deal. Sometimes we are told or given a speech topic and other times the choice is left entirely up to us. This latter option can leave people feeling completely stuck. Selecting a speech topic sometimes feels like shooting an arrow in a random direction and hoping that it hits a target. If this is our approach, we are probably quite frustrated.

This may seem like an easy task, but there are infinite public speaking topics. How do we choose the right one? How do we select a topic which is a perfect fit between us and our audience? There are many strategies for choosing a good topic.

For example, it is recommended that we choose a topic that is exciting or interesting to us, so that we can be enthusiastic about the topic while delivering our speech. Furthermore, it helps to have some prior knowledge about the topic, or at least we are motivated to research more on the topic.

2.1.1   How to Select a Topic?

Before considering a speech topic, ask yourself the following three questions:

1) Am I an expert on this topic?

It isn't necessary to know everything about a topic, but you do need to know more about the topic than your audience so as to be seen as a credible speaker. Your knowledge must cover not only what you plan to say, but also go beyond that so that you are able to comfortably handle questions afterward.

2) Am I passionate about this topic?

Passion for spreading your knowledge about a topic is the fuel that will power your speech delivery. Your posture, your gestures, your eyes, your facial expressions, and your energy level are all elevated when you speak on topics you enjoy. Likewise, all of these suffer when you talk about topics that you find mundane.

3) Does my audience care about this topic?

If your audience doesn't see value for themselves in your topic, there are two possibilities. Either they don't show up, or they show up and tune out. In either case, you are wasting your breath. Every successful speech must contain explicit value for your audience.

Imagine you have an encyclopedia full of potential speech topics. Based on the answers to the three questions above, you could sort a potential topic into one of eight speech topic zones. Seven of these zones are flawed, but one is golden!

Zone 1: Perfect Speech Topics

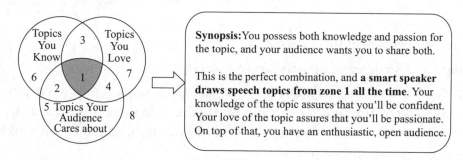

Synopsis: You possess both knowledge and passion for the topic, and your audience wants you to share both.

This is the perfect combination, and **a smart speaker draws speech topics from zone 1 all the time.** Your knowledge of the topic assures that you'll be confident. Your love of the topic assures that you'll be passionate. On top of that, you have an enthusiastic, open audience.

Whether you end up speaking about topics in this zone by strategy or by luck, you're in a great position to succeed. Speak and change the world!

However, what if you have to give a speech and your topic isn't in Zone 1? Does this mean you are destined to fail? Sometimes you are, and sometimes you aren't. Read on to find what you can do to move topics into Zone 1 before you deliver them.

Zone 2: Content-Rich, but Passion-Free Speech Topics

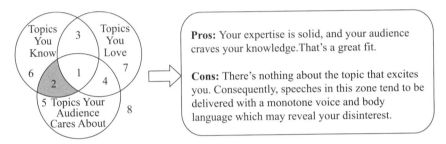

Pros: Your expertise is solid, and your audience craves your knowledge. That's a great fit.

Cons: There's nothing about the topic that excites you. Consequently, speeches in this zone tend to be delivered with a monotone voice and body language which may reveal your disinterest.

Can you transform this into a Zone 1 Topic?

Rediscover what can motivate you to become an expert in the topic, and find your passion again. Try to see the topic from the audiences' perspective and ask potential audience members what interests them about the topic. Their responses may rekindle your passion by reminding you that the topic is full of questions that need to be answered—and you have the answers!

Zone 3: Great Speech Topics for Indifferent Audience

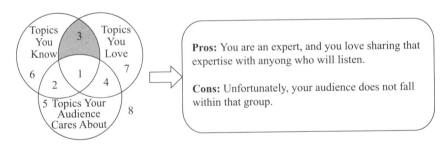

Pros: You are an expert, and you love sharing that expertise with anyone who will listen.

Cons: Unfortunately, your audience does not fall within that group.

Can you transform this into a Zone 1 Topic?

There are two different approaches you can take:

(1) You have to find the value for your audience. A great way to do this is by finding some common ground between your speech topic and a subject that the audience does care about. Drawing parallels or crafting metaphors can make this speech topic interesting to your audience.

(2) Save this speech topic for a different audience. Out there, somewhere, there's

an audience that shares your passion and wants to hear what you have to say. You've just got to find them.

Zone 4: Fascinating Speech Topics You Know Nothing About

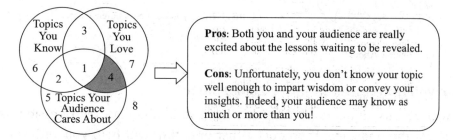

Pros: Both you and your audience are really excited about the lessons waiting to be revealed.

Cons: Unfortunately, you don't know your topic well enough to impart wisdom or convey your insights. Indeed, your audience may know as much or more than you!

Can you transform this into a Zone 1 Topic?

With these speech topics, you are standing on extremely fertile ground. There are two approaches you can take:

(1) Develop your expertise. It won't happen overnight, but through hard work you can make it happen. Your passion and eager audience provide excellent motivation for you to succeed.

(2) Admit the limits of your expertise, and ditch the traditional speech format for one where you are facilitating discussion instead. Under your leadership, the discussion can lead the audience to explore issues, brainstorm new ideas, and discover solutions collectively.

Zone 5: Speech Topics Someone Else Should Deliver

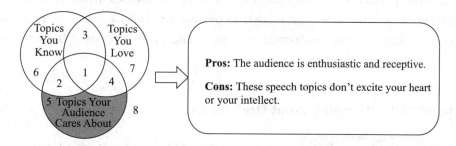

Pros: The audience is enthusiastic and receptive.

Cons: These speech topics don't excite your heart or your intellect.

Can you transform this into a Zone 1 Topic?

Probably not. You need to develop some expertise, but that's hard to do without passion for the topic. Cultivating passion is difficult without minimal expertise. You might eventually get there, but you would be more effective in digging into other speech topics. Leave this topic for someone else to deliver. Whatever you do, don't try to bluff your way through a Zone 5 speech. The audience will sense your lack of knowledge and passion, and your credibility will be shattered.

Zone 6: Speech Topics That Don't Even Interest You

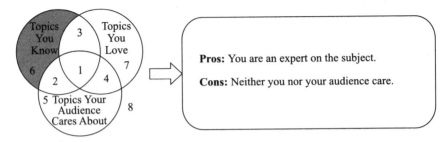

Can you transform this into a Zone 1 Topic?

It will be very difficult. You'll either have to kindle your own passion, or find meaning for the audience. If you get either one, that will help you with the other. But, as with Zone 5, you should probably devote your energy elsewhere.

Zone 7: Personal Hobbies, Not Speech Topics

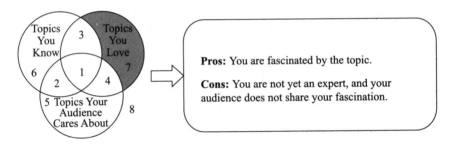

Can you transform this into a Zone 1 Topic?

Surprisingly, maybe. Having passion for a topic provides great motivation, and can motivate you to develop your own expertise, as well as seek out reasons why the audience should care. Compared to Zone 5 and Zone 6, Zone 7 is most likely to produce useful speech topics for you.

Zone 8: "Like-Watching-Paint-Dry" Topics

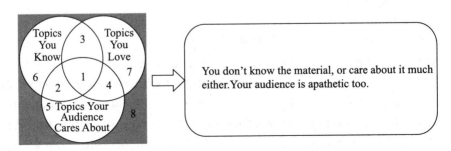

Can you transform this into a Zone 1 Topic?

No, you can't. You are suggested to choose another one.

Tips for speech topic selection

- Put yourself in your audience's shoes and consider what they would like to hear and why. Who are you speaking to? What do they care about? Once you have decided the criteria of your speech, look for topics in the particular category. If you have an idea for a topic, look for a way to relate it to your audience. Don't just talk about a topic in general—try to help your audience see the value of the topic.

- Choose a topic that interests you. If you are interested in current affairs or sports, look for a speech topic related to your field. You will sound convincing and interesting only when you select a topic of your choice! Don't forget to consider your own knowledge and background. What do you care about? The easiest speech to deliver is the one on a topic that you know inside and out. Your own passion and knowledge about a subject will come through in your presentation with very little effort.

- Look for timely topics. Check news headlines from a variety of new media platforms. Sometimes an interesting story can spark your creativity. In addition, it gives you a great way to open your speech.

- Consider the purpose. Reflect carefully on the purpose of your talk before settling on a topic and title. What is it you want the audience to learn? Do you want to motivate them into personal actions, or muster moral support for your latest project? Perhaps you want to deliver bad news with minimal upset, or shed positive light on an unfortunate turn of events.

- Bear your audience's needs in mind. Once you've chosen a topic, plan its contents from your audience's perspective. Were you to attend a talk on the subject in question, what would you expect to learn, and by what means? It may be that the use of props, animation or a quiz could prove most helpful.

2.1.2   How to Generate Ideas?

1) Make a list

(1) Ask yourself some broad questions and write down some responses.

Example Questions	Possible Answers
What is your major? What aspects of your major interest you?	• Education—preschool education in China • Agriculture—feeding the world • Graphic design—how color influences mood
What hobbies or special interests do you have?	• skiing/painting/yoga/playing video games

(to be continued)

(continued)

Example Questions	Possible Answers
Is there a topic that you think your classmates should know about?	• the dangers or risks of online dating • the time management skills in college • the social benefits of enhancing public speaking skills
What topics have been in the news lately?	• 2020 National Day box office bonanza pushes China close to world's top market • the vaccine research about COVID-19 in the world • 2020 US presidential election

By broadly answering these questions, you will find yourself with a wealth of possible topics to choose from. When selecting a topic, start by casting a broad net because it will help you limit and weed out topics quickly.

(2) Find background information.

Look at your list of topics. Once you have two to three topics in mind, it is time to do some research to look at some general background information about these topics. By simply typing the chosen topics into a search engine (Google, Bing, Baidu, etc.), you will be able to read some pertinent information about the topics to better judge if that certain topic would be suitable for your speech. When gauging this, keep in mind yourself, your audience, and the message that you are attempting to convey. Choose one or two that may interest you and the audience as potential topics. A good way to decide on a more specific topic is to look for information in the encyclopedia about the subject.

As you read the encyclopedia entries, note interesting facts or ideas. (Write down some answers to these questions mentioned above.) The example below shows how you can move from a simple idea (e.g., Chinese tea) to an actual topic. Be sure to include the source(s) of your information, since you will need this information for your bibliography.

Questions	Possible Answers
What new things have you learned about the topic?	• According to the legend, tea was discovered by Chinese Emperor Shen Nong in 2737 BC when a leaf from a nearby shrub fell into water the emperor was boiling. • Chinese tea can be classified into six distinctive categories: white, green, yellow, oolong, black and post-fermented.

(to be continued)

(continued)

Questions	Possible Answers
What aspects of the topic might be interesting to include in your speech?	• China's top tea culture cities • the best option for office workers (green tea) • the historical evolution of tea
What new questions do you have about the topic as a result of reading the encyclopedia entry?	• How has tea culture evolved historically? • How is tea traded internationally? • What is the chemical structure of tea leaves? • How is the core of our nation reflected by tea lore? (e.g., Philosophy, ethics and morality are blended into tea activity. People cultivate their morality and mind, and savor life through tasting tea, thereby attaining joy of spirit.)

Note: While the encyclopedia is a great starting place, you'll definitely want to use more sources in preparing your research, such as books or journal articles, in order to have a well-balanced examination of facts and issues.

2) Narrow the topic

When you have identified a subject area or a topic, it's simply a matter of narrowing it enough so that it fits your allotted time. Do not make the mistake of trying to cover every aspect of a topic. To accomplish this, you will need to start with your main topic and systematically break it down into smaller and smaller parts until you arrive at a topic that is manageable for the occasion. Take a look at the questions that you answered about your topic and brainstorm what some narrower aspects of the topic might be. Write down your ideas.

Here's a list following the example of the topic of *Chinese tea*:

• history of Chinese tea;

• popularity of Chinese tea;

• impact of Chinese tea on the world economy;

• tips on how to drink tea effectively;

• the highest ambit—tea lore.

Review the list that you just made. Choose one or two narrower topics. Keep the following in mind:

• Who is your audience? Which of these narrower topics will be most interesting to both you and your audience? Which topics will be understood by the audience? (Is the audience a professor or students listening to a presentation?)

- What are the specifics of the assignment? Which topics will fit? (Note that the above examples are all informative in nature, perhaps not good for a persuasive speech. A related topic focused on chemistry might interest you, but may not be appropriate for an economics course.)

- How long do you have to cover the topic? Is it still too broad?

- Which of these narrower topics interests you the most? After all, you need to do further research on this topic. It will be more difficult if it doesn't interest you.

2.2 Determining the Purpose of a Speech

2.2.1 Formulate a General Purpose

Once you have chosen and narrowed down a topic, it is time to decide exactly what the purpose of your speech will be. Specifically, you must determine your purpose for speaking and what you hope to accomplish. (What type of response do you want from the listeners? What do you want them to know, think or do as a result of your speech?)

Speeches have traditionally been seen to have one of three broad purposes: to inform, to persuade, or to entertain. These broad goals are commonly known as a speech's general purpose, since, in general, you are trying to inform, persuade, or entertain your audience without concerning specifically what the topic will be. Perhaps you could think of them as appealing to the understanding of the audience (informative), the will or action (persuasive), and the emotion or pleasure (entertaining).

2.2.2 Formulate a Specific Purpose

Now that you know your general purpose (to inform, to persuade, or to entertain), you can start to move in the direction of the specific purpose. Basically, this is a written summary of what you hope to accomplish with your speech, and it will guide you and keep you on track as you begin to decide upon the main points of your speech. A specific purpose statement builds on your general purpose (to inform) and makes it more specific (as the name suggests). For example, if your first speech is an informative speech, your purpose will be to inform your audience about a very specific realm of knowledge. You should state your specific purpose in a single infinitive phrase. The specific purpose of an informative or a persuasive speech is often stated in the following patterns:

- To inform my audience about...
- To inform my audience that...
- To persuade my audience to...
- To persuade my audience that...

If you want to inform the audience of the quality of different news websites, then your specific purpose would be: To inform my audience about the quality of different news websites. If you want to persuade the audience to visit a particular website, then the specific purpose would be: To persuade my audience to visit _____ (a particular news website).

Examples of the specific purpose for informative speeches are as follows:

(1) Topic: Communications

General Purpose: To inform

Specific purpose: To inform my audience about the value of informed intercultural communication.

(2) Topic: Qixi Festival

General Purpose: To inform

Specific purpose: To inform my audience about the traditions and customs of Qixi Festival

Examples of the specific purpose for persuasive speeches are as follows:

(1) Topic: Cell Phone

General Purpose: To persuade

Specific Purpose: To persuade my audience to change unhealthy habits of using mobile phones.

(2) Topic: Capital Punishment

General Purpose: To persuade

Specific purpose: To persuade my audience to believe that capital punishment is morally wrong.

Here are some tips for formulating the specific purpose statement:

(1) Write the purpose statement as a full infinitive phrase, not as a fragment.

Ineffective: Calendars.

More Effective: To inform my audience about the four major kinds of calendars used in the world today.

(2) Express your purpose as a statement, not as a question.

Ineffective: Is the China space program necessary?

More Effective: To persuade my audience that the China space program provides many important benefits to people on earth.

(3) Avoid figurative language in the purpose statement.

Ineffective: To inform my audience that yoga is extremely cool.

More Effective: To inform my audience how yoga can improve their health.

(4) Make sure your specific purpose is not too vague or general.

Ineffective: To inform my audience about one of China's Four Great Classical Novels: *Dream of the Red Chamber.*

More Effective: To inform my audience about the love and compassion in *Dream of the Red Chamber.*

2.2.3 Compose a Thesis Statement

A thesis statement is a complete sentence that expresses the speaker's most important idea, or key point, about a topic. A thesis statement guides the development of a speech. To create a thesis statement helps because: (1) You will use it in the introduction and conclusion of your speech. (2) It will help the audience to remember the overall idea of your speech. (3) It helps you narrow down your topic and maintain a focus for your speech. (4) It identifies your position in a persuasive speech.

Examples of the specific purpose with a thesis statement for an informative speech is as follows:

(1) Topic: Show Dogs

General Purpose: To inform

Specific purpose: To inform my audience about the six major classifications of show dogs.

Thesis Statement: Show dogs are classified according to their characteristics as hounds, terriers, working dogs, toys, sporting dogs, and non-sporting dogs.

(2) Topic: Recommendation of a Novel

General Purpose: To persuade

Specific purpose: To persuade my audience to read the science fiction entitled The Three-Body Problem.

Thesis Statement: The Three-Body Problem is an excellent book to read because it features interesting characters, thought-provoking issues, and an exciting plot.

You will rely on your thesis statement to guide you and help keep you committed and focused on the topic at hand. The thesis statement should be as specific as possible to your chosen topic with detailed language that grabs the attention of the audience and allows them to know exactly about what your speech will discuss. The thesis statement is the first thing that your audience will hear, and in the short amount of time that it takes to deliver this first sentence, the audience will have already made the judgment as to whether they want to listen or tune out the remainder of your speech. The importance of creating an intriguing thesis statement is essential to the success of your speech.

It might also be helpful to think of your speech in terms of what you want your listeners' response to be as a result of having heard your speech, be it informative or persuasive in nature. Along with purpose statements, identifying specific behavioral objectives for the audience helps you focus on your efforts and clarify your goals for the speech. Examples of behavioral objectives you might identify for an audience are: "After listening to this presentation the audience will be able to list 4 essential pieces of ski equipment for beginners and their uses." "After listening to this speech the class will be able to name the top 3 ski resorts in China and what activities are available at each." "After hearing my speech the audience will stop being a mouse potato."

As you can see, the process of topic selection makes it easy to select a theme to develop a one-of-a-kind speech. By allowing yourself to creatively answer each question via brainstorming, you may generate ideas, set the overall tone of your developing speech. As you initiate background information, the topics begin to "come alive", creating some interesting themes to speak about. During the narrowing phase, the actual topic for your speech emerges and allows you to create an alluring thesis statement that gives worthiness to your speech.

2.2.4　Support a Thesis Statement

Aristotle said, "There are only two parts to a speech: you make a statement and you prove it." Supporting materials prove your assertions. You need to find information to support your main idea expressed in your thesis statement. The term *supporting materials* refers to the information a person provides to develop and/or justify an idea that is offered for a listener's consideration. Supporting materials are the basic building blocks of speeches, and thus provide the substance of speeches.

Supporting materials serve a variety of functions in oral presentations, for example, to clarify the speaker's point, to emphasize the point, to make the point more interesting, and to furnish a basis that enables others to believe the speaker's point. Without supporting materials, a speech is little more than a string of assertions (claims without backing).

There are several kinds of supporting materials that you might choose to use in your speeches. You should use several different kinds in the same speech. Remember, well-chosen, carefully researched, and strategically placed, supporting materials form the backbone of effective speeches. The commonly used supporting details include facts, opinions, examples, illustrations, anecdotes, statistics, comparisons, definitions, descriptions, and quotations.

1) Facts and opinions

Statements of fact contain information that can be proved, or verified, by testing, by observing, or by consulting reference materials. Statements of opinion express personal beliefs or attitudes. Such statements contain personal judgments, which include information that cannot be proven. In some situations, you may seek an expert opinion, which is a statement of belief about a subject from a person who is recognized as an authority on that subject. For example, a rocket scientist could offer an expert opinion on space travel. Experts can also supply facts. For instance, Jack Ma, the CEO of Alibaba can report on how many online shoppers have visited Taobao during 2018.

2) Examples and illustrations

An example is a single instance that supports or develops a statement. An illustration is a detailed/lengthy/extended example.

3) Anecdotes

Anecdotes are brief and amusing stories. The purpose of an anecdote is to give information in a form that the audience will remember. Because anecdotes are often entertaining, they can help make your speech more interesting and enjoyable as well as informative.

4) Statistics

Statistics are numerical representations of information. They are very credible in our society, as evidenced by their frequent use by news agencies, government offices, politicians, and academics. Using statistics in public speaking is a powerful way to add a quantifiable and persuasive aspect to your message. It provides a basis on which you can build an argument, prove a statement, or support an idea. As a speaker, you can capitalize on the power of statistics if you use them appropriately. When you give the audience a large number that they would expect to be smaller, or vice versa, you will be more likely to engage them, as the following example shows: *"Did you know that 1.3 billion people in the world do not have access to electricity? That's about 20 percent of the world's population according to a 2016 study on the International Energy Agency's official website."* Remember to always mention the source for data and never give a nonspecific source for statistics. Do not say, "Research shows..."

What research? Who did it? Or "An informed source said that..." Be specific. This information provides credibility for you and will strengthen the impact of the information the statistics provide. You may also use statistics carefully to add interest or to emphasize a point.

5) Comparisons

A comparison is a statement that shows the similarities between people, places, things, events, or ideas. Comparisons help listeners relate new ideas to familiar concepts. A figurative comparison imaginatively shows similarities between things that are essentially not alike. For example, you may say someone is "as tall as a giraffe" to point out that the person is very tall. In contrast, a literal comparison shows the real similarities between things that are essentially alike. For example, "Tom runs slower than Jorge." Occasionally, a comparison is phrased as a contrast, highlighting the differences between two things. For instance, you might say, "Unlike last year's ecology club, which consisted primarily of seniors, this year's club has mostly sophomores and juniors as members."

6) Testimony

Testimony is quoted information from people with direct knowledge about a subject or situation. Expert testimony is from people who are credentialed or recognized experts in a given subject. Lay testimony is often a recounting of a person's experiences, which is more subjective. Both types of testimony are valuable as supporting materials.

7) Descriptions

A description is a word picture of a person, place, thing, or event. Accurate descriptions help people in your audience form mental pictures that correspond to the actual thing described.

8) Quotations

A quotation expresses someone's exact words. Usually, you express your ideas in your own words. However, in some cases, you will use a quotation to express the opinion of authority or to include a particularly well-stated idea. When you use quotations, you must give credit to the source from which the words were taken.

Among these eight types of supporting materials, using examples, statistics and testimony are the three most preferred and commonly used ones in speeches. Thus, some sample speech excerpts that use these supporting materials are provided.

Sample Analysis for Using Examples

- (1) The vast distance is one we have now crossed. (2) We have communication, cooperation, trade, investment, tourism, cultural and scientific exchanges. (3) For example, in 1972, there were no American tourists in the P.R.C.; last year there were over 100,000. In 1972 no students from the P.R.C. were studying in the United States; last year there were over 12,000. In 1972, there was no trade between the P.R.C. and the United States; last year trade exceeded six billion dollars.

—Richard Nixon

Analysis: This is taken from the speech by former President Nixon of the USA at the University of International Business and Economics in Beijing in 1985. (1) is the main head or point the speaker intends to support. In (2), there is a brief mention of several items, as a transition to the following more specific examples. Notice (3) is an explicit indicator introducing a series of examples to back up the point "The vast distance is one we have now crossed."

- So often, we see individual actions of courage and love in everyday life that give us faith in ourselves and hope for a better future (1) In 1981, a bright, young American student, John Zeidman came here to study in China and seek new friends. (2) He was a boy of great heart and enthusiasm, and riding his bicycle on Beijing's streets, conversing and camping with artists and students, and he fell in love with your country. Tragically, he was struck ill on his 20th birthday and later died. But his tragedy brought forth new life.

  Analysis: This is an extended example, telling in more detail about a young American student who contributed to the friendship between Chinese and Americans but unfortunately died of illness. (1) is the main head, and (2) tells the story about the boy, which supports the idea that some individual actions enable us to be confident of a better future. Notice how naturally the speaker turns from the point o the supporting example. This kind of example can also be regarded as an anecdote, which has a point of moral.

- (1) I say to you today, my friends, even though we face the difficulties of today and tomorrow, I still have a dream. It is a dream deeply rooted in the American dream. I have a dream that one day this nation will rise up and live out the true meaning of its creed: "We hold these truths to be self-evident, that all men are created equal." (2) I have a dream that one day on the red hills of Georgia, the sons of former slaves and the sons of former slave owners will be able to sit down together at the table of brotherhood.I have a dream that one day even the state of Mississippi, a state sweltering with the heat of injustice, sweltering with the heat of oppression, will be transformed into an oasis of freedom and justice. I have a dream that my four little children will one day live in a nation where they will not be judged by the color of their

skin but by the content of their character. I have a dream that one day...
(3) This is our hope. This is the faith with which I return to the South... With
this faith we will be able to hew out of the mountain of despair a stone of
hope... knowing that we will be free one day.

—Martin Luther King, Jr.

*Analysis: The hypothetical illustration or example can be found in this sample since
the illustration in not actual but imaginative. Part (1) including two paragraphs,
states the main head: the racial injustice the black Americans were suffering and
the determination to win equality they should adopt. Part (2) is where we can find
the extended hypothetical illustration expressed in the parallel structure. In order to
make the black Americans more confident and courageous in the peaceful struggle
for racial equality, the speaker elaborately depicted a bright future based on his
imagination. This description would be definitely illustrative and appealing to the
large audience. Part (3) Indicates the application of the illustration to the main
head.*

Sample Analysis for Using Statistics

- The number of Singaporeans visiting China has increased from 18,000 in
1982 to 32,000 in 1984. With the establishment of direct air service between
China and Singapore this year, this flow of tourists will increase.

—Lee Kuan Yew

*Analysis: This is taken from the speech by Lee Kuan Yew, former Prime Minister of
Singapore in Beijing in September 1985. The growth of the number of Singaporean
tourists in China evidently illustrates, in one respect, the development of the friendly
exchange between these two counties.*

- In 1962, fewer than 4 million Americans had ever experimented with illegal
drugs. Today, more than 100 million have.

*Analysis: It is the use of figures that makes an appalling contrast, and warns
American and other people of the menace from drug abuse to human health. Such
a persuasive effect could not be achieved without the numbers.*

Sample Analysis for Using Testimony

- As we enter the twenty-first century, we should be reminded of the warning
Aristotle issued in his Politics: "For man, when perfected, is the best of
animals; but when separated from law and justice, he is the worst of all...
therefore, if we have no virtue, he is the most unholy and the most savage of
animals." With this in mind I would like to discuss my topic "The widening

gaps between the rich and the poor—the challenge of the twenty-first century".

—Andrew R. Cecil

Analysis: The great philosopher, Aristotle, is known to everyone. Quoting from a resourceful man like him can absolutely enhance the speaker's credibility and the persuasiveness of the speech. The topic the speaker intends to discuss is the gap between the rich and the poor, but it is related to a question about morality, that is, what role virtues such as generosity and compassion play in human relationships today and tomorrow. On this point, Aristotle's witty remarks are well-chosen and forceful. They work quite well at initiating and supporting the entire speech.

- Our passion for freedom led to the American Revolution, the first great uprising for human rights and independence against colonial rule. We knew each of us could not enjoy liberty for ourselves unless we were willing to share it with everyone else. And we knew our freedom could not be truly safe, unless all of us were protected by a body of laws that treated us equally. George Washington told us we would be bound together in a sacred brotherhood of free men. Abraham Lincoln defined the heart of American democracy when he said, "No man is good enough to govern another man without other's consent." These great principles have nourished the soul of America ...

—Ronald Reagan

Analysis: Notice both George Washington and Abraham Lincoln are cited: the remarks of the former are paraphrased while those of the latter are quoted directly. Because of their great reputation and historical influence, the remarks of the two presidents obviously enhance the speaker's idea, the idea traditionally held by Americans—all men are created equal.

With these illustrations, it is apparent that the use of supporting materials can convincingly show your listeners that you know well about your topic. The followings are the steps that may guide you to use support in your speech.

STEP 1. State the point (assertion) you wish to make/prove/illustrate.While this seems obvious, sometimes speakers begin with statistics or a story without indicating what their point is, assuming the audience will draw the right conclusion. The problem is that your audience may not see the point which you assume is obvious. You need to be clear, and make your point stand out as you deliver it, so the audience will recognize it as important.

STEP 2. Present supporting materials (one or more items) which clarify, illustrate, or prove (convince) your assertion. Use the support to develop your idea and take enough time to let the point "soak in".

STEP 3. Show how the supporting materials clarify or prove your assertion by summarizing the point, or explaining the link between support and assertion. At the very least you should remind listeners of your point after you present the support materials to reinforce what you want them to remember. This may seem repetitive to you but not to your audience. They may not get the assertion in step 1 and need a summary. Sometimes you may need to do more than just summarize. The audience may not be able to see how your support proves your point (This is especially true when the support is statistical). When that is possible, you should be sure to explain the link as well as summarize.

An example from a classroom speech using the 3 steps

Step 1. Cardiovascular disease, the nation's leading cause of death, is caused by inactivity.

Step 2. Clogged arteries and veins are a result of inactivity (example). Excess fat also caused by inactivity leads to a higher incidence of heart disease (explanation and example).

Step 3. Statistically, then, you will die at an earlier age if you do not exercise (internal summary).

 # 2.3 Analyzing Your Audience

2.3.1   Why Is Audience Analysis Important?

For of the three elements in speech-making—speaker, subject, and person addressed—it is the last one, the hearer that determines the speech's end and object.

—Aristotle

Speakers all know the importance of properly preparing materials in advance, but this is not enough to ensure that the speech or presentation is well received. When preparing a speech, one must also gather information about the audience members and their needs. A well-prepared speech given to the wrong audience can have the same effect as a poorly prepared speech given to the right audience. They can both fail terribly.

It is critical that your preparation efforts include some amount of audience analysis. Audience analysis is the process of examining information about the listeners who will hear our speech. Proper audience analysis will ensure that we give the right speech to the right audience. We analyze audiences every day as we speak to others or join in group conversations. Here's an example of how analyzing audience may work: Mike spent a glorious spring break at Daytona Beach. He and three friends piled in a car and headed for a week of adventure. When he returned from the beach, sunburned and fatigued from merrymaking, people asked how his holiday went. He described his escapades to his best friend, his mother, and his professor. To his best friend, he bragged, "We partied all night and slept on the beach all day. It was great!" He informed his mother, "It was good to relax after the hectic pace of college." And he told his professor, "It was mentally invigorating to have time to think things out." It was the same vacation, but how different the messages were! Mike analyzed his audiences and adapted his message to the different people he addressed.

The more we know and understand about our audience and their needs, the better we can prepare our speech to meet their needs. Actually, the stage fright or speech anxiety experienced by many speakers is due to lack of knowledge about the audience. The more we know about who we will be talking to, the more relaxed we will be when delivering our speech.

Using the word "A-U-D-I-E-N-C-E" as an acronym, some aspects of audience analysis categories can be defined.

Analysis—Who are they? How many will be there?

Understanding—What is their knowledge of the subject?

Demographics—What is their age, sex, educational background?

Interest—Why are they there? Who asks them to be there?

Environment—Where will you stand? Can they all see and hear you?

Needs—What are their needs? What are your needs as a speaker?

Customized—What specific needs do you need to address?

Expectations—What do they expect to learn or hear from you?

Your audience is not an innocent bystander who just happens to be in the room when you deliver your speech. They are an integral part of the communication path. Great delivery by a speaker does not guarantee a successful speech; **a successful speech is one where the audience receives the message.**

In order to elicit the best response from them, you need to determine (to the best of your ability) their interests and existing knowledge on the subject matter. You need to know your audience—at least enough to be able to predict how they think and what will connect with them. Taking the time to tailor a presentation early on during the planning stage will save you a lot of headaches in the long run as you prepare your speech.

2.3.2   How to Analyze Audience?

There are some key audience analysis factors.

1) Demographic information

Demographic information includes factors such as gender, age range, marital status, race and ethnicity, and socioeconomic status. These categories often underpin the individual's experiences and beliefs, so you should tailor your speech accordingly. In your public speaking class, you probably already know how many students are male and female, their approximate ages, and so forth. But how can you assess the demographics of an audience ahead of time if you have had no previous contact with them? In many cases, you can ask the person or organization that has invited you to speak; it's likely that they can tell you a lot about the demographics of the people who are expected to come to hear you. Of course, Using demographic factors to guide speech-making does not mean changing the goal of the speech for every different audience; rather, consider what pieces of information will be most important for members of different demographic groups.

2) Knowledge of the topic

You need to determine how much your audience already knows about your topic as an audience's knowledge can vary widely. Never overestimate the audience's knowledge of a topic. If you start speaking about complex algorithms for robotics, but the listeners are not familiar with technical concepts, they'll quickly lose interest and find something to distract themselves with. On the other hand, drastically underestimating the audience's knowledge may result in a speech that sounds condescending. Remember when you speak to an audience that is cognitively complex, your strategy must be different from the one you would use for an audience that is less educated in the topic. With a cognitively complex audience, you must acknowledge the overall complexity while stating that your focus will be on only one dimension. With an audience uninformed about your topic, that strategy in a persuasive speech could confuse them; they might well prefer a black-and-white message with no gray areas. You must decide whether it is ethical to represent your topic this way.

3) Audience size

Your speech will change depending on the size of the audience. In general, the larger the audience the more formal the presentation should be. In a typical class, your audience is likely to consist of twenty to thirty listeners. This audience size gives you the latitude to be relatively informal within the bounds of good judgment. It isn't too difficult to let each audience member feel as though you're speaking to him or her. However, with larger audiences, it's more difficult to reach out to each listener, and your speech will tend to be more formal, staying more strictly within its careful outline. Large audiences often require that you use a microphone and speak from an elevated platform.

4) Audience expectation

This is just as important as asking what core message you want to deliver. If you are passionate, but your audience doesn't care, your presentation will fail. (They will tune out.) If you deliver what the audience desires, but you don't care, your presentation will fail. (Your delivery will be flat.) If you attempt to speak on a topic where you have no expertise or experience to draw from, your presentation will fail. (Your content will be empty and shallow.) However, if you find a topic where you have both expertise and passion, and the audience is interested, you will succeed.

5) Physical setting

Presentation setting, such as what time you are presenting and the style of the conference room, will influence audience's ability and desire to listen. Finding out ahead of time the different environment and situational factors. In your classroom, conditions might not be ideal, but at least the setting is familiar. If you will be giving your presentation somewhere else, it is a good idea to visit the venue ahead of time if possible and make note of any factors that will affect how you present your speech. In any case, be sure to arrive well in advance of your speaking time so that you will have time to check if the microphone works, to test out any visual aids, and to request any needed adjustments in lighting, room ventilation, or other factors to eliminate distractions and make your audience more comfortable. In addition, take into account the way that the setting will affect audience attention and participation. If you're scheduled to speak at the end of the day, you'll have to make the speech more entertaining and appear more enthusiastic to keep their attention.

2.3.3 How to Adapt to Audience?

Audience adaptation is the process of ethically using the information you have gathered when analyzing your audience to help your audience clearly understand your message. If you only analyze your audience but don't use the information to customize your message, the information you've gathered will be of little value. Using your skill to learn about your listeners and then to adapt to them can help you maintain your listeners' attention and make them more receptive to your ideas.

When you think of your audience, don't think of some undifferentiated mass of people waiting to hear your message. Instead, think of individuals. Public speaking is the process of speaking to a group of individuals, each with a unique point of view. Your challenge as an audience-centered public speaker is to find out as much as you can about these individuals. From your knowledge of the individuals, you can then develop a general profile of your listeners.

When you are speaking in public, you should ask audience-centered questions. Several key questions can help you formulate an effective approach to your audience:

To whom am I speaking?

What does my audience expect from me?

What topic would be most suitable for my audience?

What is my objective?

What kind of information should I share with my audience?

How should I present the information to them?

How can I gain and hold their attention?

What kind of examples would work best?

What language or linguistic differences do audience members have?

What method of organizing information will be most effective?

The audience-centered speaker will adjust his or her topic, purpose, central idea, main ideas, supporting materials, organization, and even delivery of the speech so as to get the message across Remember that audience adaptation goes through the whole speech process.

1) Audience adaptation before the speech

Keeping your audience in mind basically involves two things: (1) assessing how your audience is likely to respond to what you will say in your speech and (2) adjusting what you are saying to make it as clear, appropriate, and convincing as possible.

2) Audience adaptation during the speech

Even when you did the perfect preparation work, you still will have many kinds of emergencies and changes in the audience. In this kind of situation, be calm. Then try to adjust to the new environment (size, visual aids, time limit). Finally, be sure to pay attention to the audience's reactions during the speech.

3) Audience adaptation after the speech

After you have given your speech, you're not finished adapting to your audience. It is important to evaluate your audience's positive or negative response to your message. Why? Because this evaluation can help you prepare your next speech. Post-speech analysis helps you polish your speaking skill, regardless of whether you will face the same audience again. From that analysis, you can learn whether your examples were clear and your message was accepted by your listeners. Some speakers keep journals of their speeches, audiences and responses. This kind of post-speech reflection will, without any doubt, help you to become a more effective speaker next time.

Examples of Adapting Your Message to Different Types of Audiences

Type of Audience	Example	How to Be Audience-Centered
Captive	Students in a public speaking class	Find out who will be in your speaking class and use this knowledge to adapt your message to them.
Uninterested	Junior high students attending a lecture on retirement benefits	Make it a high priority to tell your listeners why your message should be of interest to them. Remind your listeners throughout your speech how your message relates to their lives.
Unfavorable	Students who attend a lecture by the university president explaining why tuition fees will increase 15 percent next year	Be realistic in what you expect to accomplish; acknowledge their opposing point of view; consider using facts to refute misconceptions they may hold.

Key Takeaways of This Chapter

★ Selecting a topic is a process. We often start by selecting a broad area of knowledge and then narrowing the topic to one that is manageable for a given speech situation.

★ When finalizing a specific purpose for your speech, always ask yourself four basic questions: (1) Does the topic match my intended general purpose? (2) Is the topic appropriate for my audience? (3) Is the topic appropriate for the given speaking context? and (4) Can I reasonably hope to inform or persuade my audience in the time frame I have for the speech?

★ The reasons to use support are: to clarify content, to increase speaker credibility, and to make the speech more vivid. A good piece of support should be accurate, authoritative, current, and unbiased.

★ Systematically think through the support you have accumulated through your research. Examine the accumulated support to ensure that a variety of forms of support are used. Choose appropriate forms of support depending on the speech context or audience. Make sure all the support is relevant to the specific purpose of your speech and to your audience. Don't go overboard using so much support that the audience is overwhelmed. Finally, don't manipulate supporting materials.

★ Audience analysis should guide your choice of a topic so that you select a topic that is relevant and useful to them. In addition, audience analysis requires that you adapt to the needs of your audience; this includes considering cultural diversity, making your message clear, avoiding offensive remarks, and speaking with sincerity.

Part II

Exercises

I. Discuss the following questions.

1. Discuss the principles of choosing a good speech topic. How do they best relate to the speech you previously presented in class?

2. It is important to evaluate your audience's response to your message. Name four audience responses you can use to analyze your audience after your speech. Describe different strategies for evaluating these four types of responses and how each would aid you in preparation for your next speech.

3. Think about your audience in your public-speaking class. What is this audience's demographic composition, and how would this influence your speech-making process?

4. What are two advantages and two potential drawbacks of using the Internet for researching your topic?

II. Choose the correct answer.

1. Selecting a speech topic is often the _____ part of preparing a speech.
   A. easiest   B. most difficult
   C. least important   D. least time-consuming

2. Which of the following is NOT a question to ask when selecting a speech topic?
   A. What does this audience expect me to talk about?
   B. What is my thesis statement?
   C. What topics should I avoid with this audience?
   D. What topics will be most appropriate for my audience?

3. Which of the following is good advice when selecting a topic?
   A. Be careful that there are many boring topics.
   B. Choose a complex topic so the audience won't get bored.
   C. Choose a historical event that you are quite familiar with.
   D. Make sure you are interested in the topic.

4. After you have determined your general purpose, your next step in the process of selecting a speech topic is to _____.
   A. formulate your specific purpose   B. generate a list of possible topics
   C. focus on the topic   D. word your thesis statement

5. Which of the following is NOT one of the questions to consider when selecting a topic?
   A. Is this topic of interest or importance to people in general?
   B. Am I interested or likely to become interested in this topic?
   C. Am I likely to find enough authoritative supporting material in the time I have to work on the speech?
   D. Do I understand the topic well enough to undertake and interpret my research?

6. A speech in which a speaker tells the audience how fiber optics work has a general purpose to _____.
   A. convince   B. persuade   C. inform   D. actuate

7. A speech in which a speaker wants the audience to agree that capital punishment deters crime has as its general purpose to _____.
   A. entertain   B. convince   C. persuade   D. inform

8. "To persuade the audience of the harms of sexist language" is an example of

   _____.
   A. a speech title   B. a thesis statement
   C. a general purpose statement   D. a specific purpose statement

9. Which of the following is NOT suggested as one of the ways to find out the interests of your classmates for a speech?
   A. Brainstorm.
   B. Issue surveys.
   C. Interview them.
   D. Use audience analysis strategies.

10. Which of the following is NOT one of the three parts of a specific purpose?
    A. The general purpose.
    B. What you want the audience to do.
    C. The individuals to whom the speech is addressed.
    D. What you want to accomplish in the speech.

11. Which of the following is NOT appropriate when choosing support for a speech?
    A. Making sure sources are credible.

B. Conducting interviews or contacting experts.

C. Making use of the library.

D. Using strong but unidentified evidence.

12. The first source of information for a presentation is usually _____.

    A. oneself   B. the library

    C. another person   D. an expert

13. A speech on Gillette Industries' testing of animals would NOT be appropriate for _____.

    A. scientific researchers

    B. kindergartners

    C. PETA (People for the Ethical Treatment of Animals) members

    D. a college class

14. Which of the following is NOT a purpose that supporting materials for speeches should accomplish?

    A. Support claims.   B. amplify ideas

    C. Clarify points.   D. add interestingness

15. A pharmaceutical researcher testifies about the effects of a specific medication. What type of testimony is this?

    A. Expert testimony.   B. Peer testimony.

    C. Hypothetical testimony.   D. Medical testimony.

III. Each of the following statements violates at least one of the criteria for effective supporting materials. Identify the flaw or flaws in each statement.

1. A random poll of 265 people taken recently in Washington, D.C, showed that 78 percent of those interviewed opposed term limitations on U.S. senators and representatives. Clearly, then, the American people opposed such limitations.

2. It is just not true that violence on television has an influence on crimes committed by young people. All my friends watch television, and none of us have ever committed a violent crime.

3. As Harrison Ford said in a recent interview, America must act now to protect its national parks. If we do not take actions right away, Ford said, the park system may be permanently destroyed.

4. According to a survey conducted on Chinese people's online shopping behavior, most people prefer Tao Bao's service, compared to Jing Dong or other service providers.

IV. **The following specific purpose statements are not appropriate. Write an appropriate one for each.**

1. Inappropriate: Art collection.
    More appropriate: _____

2. Inappropriate: Is recycling necessary?
    More appropriate: _____

3. Inappropriate: To persuade my audience that they need to live a healthy life and become volunteers.
    More appropriate: _____

4. Inappropriate: To inform my audience about my hometown.
    More appropriate: _____

5. Inappropriate: To inform my audience about some knowledge of coffee.
    More appropriate: _____

V. **Read the five statements given and indicate those with which you agree and disagree. Discuss the type(s) of supporting materials you would like to use to support your positions.**
   A. The fear of giving a speech can be reduced.
   B. IQ is more important than EQ.
   C. Life in the country is more fun than that in the city.
   D. Beijing is an excellent place to visit.
   E. E-books will replace library books in the future.

VI. **Read the following article on surveillance cameras. Locate passages from the article which would prove/support the following claims.**
   A. Electronic surveillance is easier than ever before.
   B. Much electronic surveillance is unethical.
   C. Businesses use electric surveillance frequently.
   D. Electronic surveillance is common around the world.
   E. Fear of violent crimes makes Americans willing to accept electronic surveillance.
   F. Electronic surveillance is unregulated.
   G. Electronic surveillance invades one's privacy.
   H. Electronic surveillance is an effective crime fighter.

Surveillance cameras move into locker rooms, money machines, and lawsuits.

A male security guard uses store surveillance cameras to zoom in on the cleavage of an unsuspecting JC Penney sales manager as she works the floor. Police in the Chicago suburb of Rosemont can now spy 24 hours a day on visitors to the town's prized fountain and gardens who may be stealing random wallets ... or moonlit smooches. More and more Americans are blindly mugging for hidden cameras as they sit in their offices, ring their neighbors' doorbells, or drive through traffic lights and tollbooths. As the electronic eyes shrink in size, Big Brother grows even bigger, leaving citizens with a dilemma: is more security worthless privacy? Are Americans willing to let government poke its lens into their business if it means more streets are safe for shopping?

The simple answer is, yes, at least for now. The fear of violent crime is too great, and the memory of terrorist attacks is too fresh. A bank ATM camera filmed a Ryder truck outside Oklahoma City's federal office building just before the blast last April that killed 167 people. That cue helped police track down Timothy McVeigh. The same month a store camera captured the brutal slayings of two pawnshop employees in Wheat Ridge, Colorado. Within 24 hours after the film was aired on a local television station, the killer was identified. He was caught a week later. In an ironic twist, the convicted killer was ordered to live out consecutive life sentences with a copy of the videotaped murder in his cell, to conceivably be viewed over and over and over again. "A video camera can't change its testimony, "says Brian Terrett, a spokesman for the county's office of the district attorney. "A video camera can't forget what somebody looks like."

But if cameras help snag violent criminals, they can also turn into instruments of abuse. Workers at Boston's Sheraton Hotel discovered that a tiny lens lodged in a pin-size hole in one of their personal lockers was recording their every move. Bradley Fair, a waiter filmed with nothing on but his jockstrap, is one plaintiff in a pending lawsuit against the company for invasion of privacy. "I worked really hard for them and went the extra mile," says Fair. "Then I was spied upon. This really soils it all." A lawyer for Sheraton defends the company's action, saying that it was investigating suspected drug use by its workers.

In Concord, California, Katheryn Hernandez, the JC Penney sales manager, filed suit in August 1993 against the company when she discovered that a guard had shown a tape he made of her using the store ceiling cameras. The case was settled out of court. Says Cliff Palefsky, Hernandez's attorney: "They were zooming in on her breasts. It was like watching 'Animal House', so childish. Enough to give any woman the creeps."

Creeping phenomenon: The wired workplace is a creeping phenomenon, say critics, because there are no federal regulations, and no state statutes, no labor laws to protect workers against video surveillance. A bill was introduced in the U.S. Senate two years ago that would require employers to inform workers about cameras in the bathrooms or locker rooms. It was first attacked by the business community and later stymied by congress. "This is all leading to a total-surveillance society," says Craig Cornish, of the National Employment Lawyers Association.

That's an exaggeration, but the industry is thriving. Closed-circuit television businesses will pull in an estimated $2.1 billion in 1995, according to STAT Resources, Inc., a Brookline, Massachusetts research firm. Revenues by companies that make, install and service cameras are expected to increase 62 percent by the year 2000.

The business is growing, and the cameras are shrinking. Once fairly large and clunky, surveillance cameras now can be as small as a pair of dice. Like gadgets from James Bond's cache, they can be lodged almost anywhere—in plants, books, fire detectors, exit signs and overhead in department store domes. Common household items like baseball caps, purses, ties, and flip-up cellular phones can also house the detective devices. Imminently available are badge-size cameras, like the PVSS (Personal Video Surveillance System), which projects images of arrests to video recorders in a patrol car.

The small cubes are no longer stationary. They can pan, tilt, and zoom. The units are like motion detectors. When activated, they click on the cameras that then feed images to monitors in another room. The next challenge is to shrink the camera even more—to the size of a computer chip—so it can be stuck in ever more private places. But the smaller cameras make for blurrier images. According to Albert Janjigian of STAT Resources, the software is being developed to bring those fuzzy pictures into sharp focus.

This is not just an American phenomenon. In England, police use surveillance cameras in more than 90 town centers. Last week police in Liverpool switched on an elaborate system, featuring 20 cameras that can produce nighttime color pictures, magnified up to 15 times. Police Superintendent Howard Parry told The Times of London that this "system's like 20 officers on duty 24 hours a day will make a note of everything, never take a holiday and are very rarely off sick." This is no surprise to listeners of soft-rock radio. As Sting sang when he was with the group Police, "Every breath you take, every move you make, I'll be watching you."

VII. Never neglect speaking ethical issues. Discuss the situation with your partner and provide your thoughts on the questions given.

Mary has just received an e-mail from her boss. It was read like this: "Mary, I need you to prepare a presentation on what our company has done in the past year for Mrs. Green. She's old, keep it simple. Leave out any of the complex material because it will probably just bore her anyways. —John."

Mary stared at her screen and wondered to what extent she should follow John's advice and "keep it simple". She only met Mrs. Green twice, but she always seemed to be pretty knowledgeable about the inner workings of the firm. Sure Mrs. Green wasn't an expert in the field, but should she be treated like a helpless little old lady? Not only is that sexist, it's completely ageist! On the other hand, John's words may have been chosen poorly, but maybe all Mrs. Green really wanted was a quick snapshot of what's going on here?

Mary sat in silence for a few minutes, opened up PowerPoint, and tried to figure out the best way to proceed.

(1) Do you think John's e-mail to Mary expressed unethical audience analysis? Why or why not?

(2) How do you think Mary should proceed?

Chapter **3**

Speech Organizing and Outlining

Part I

How to Organize and Outline a Speech

1. The one who is incapable of making an overall arrangement is incompetent to cope with any constitutional part.（不谋全局者，不足谋一域。）

——陈澹然《寤言二·迁都建藩议》

2. Good design is making something intelligible and memorable. Great design is making something memorable and meaningful.

—*Dieter Rams*

In order to make your speech as effective as possible, it needs to be organized into logical patterns. Information will need to be presented in a way your audience can understand. Arguably, an organization of a speech allows you and your listeners to see what ideas you have and to put mental "hands" on the most important ones. In fact, when students explain what they hope to learn from their speech classes, they almost always put "the ability to organize my ideas more effectively" near the top of the list. This ability is especially vital for speech-making.

A **well-organized speech** can:

- make it easier for you to remember what you want to talk about. When you use a predictable pattern, the next thing to talk about seems more natural.

- make it easier for the audience to follow your message. They're able to predict, in general, what will come next and make sense of it, so they can spend their time listening to your speech rather than trying to figure out how your ideas fit together.

- help to enhance your credibility. The consensus of research is that audiences think speakers with clearly organized presentations know what they're talking about better than disorganized speakers. Your credibility is very important to your success as a speaker, and you ought to do whatever you can to enhance it.

In a word, a well-structured speech can usually balance information, knowledge, and wisdom as you are building a house: lay a strong foundation of information, build knowledge on top of it, and finish the house with a roof of wisdom.

3.1   Three Major Parts of a Speech

Most good writing must have structure and a good speech is no exception. The first step in developing a strong sense of speech organization is to gain command of the three basic parts of a speech. i.e., introduction, body, and conclusion and the strategic role of each. In the introduction, the topic is introduced to the audience and you put before the audience the main points of your speech. You inform them what areas related to the topic will be covered in the speech. In the body of the speech, each issue is discussed in detail. In the conclusion, you summarize the main points of the speech and emphasize the take-home points again.

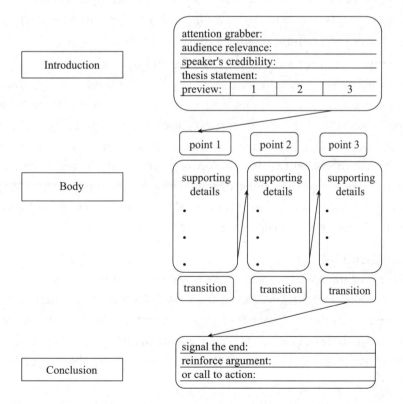

1) Introduction

The introduction section of a speech sets the tone for the entire speech and lets the listener know what the speech is about. In the first thirty seconds of your speech, you must grab the attention of the audience, and engage their interest in what you will say in your speech. This can be achieved in several ways. For example, you could raise a thought-provoking question, make an interesting or controversial statement, recite a relevant quotation or even recount a joke.

The following are the steps usually found in an introduction.

(1) Attention Step: This step is used to grab the attention of the audience through the use of attention grabbers, such as a shocking statement, a funny story or joke, etc.

(2) Benefit Step (audience relevance): This could be a statement outlining how the speech will benefit the listeners. For example, it will make them gain some new knowledge or help them live healthier.

(3) Thesis Statement & Preview Step: This could be a sentence or two encapsulating the important points of a speech to give audiences a quick preview of what the entire speech will be about.

2) Body

The body of a speech is your main text, and the area where you deliver the major points of your speech. The body of your speech will consume the largest amount of time to present and it is the opportunity for you to elaborate on facts, evidence, examples, and opinions that support your thesis statement.

In the context of your speech, a "point" could be a statement about a product, a joke about the bridegroom or a fond memory of the subject of a eulogy. The points should be organized so that related points follow one another and each point builds upon the previous one. This will also give your speech a more logical progression, and make the job of the listener a far easier one. Don't try to overwhelm your audience with countless points. It is better to make a small number of points well than to have too many points, none of which are made satisfactorily. Keep in mind that when moving from one point to another, transitions should be applied among different points to make the speech more cohesive.

3) Conclusion

The closing of the speech is where the speaker wraps up the speech and, in some instances, provides a conclusion. Presenting a well-thought-out conclusion to make a lasting impression on the audience is of vital importance. In the closing, speakers are expected to recap all of the earlier points made in the body of the speech and outline them in the order they were given, so they remain fresh in the listener's mind. You can also provide a concluding thought or moral here, to leave the audience with one resounding message from your speech.

Like your opening, the closing of your speech must contain some of your strongest material. You should view the closing of your speech as an opportunity to:

- summarize the main points of your speech and signal the end.

- reinforce argument by providing some further food for thought for your listeners and leave them with positive memories of your speech (e.g., with good wishes to the Bride and Groom, with fond memories of a departed friend, with admiration for winners and losers at an awards ceremony).

- call to action with a final thought/emotion.

3.2   Organizing Main Points

3.2.1   Determine Your Main Points

The main points of any speech are the key pieces of information or arguments contained within the talk or presentation. In other words, the main points are what your audience should remember from your talk. Unlike facts or examples, main points are broad and can be encapsulated in just a sentence or two and represent the big ideas you want to convey to your audience.

The process of organizing the body of a speech begins when the main points are determined. The main points are the central features of your speech. You should select them carefully, phrase them precisely, and arrange them strategically.

For example, here are the main points of a student speech about the medical uses of hypnosis:

Specific purpose:

To inform my audience about the major uses of hypnosis.

Central Idea:

The major uses of hypnosis today are to control pain in medical surgery, to help people stop smoking, and to help students improve their academic performance.

Main points:

Hypnosis is used in surgery as an adjunct to chemical anesthesia.

Hypnosis is used to help people stop smoking.

Hypnosis is used to help students improve their academic performance.

As revealed from this example, the three main points form the skeleton of the body of the speech. If there are three major uses of hypnosis for medical purposes, then logically there can be three main points in the speech.

Sometimes main points are evident from your specific purpose statement and they may be easy to project from the statement. In other words, they will emerge as you research the speech and evaluate your findings. Suppose your specific purpose is "to persuade my audience that China should not approve proposals for online voting", you know that each main point in the speech will present a reason why online voting should not be instituted in China, but you aren't sure how many main points there will be or what they will be. As you research and study the topic, you decide there are two major reasons to support your view and then each of these reasons will become a main point in your speech.

Tips for Preparing Main Points

- Limit the number of main points: The number of major points you can develop in a speech depends on the time you have, the complexity of the topic, and the audience's knowledge of the subject. But many speakers find that a three-point structure works best. If your speech has too many points, your audience will struggle to recognize the most important ideas.

- Keep main points separate: Each main point in a speech should be clearly independent of the other main points.

- Make sure each main point contributes to the topic: The main points should not go beyond the focus of the speech. For example, if your speech concerns with the local specialty of your hometown, don't introduce irrelevant information such as the climate or historical changes there.

- Balance the amount of time devoted to main points: Because your main points are so important, you want to be sure they all receive enough emphasis to be clear and convincing. However, the time devoted to each main point may not be exactly the same. Balance among the main points of your speech is another good technique.

- Use concise and simple language to phrase main points: The audience of a speech has only a limited opportunity to process information. If you phrase your main points as complex sentences, you may lose your audience.

3.2.2 Organizational Patterns of Speeches

Giving a well-received and clearly understood speech is the goal of every public speaker. For that to happen, you need to have a clear road map leading to your destination. How are you going to organize the main points? Here several basic patterns are introduced.

(1) Chronological or Time Sequence

(2) Spatial or Geographical

(3) Logical or Topical

(4) Comparative

(5) Problem-Solution

(6) Cause-Effect

Patterns	Explanations	Examples
Chronological/ Time Sequence pattern	Use this pattern when your main points are connected by "time" or you want to tell about events in the order in which they happen, from the earliest to the latest.	**Specific purpose**: to inform the audience of the steps for a successful job interview **Main points**: (1) Prepare thoroughly. (2) Communicate effectively. (3) Follow up immediately.
Spatial/ Geographical pattern	Use this pattern when your main points cover a certain physical space. This involves organizing things or events according to their position in space or to simplify it, from top to bottom, or bottom to top. Note: The spatial style is an especially useful organization style when the importance of main points is derived from its location or directional focus.	**Specific purpose**: to inform the audience about the design of the Eiffel tower **Main points**: (1) The lowest section of the tower contains the entrance, a gift shop, and a restaurant. (2) The middle section of the tower consists of stairs and elevators that lead to the top. (3) The top section of the tower includes an observation deck with a spectacular view of Paris.

(to be continued)

(continued)

Patterns	Explanations	Examples
Logical/Topical pattern	Use this pattern when you have several ideas to present and one idea naturally follows on from another. You may break your topic down into parts and place them in the order that you decide on. Since this pattern of organization does not require a time sequence, you decide what you tell first. Note: This is a useful pattern for informative speeches.	**Specific purpose**: to inform the audience about the composition of a Newspaper Company **Main points:** (1) The advertising department sells display advertisements to local and national businesses. (2) The editorial department produces the written content of the newspaper, including feature stories. (3) The production department lays out the pages and manages pre-press work such as distilling the pages and processing colors. (4) The business department processes payments from advertisers, employee paperwork, and the bi-weekly payroll.
Comparative pattern	Use this pattern when you need to discuss the similarities and differences between two or more things. Some topics that are routinely comparatively spoken about include different cultures, different types of transportation, and even different types of tea.	**Specific purpose**: to inform the audience about differences between Eastern and Western cultures **Main points:** (1) Eastern cultures tend to be more collectivistic. (2) Western cultures tend to be more individualistic. (3) Eastern cultures tend to treat health issues holistically. (4) Western cultures tend to treat health issues more acutely.

(to be continued)

(continued)

Patterns	Explanations	Examples
Problem-Solution pattern	Use this pattern when you have two main points: one point is about a problem, and the second is the solution to the problem. Note: This pattern is often used in persuasive speeches.	**Specific purpose**: to persuade the audience to vote for a political candidate **Main points:** (1) The United States is facing an energy crisis because we cannot produce enough energy ourselves to sustain the levels of activity needed to run the country (problem). (2) The current administration has failed to invest enough resources in renewable energy practices (problem). (3) We can help create a more stable situation if we work to produce renewable forms of energy within the United States (solution). (4) If you vote for me, I will ensure that renewable energy creation is a priority (solution).
Cause-Effect pattern	Use this pattern when you have two main points: the first point is about the cause of a problem, and the second is the effects of the problem. Note: This pattern is useful when you need to share the results of a new program, discuss how one act leads to another, or discuss the positive/negative outcomes of taking some action.	**Specific purpose**: to persuade my audience to quit smoking **Main points:** (1) Smoking causes several health problems (cause). • Smoking causes lung cancer. • Smoking causes emphysema. • Smoking causes heart disease. (2) If you quit smoking, you will reduce your risk of health problems (effect). • Lung cancer risk is lowered for those who stop smoking. • Emphysema risk is lowered for those who stop smoking. • Heart disease risk is lowered for those who stop smoking.

Monroe's Motivated Sequence

In addition to the above-mentioned patterns, Monroe's Motivated Sequence (MMS) is an organizational pattern used to develop a sense of want or need in the audience, satisfy that want or need, and to help the audience become enthused about the advantages of that solution. Developed by American psychologist Alan Monroe at Purdue University in the mid-1930s, Monroe's Motivated Sequence is a five-step speech outline that aims to inspire or persuade the audience to take action. This pattern is simple and has a clear structure, making it an effective method to organize and deliver persuasive speeches.

The five steps of MMS are as follows:

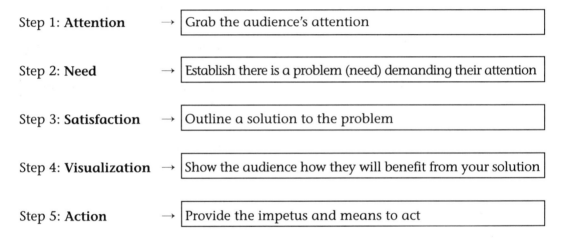

Step 1: **Attention** → Grab the audience's attention

Step 2: **Need** → Establish there is a problem (need) demanding their attention

Step 3: **Satisfaction** → Outline a solution to the problem

Step 4: **Visualization** → Show the audience how they will benefit from your solution

Step 5: **Action** → Provide the impetus and means to act

3.2.3 Using Connectives

Connectives are broad terms that encompass several types of statements or phrases. They are generally designed to help "connect" parts of your speech to make it easier for audience members to follow. Connectives are tools that add to the planned redundancy, and they are methods for helping the audience listen, retain information, and follow your structure. In fact, it is one thing to have a well-organized speech and it is another for the audience to be able to "consume" or understand that organization. When a speaker uses connectives properly, the speech will flow smoothly and make complex ideas understandable. Connectives can include the following four types: **transitions**, **internal previews**, **internal summaries**, and **signposts**. Connectives, when combined effectively, allow a speech to flow smoothly through each idea.

1) Transitions

Transitions are words or phrases that prepare your audience for understanding the relationship between what you just said and what you are going to say. The following examples indicate the use of this connective.

(1) *In addition to* being a problem nationwide, suicide is *also* a problem on our campus.

(2) *So much for* the problem; *what about* the solution?

(3) *Now that you have seen* what a serious problem illiteracy is, *you may be asking yourself*: "How can I help?"

(4) *Since we know* a little more about what memory is, *let us turn to* the relationship between the human brain and the process of memory.

(5) *This next point* will be of special interest to all parents.

2) Internal Previews

Internal previews direct the audience to what areas will be covered next. Internal previews generally appear once the speaker has finished a transition and after a new main point. The speaker simply previews the subpoints which make up the point being addressed. The following examples show how internal previews lead the audience into the areas to be discussed.

(1) We can help solve the problem by *knowing how to identify the symptoms and knowing whom to contact for help.*

(2) Experts agree that *there are three main causes of amusement park tragedies: equipment failure, operator failure, and rider failure.*

(3) Once your resume is prepared, the next step in job seeking is to prepare a list of specific job openings. *The three best sources here are newspaper listings, your campus placement service, and word-of-mouth recommendations.* We will examine the pros and cons of each of these.

3) Internal Summaries

Internal summaries are the flip side of internal previews. Rather than indicating what subpoints are to follow in the speech, internal summaries remind the listeners what subpoints have been discussed. Internal summaries are excellent ways to reinforce and clarify ideas which are essential for the audience to remember. The following are examples of internal summaries.

(1) Therefore, anyone can help solve the problem by *knowing how to identify the symptoms, and knowing whom to contact about helping them.*

(2) I've told you *why we need to reduce our dependence on the automobile,* and I hope I've convinced you that *a light rail system is the best alternative for our city.*

(3) So far I have shown *how the designers of King Tut's burial tomb used the antechamber to scare away intruders* and the *second chamber to prepare royal visitors for the experience of seeing the sarcophagus.*

4) Signposts

Signposts are phrases within a main point indicating the speaker is moving from one subordinate point to the next short statement and tell the audience where the speaker is in the speech. Oftentimes, signposts are numbers of words which suggest that what the speaker is about to say is important. Generally speaking, enumerating the subordinate points (that is, saying "First... Second... Third") is more clear than using words such as "another" or "next", because the numbers provide a more noticeable cue to the audience that you're changing ideas. When you say "another" or similar words it often seems like you're still explaining the previous point when you're really moving to the next. Better signposts will include both a number and a reminder of the general category of which the ideas are part. So, instead of just saying, "Third..." it is more clear to say, "The third way you can save money while going to school is..." The following are examples of signposts.

(1) Let's **first** take a look at the nature of the problem.

(2) The **third** warning sign is giving away one's possessions.

(3) And **first, the most important thing** to remember is child custody battle injures the children.

(4) **To begin with**, we must examine the engine of the car.

(5) **The final point** we should consider is...

3.3 Outlining a Speech

An outline is a way to organize your ideas logically and clearly. It is a blueprint for your speech and has very important functions. It can:

- highlight the key logical elements and the key structural elements;
- link these elements together in a sequence;
- map out the transitions between elements;
- test the scope of a speaker's content and the logical relations among parts of the speech;
- test relevance of supporting ideas;
- check balance of proportion of speech;
- serve as notes during delivery of speech.

3.3.1 Six Main Parts of a Speech Outline

1) The statement of the specific purpose and central idea
These are important so that you are clear on your purpose.

These typically belong to the top of your outline to keep you focused.

2) Introduction

The introduction has five main parts:

- attention-getter
- statement of relevance/audience significance
- establishment of credibility
- orientation to central idea
- preview of points

The introduction may be written in paragraph form or using the five points.

3) Transition and summaries

Transitions help your audience see the connection between major points of the speech.

Summaries remind the audience what you've said so far.

4) Body

The body should contain the central idea of your speech.

- The body is often considered the central part of the speech.
- The body should be clearly organized.

It should be divided into two to five distinct points connected by transitions.

- The main points should be of roughly equal length.
- If you give too much time and space to one point, your speech will seem lopsided and unbalanced to listeners.

5) Conclusion

The conclusion should summarize your main points.

The conclusion should end on a note of finality.

The conclusion can refer back to the introduction.

6) List of works cited

This should follow an accepted citation format (e.g., MLA or APA).

This should contain all sources used in the speech itself.

3.3.2   Steps of Organizing a Speech

Step one: to **identify ideas that could go into your speech.** You would like to create a list you can choose from. The list can involve general ideas, specific evidence, stories, definitions, analogies, and almost anything else to do with your topic and the way it relates to the audience.

Step two: to **identify the major subdivisions or facts of the topic**. You should separate the materials listed in the first step and put them into groups. You might have lots of groups or only a few, but you try to group all the aspects of the topic that you could talk about in your speech into a few major ideas.

Step three: to **decide which subdivisions are essential to your purpose**. You have to decide which ideas help you achieve your purpose and eliminate those you don't need. If you have too little material, you may want to expand your goal and if you have too much, you may want to focus on your purpose more.

Step four: to **organize the major subdivisions and supporting material**. You should choose the pattern that you believe will help you communicate with the audience and achieve your purpose the best, and decide where each major subdivision should go. One idea you should know about choosing a pattern is that a particular speech might include more than one type of pattern, but one pattern should dominate.

Step five: Once you have the major subdivisions and supporting material in a general order, the fifth step in organizing your speech is to **outline your speech**.

Step six: After you've outlined your speech you are ready to go back through it and complete the sixth step in organizing your speech, which is to add transitions and signposts.

3.3.3 Sample Preparation Outline

An Example of Informative Speech Outline Using Topic Pattern

Topic: The Kentucky Fried Rat and Other Tall Tales
Specific Purpose: To inform my audience what urban legends are and why they exist.
Central Idea: An urban legend is a story spread through word of mouth that serves a purpose in our society.
Introduction   (1) **(Introducing the topic)** Have you heard the one about the fried rat found at Kentucky Fried Chicken?   (2) **(Establish credibility)** I have studied urban legends for the last few years because they are so fascinating.   (3) **(Central idea, preview)** In order to better understand this phenomenon, let me explain what an urban legend is and what purpose it serves in our society.   **(Transition:** First, let me explain what urban legends are.)

(to be continued)

(continued)

Body

(1) Urban legends are stories which are spread primarily through word of mouth and they are widespread.

- Urban legends are spread by word of mouth.

    a. Friend of a Friend (FOAF)

    b. Usually not recorded

- Urban legends are widespread.

    a. Occur throughout the country

    b. Situation may change slightly

(**Transition**: Now that you know what we are dealing with, you are probably wondering why these stories exist.)

(2) Urban legends serve four main functions.

- They teach us a lesson.
- They allow us to discuss common fears in a non-threatening way.
- They give us the opportunity to have villains and heroes.
- They provide traditional entertainment, i.e., storytelling.

(**Transition**: So obviously there are some fairly important reasons for the existence of these stories.)

Conclusion

(1) To summarize, urban legends, which are spread by word of mouth and frequently involve violence or tragedy. They also serve four main functions: teaching lessons, allowing discussion of fears, allowing discussion of villains and heroes, and providing entertainment.

(2) After this, I hope you'll never react to the Kentucky Fried Rat story the same way!

References

List your references such as books consulted, websites visited or any material cited from a source.

An Example of Persuasive Speech Outline Using MMS Pattern

Topic: Random Acts of Kindness

Specific Purpose: To persuade my audience to partake in random acts of kindness.

Central Idea: Partaking in random acts of kindness can brighten someone's day, save someone's life, and even change the world.

(to be continued)

(continued)

Introduction

The Attention Step

(1) **(Introducing the topic)** So how many times have you stopped to help someone pick up the books they dropped? Or paused to thank a housekeeper for keeping your hall so clean? Asked to speak to the manager of a restaurant because you had a great waitress?

(2) **(Establishing credibility)** I have recently become interested in random acts of kindness and by reading several books on the subject, I have learned more about the impact these acts can have on people's lives.

(3) **(Previewing)** Random acts of kindness can brighten someone's day, save someone's life, maybe even change the world.

(**Transition**: So why do we need random acts of kindness?)

The Need Step

(1) Throughout the nation, throughout the world, people are having bad days.

- In fact, 17.5 million Chinese suffer from depression each year.
- How many times have you heard about people in the news who were so distraught or depressed that they decided to kill a few people?
- And I'm sure all of you can recall having a bad day or feeling unhappy.

(2) As college students, we tend to get wrapped up in the stress and deadlines of our everyday life.

- We forget to take the time to offer a compliment to others.
- We are often in too much of a hurry to stop and help someone in need.
- When we are in need of help and can't get it, we may become unhappy.

(**Transition**: Now that you know what we are dealing with, you are probably wondering why these stories exist.)

(3) Unhappiness leads to more unhappiness.

- For instance, a teacher having a bad day might yell at a student.
- The student may then go back to the dorm and yell at his/her roommate.
- The roommate then yells at his/her friend. It's a chain reaction.

(**Transition**: But there is a way to break a link in this chain. The smallest effort can stop this chain reaction in its tracks and even reverse it. And every one of you can do it.)

The Satisfaction Step

(1) By partaking in random acts of kindness, you can change someone's day for the better, give someone a boost of confidence, possibly even save a life or eventually change the world.

- There are so many ways to be kind.

    a. You could tell the next worker you see what a great job he/she's doing.

    b. Pick up and return that pen the person walking in front of you dropped.

(to be continued)

(continued)

c. Thank the cafeteria worker for the superior service.

d. Compliment a friend on a quality or a classmate on his/her speaking performance.

- Just think of the things you could do for others or say to others that will brighten their day.

(Transition: These are only a few examples of kind acts that you can do.)

(2) According to a Greek proverb, "Kindness begets kindness."

- It's true! Kindness is also a chain reaction.
- One act of kindness leads to another.

   a. Example: A teacher compliments you on the strong points of your speech.

   b. With the boost of confidence, you will go to your room and thank your roommate for the cleaning last weekend.

   c. He/She'll compliment a friend and so on. And it all started with a teacher's simple comment on a speech.

(Internal Summary): Now you know how you can use random acts of kindness everyday to benefit yourself and everyone around you.

(Transition: Envision yourself partaking in Random Acts of Kindness on a daily basis.)

The Visualization Step

(1) Imagine yourself thanking your professor for his/her enthusiasm.

- How would that make him/her feel? Probably terrific.
- And the next class that comes in that day will be in for the most enthusiastic lecture ever.

(2) Or imagine commenting on a classmate's talent, only to find out later that you saved his/her life.

(3) There are no disadvantages. It is a win-win situation.

- It doesn't cost anything, and we definitely don't lose anything by doing it.
- In fact, random acts of kindness will not only cheer other people up, they will make you feel good too.
- Let's admit it, when we compliment someone or lend a helping hand, we feel good about ourselves.

(Transition: But don't just think about what you can do. Go to do it!)

Conclusion

The Action Step

(1) **(Summary)** With all of the problems in the world, and the bad days that people are having, sometimes all it takes to turn a problem into an opportunity, and a bad day into a smile is a simple act of kindness.

(2) **(Call to Immediate Action)** According to William Wordsworth, "nameless, unremembered acts of kindness" are "the best portion" of a person's life, so go out and demonstrate it in every way that you can.

(to be continued)

(continued)

> - I'm going to hand out some cards that have a suggestion for a random act of kindness you can do today.
>
> - Try one of the random acts on the card you receive, or try one of your own ideas.
>
> - Be honest, sincere, generous and kind.
>
> 3) **(Memorable Close)** Who knows, the world may slowly become a better place because of a single random act of kindness. Let it be yours.
>
> **References**
>
> List your references such as books consulted, websites visited or any material cited from a source.

Key Takeaways of This Chapter

★ An organization of a speech is of great importance. A good organization can make it easier for the speaker to remember and the audience to follow and it also can enhance the speaker's credibility.

★ An organization of a speech includes three parts: introduction, which sets the basic tone of the speech; body, which is your main text and conclusion which is used to wrap up your ideas and give some predictions in some cases.

★ The main points in your body part should be well prepared. The number of main points should be limited; different main points should be separated. In addition, make them serve your topic using concise and simple language, put them in the same pattern of wording, and balance the amount of time devoted to each main point.

★ An outline is a framework that helps the speaker to organize ideas and tie them to the main structural elements of the speech. The six steps to prepare for an outline are very helpful and useful before your working on the speech. Firstly, you need to identify ideas related to the topic and identify subdivisions which are essential. Then you need to organize the ideas and find supporting materials. The next step is to write your outline and add some transitions to make it sound coherent.

★ Connectives are essential to help the audience focus on main ideas without making them guess which ideas the speaker thinks are important. The audience is able to tune into what points the speaker has talked about and what point the speaker is presently talking about. When a speaker uses connectives properly, the speech will flow smoothly and make complex ideas understandable.

Part II

Exercises

I. Discuss the following questions.

1. Why is outlining a speech important? How does outlining help you test the logic of your speech?

2. What is the function of connectives in a speech? Discuss the function of each kind of connectives and share your thoughts with the entire class.

3. Using the hypothetical topic "What we can do about campus bully", select an organizational pattern from the ones described in your textbook. Then defend why this pattern would be most suitable for this particular topic.

II. Choose the correct answer.

1 How well a speech is organized will likely influence _____.
A. how clearly the audience understands the speech
B. how the audience views the competence of the speaker
C. how confident the speaker feels about his or her delivery
D. all of the above

2. The _____ is the longest and most important part of the speech.
A. body　　　　B. blueprint　　　　C. introduction　　　　D. conclusion

3. What is the MOST important reason for limiting the number of main points in a speech?
A. It is hard to maintain parallel wording if there are too many main points.
B. It is hard to phrase the central idea if a speech has too many main points.
C. It is hard to organize supporting materials if there are too many main points.
D. It is hard for the audience to keep track of too many main points.

4. Which organizational pattern would probably be most effective for arranging the main points of a speech with the specific purpose "to inform my audience how to start an online business"?

    A. Spatial.   B. Chronological.

    C. Causal.   D. Comparative-advantages.

5. What organizational pattern would probably be most effective for arranging the main points of a speech with the specific purpose "to inform my audience about three major ways to block junk mail from their e-mail system"?

    A. Topical.   B. Logistical.

    C. Chronological.   D. Causal.

6. Here are the main points for a speech about the major steps involved in a successful job interview:

(1) The first step is preparing for the interview before it takes place.

(2) The second step is presenting yourself well during the interview itself.

(3) The third step is following up after the interview.

These main points are arranged in _____ order.

    A. topical   B. spatial

    C. chronological   D. causal

7. Which organizational method is used in a speech with the following main points?

(1) Many citizens are victimized every year by incompetent lawyers.

(2) A bill requiring lawyers to stand for recertification every 10 years will do much to help solve the problem.

    A. Legal.   B. Topical.

    C. Chronological.   D. Problem-solution.

8. If the following transition were used in a persuasive speech, the speech would most likely be organized in _____ order.

"Now that I've told you about declining voter involvement in this country, let's look at what we can do about it."

    A. causal   B. spatial

    C. comparative   D. problem-solution

9. If the following internal summary was used in an informative speech, the speech would most likely be organized in _____ order.

"On our tour of campus thus far, we have moved from the student union on the east side of campus and around the perimeter. We've taken in the engineering campus on the north, the design college on the west side, and the school of education on the south."

    A. causal   B. topical

    C. spatial   D. chronological

10. Words or phrases that indicate when a speaker has completed one thought and is moving on to another are called _____ .

    A. transfers   B. internal summaries

    C. signposts   D. transitions

Ⅲ. Decide whether the following statements are true or false. Write T/F in the brackets.

1. ( ) Clear organization is usually less important in speaking than in writing.
2. ( ) Audiences find well-organized speakers to be more credible than poorly organized speakers.
3. ( ) The time given to each main point in the body of a speech should be exactly the same.
4. ( ) You should have no more than five main points in your speech.
5. ( ) The organizational pattern you choose will determine the order of your main points.
6. ( ) Because section transitions seem repetitive, they should only be used when the audience isn't very familiar with the topic.
7. ( ) In topical order the main points proceed from top to bottom, left to right, front to back, east to west, or some similar route.
8. ( ) Speeches arranged in chronological order follow a time sequence.
9. ( ) A public speaker should avoid using transitions and internal summaries together.
10. ( ) According to your textbook, the following statement is an example of a transition: "So much for the present; now let's turn our attention to the future."

Ⅳ. Fill in the blanks according to the instructions provided.

1) Provide the specific purpose, and main points for a speech with the following central idea:

Specific Purpose: _____

Central Idea: The four stages of alcoholism are the warning stage, the danger stage, the crucial stage, and the chronic stage.

Main Points: (1) _____

                 (2) _____

                 (3) _____

                 (4) _____

2) Provide the specific purpose, and main points for a speech with the following central idea:

Specific Purpose: _____

Central Idea: Handwriting analysts try to determine personality traits by examining the consistency, angularity, and size of a person's writing.

Main Points: (1) _____

(2) _____

(3) _____

V. Identify the main point and supporting material used in an outline.

Below is a disorganized outline for a main point speech on campus suicide. Where do you think each piece of information should go to make it more organized?

A. Even on our campus, the rate of suicide and attempted suicide is quite high.

B. Suicide among college students has become a serious problem that cannot be neglected.

C. In an interview with Michael Zhang, the Associate Dean of Students' Office, I learned that last year there were over 10 known suicide attempts on our campus.

D. Last year, 10,000 young Chinese students committed suicide.

E. The Dean, Michael Zhang also said that for every known suicide attempt, two or three more go unnoticed.

F. According to the National Institute of Mental Health, suicide is the fastest-growing cause of death for people aged 17 to 24 nationwide.

Main point: _____
Supporting material 1: _____
Supporting material 2: _____
Supporting material 3: _____
Detail 1: _____
Detail 2: _____

VI. Practice outlining.

1. Create an outline of your day, with main headings and detailed points for your main tasks of the day. At the end of the day, review the outline and write a brief

summary of your experience. Share with your classmates and comment on how to make an effective outline.

2. Diagram or create an outline for the speech entitled *How to speak so that people want to listen.* You can search for the speech on TED website. Do you notice any patterns in this talk? Share and compare your results with your classmates.

Ⅶ. Never neglect speaking ethical issues. Discuss the situation with your partner and provide your thoughts on the questions given.

George needs to turn in an outline for the speech he was assigned to deliver. The speech itself is two weeks away, but the outline is due today. George has already written the entire speech, and he does not see why he should spend time deleting parts of it to transform it into an outline. He knows exactly what he's going to say when he gives the speech. Then he discovers that the word-processing program in his computer can create an outline version of a document. Aha! Technology to the rescue! George happily turns in the computer-generated outline, feeling confident that never again will he have to hassle with writing an outline himself.

(1) Do you think George's use of a computer-generated outline fulfills the purpose of creating an outline for a speech? Why or why not?

(2) Do you think George's instructor will be able to tell that the outline was created by a word-processing program?

Chapter **4**

Beginning
and Ending of
Speech

Part I

How to Begin and End a Speech

1. A journey of a thousand miles begins with a single step. (千里之行，始于足下。)

   —Lao Zi

2. Well begun is half done.

   —A well-known saying

Similar to a piece of musical work, a speech with an attractive beginning and a functional ending can satisfy the audience fully. The beginning opens the curtain and lets the audience know what is to come, and the ending wraps up the speaker's ideas. In this chapter, we will introduce some important techniques in beginning and ending a speech, hoping to help you find the "best" way.

 ## 4.1 Beginning a Speech

4.1.1 Functions of a Beginning

The beginning of a speech is critical to its success, which functions as the first impression in a job interview. To be more specific, the functions of a beginning are as follows:

1) Grabbing the audience's attention and generating interest
Introduction is also called "grabbers" by some people because the first few

words out of your mouth should be something that will perk up the audience's ears. So the first major purpose of an introduction is to gain the audience's attention and make them interested in what you are going to say. If you do not get the audience's attention at the outset, it will only become more difficult to do so as you continue speaking.

2) Establishing credibility and goodwill

Another function of introduction is to let the audience know that you are a knowledgeable and credible source for the topic and thus qualified to speak on the subject. Essentially, credibility has two elements: external credibility and internal credibility. External credibility is the type of credibility as a speaker gained by association, for example, the use of sources that the audience finds credible. Furthermore, you could develop internal credibility as the speaker through specific actions such as appropriately attiring, making eye contact with the audience before you speak and speaking clearly, fluently and confidently. In addition, a speaker can establish credibility by demonstrating personal experience or knowledge of the topic.

Goodwill is the most important factor of credibility, which refers to the degree to which an audience member perceives a speaker as caring about the audience member. Simply put, we are going to listen to people who we think truly care for us and are looking out for our welfare. As a speaker, then, you need to establish that your information is being presented because you care about your audience and are not just trying to manipulate them.

3) Previewing main points

The last major function of an introduction is to preview the main ideas that your speech will discuss. A preview establishes the direction your speech will take. Sometimes this process is called signposting because you're establishing signs for audience members to look for while you're speaking. In the most basic speech format, speakers generally have three to five major points they plan on making. During the preview, a speaker outlines what these points will be, which demonstrates to the audience that the speaker is organized.

As a matter of fact, presenters who were unorganized while speaking are perceived as less credible than those who were organized. Having a solid preview of the information contained within one's speech and then following that preview will definitely help a speaker's credibility. It also helps your audience keep track of where you are if they momentarily get distracted. Your preview of the main points should be clear and easy to follow so as to help the audience know what to expect throughout the course of your speech and prepare them to listen.

4.1.2 Techniques to Begin Your Speech

1) Make a startling statement

Startle your listeners with an intriguing statement that will compel them to listen further.

Example: *When winter is approaching and the days are getting darker and shorter, do you feel a dramatic reduction in energy or do you sleep longer than usual during the fall or winter months? If you answered "yes" to either of these questions, you may be one of the millions of people who suffer from Seasonal Affective Disorder, or SAD. For most people, these problems do not cause great suffering in their life, but for an estimated six percent of the United States population, these problems can result in major suffering.*

Comments: The description of surroundings is used to illustrate the SAD, with which people will be startled by learning that they themselves may be one of the sufferers of SAD.

2) Arouse suspense or curiosity

An attractive story or a series of statements related to the topic will trigger your listeners' interest.

Example: *In the next 18 minutes, I'm going to take you on a journey. And it's a journey that you and I have been on for many years now, and it began some 50 years ago, when humans first stepped off our planet. And in those 50 years, not only did we literally, physically set foot on the moon, but we have dispatched robotic spacecraft to all the planets—all eight of them—and we have landed on asteroids, we have rendezvoused with comets, and, at this point in time, we have a spacecraft on its way to Pluto, the body formerly known as a planet. And all of these robotic missions are part of a bigger human journey: a voyage to understand something, to get a sense of our cosmic place, to understand something of our origins, and how Earth, our planet, and we, living on it, came to be.*

Comments: All audience will be curious about the journey the speaker talks about. As a beginning of a speech, it successfully arouses the curiosity of the audience, which keeps the audience motivated for more information until the journey is revealed.

3) Ask a rhetorical question

Rhetorical questions are designed to allow you as speaker to get the audience to think about your topic without actually providing the a answer to the question.

Example: *What is it about flying cars? We've wanted to do this for about a hundred years. And there are historic attempts that have had some level of technical success. But we haven't yet gotten to the point where on your way. Here this morning you see something that really, truly seamlessly integrates the two-dimensional world that we're comfortable in with the three-dimensional sky above us—that, I don't know about you, but I really enjoy spending time in.*

Comments: Asking a question as an attention-getter is a frequently used technique, but you need to be careful to make sure your rhetorical question relates specifically to your topic and is interesting enough so that people will listen.

4) Tell a story

In all cultures, stories are used to communicate and share values, traditions and knowledge. Stories (and anecdotes and illustrations) have a built-in structure with a beginning, middle, and ending, thus allowing the audience and the speaker to immediately share the experience.

Example: *One hot October morning, I got off the all-night train in Mandalay, the old royal capital of Burma, now Myanmar. And out on the street, I ran into a group of rough men standing beside their bicycle rickshaws. And one of them came up and offered to show me around. The price he quoted was outrageous. It was less than I would pay for a bar of chocolate at home.*

Comments: A personal story can connect the speaker and the audience very quickly. The speaker told us a story that happened in Mandalay at the beginning, which has aroused the curiosity of the audience and could keep them listening.

5) Begin with a quotation

Using a quotation is an easy and effective way to attract people's attention. You are expected to keep quotes short and relate directly to the speech topic.

Example: *"Man did not weave the web of life; he is merely a strand in it. Whatever he does to the web, he does to himself," said Chief Seattle in "How Can You Buy or Sell the Sky?" The metaphor of a web relates well with the overall concept of a community. In Burke's introduction of The Pinball Effect, he writes, "We all live on the great, dynamic web of change. It links us to one another and, in some ways, to everything in the past." America was once a place where people visited their neighbors, sat on front porches, and helped out each other at harvest, but today's culture is drastically different. Neighbors are no longer entwined in this interdependent web. With the disenfranchisement of America, schools must fill the gap of creating community in cities and towns.*

Comments: Quotations are very powerful in both starting your speech and proving your point. But you need to place the quotation in the context of your speech; do not simply find a quotation and use it to start every speech.

4.1.3 Some DO's & DON'Ts for Openings

1) DO's

(1) Do memorize your opening.

Once you have written up the beginning, memorize it, so you can free yourself from prepared notes. A memorized, polished introduction helps to establish credibility and rapport with your audience.

(2) Do keep the introduction relatively short.

The body of the speech serves as the heart of the entire speech, so the introduction which takes about 10 to 15 percent of the speech time needs to be concise and succinct.

2) SOME DON'Ts

(1) Avoid a dull and boring introduction.

Listeners need to be captivated, informed, inspired, and motivated. A speaker hopes to accomplish this from the beginning of the speech. As a result, you should stay away from a bland beginning.

(2) Avoid delaying mention of the topic. Some speakers think that delaying mention of the topic creates anticipation and arouses curiosity, but this is not the case. If the audience does not know the subject matter and purpose of the speaker's message, they will immediately lose focus.

(3) Avoid apologizing. Don't start with an apology or speak tentatively. Avoid saying, "Even though I'm not an expert…" "I rushed to prepare for this talk…" An apology is an invitation not to be taken seriously. Don't put yourself and your insecurities upfront; focus instead on the audience and your message.

4.1.4 Strategies for Preparing an Introduction

1) Prepare the introduction last

While this may seem both counter-intuitive, you really do want to leave the development of the introduction for the last part of your speech preparation. Think of it this way: until you know what you are going to say in your speech, then you can introduce your speech well.

The introduction is prepared last because it helps make sure that the body of the speech drives the introduction, not the other way around. The body of the speech contains most of the content, the arguments, the evidence, and the source material. The introduction sets up the body, but it should not overwhelm the body of the speech, nor should it dictate the content of the speech. Upon finishing the whole speech draft, you can carefully choose and craft the type of introduction that may serve the best, and concentrate on making sure that the introduction fulfills its functions.

2) Relate the introduction to the speech

As your introduction will contain the thesis statement and preview of the main points, at least part of the introduction will be relevant to the rest of the speech. Your speech will make a positive impression you desire with a close connection between the introduction and the body, otherwise, your audience will have difficulty following your main ideas, and you will lose goodwill and personal credibility.

3) Make the introduction succinct

If you are unable to complete your introduction in the first 60 to 90 seconds of most speeches, you have probably gone too long. Most audiences expect you to introduce your speech and then move quickly into the body of the speech.

4) Write out the introduction word for word

Writing your introduction out word for word can help you more easily see if the introduction could function well, and give you a very good idea about how long the introduction will be. You are recommended to memorize and then deliver the introduction word for word when rehearsing your speech because that will give you the most control over this important yet short part of your speech.

4.2 Ending a Speech

4.2.1 Functions of an Ending

Shakespeare said, "All's well that ends well." The conclusion of a speech is your last chance to make an impression on your audience. No speech is complete without the refocusing and closure a conclusion provides. When a speaker opts to end the speech with an ineffective conclusion or no conclusion at all, the speech loses the energy that has been created, and the audience is left disappointed. Instead of falling prey to emotional exhaustion, remind yourself to keep your energy up as you approach the end of your speech, and plan ahead so that your conclusion will be an effective one. Just as a good introduction helps bring an audience member into the world of your speech, and a good speech body holds the audience in that world, a good conclusion helps bring that audience member back to the reality outside of your speech.

A conclusion of a speech includes at least the following functions:

1) Signal the end

The first thing a good conclusion can do is to signal the end of a speech. When a speaker just suddenly stops speaking, the audience is left confused. We really want to make sure that audiences are left knowledgeable and satisfied with our speeches.

Throughout the speech, you have been providing the audience with verbal and nonverbal cues to where you are going in the speech. As you move to the conclusion, you need to continue to provide these cues. You can use language cues ("now that we have seen that we can solve this problem effectively, we can review the entire situation"), movement cues (physically moving back to the center of the room where you began the speech), and paralinguistic cues (slow the rate of the speech, use more pauses) to help prepare your audience for the end of the speech.

2) Aid audience's memory of your speech

Depending on the type of speech you are presenting, for example, you may be asking them to act in a certain way, or to change their attitude toward a certain person or topic, one of the tasks of the conclusion is to leave the audience motivated positively toward you and the topic you have been presenting.

3) Summarize and close

Just as the introduction should include a statement of the purpose of the speech, as well as a preview of the main ideas of the speech, the conclusion should include a restatement of the thesis and a review of the main ideas of the speech. The review and restatement are mirror images of the preview statement in the introduction. Structurally, the restatement and review bring the speech back to the top of the circle and remind the audience where we started. Functionally, they help cue the audience that the end of the speech is coming up.

4.2.2　Techniques to End Your Speech

1) Challenge Close

Challenge your audience to apply what you have told them in the speech.

Example: *And it's simple. And why should we care about this? We talk about world peace. How can we have world peace with different cultures, different languages? I think it starts household by household, under the same roof. So, let's make it right in our own backyard. And I want to thank all of you in the audience for being great husbands, great mothers, friends, daughters, sons. And maybe somebody's never said that to you, but you've done a really, really good job. And thank you for being here, just showing up and changing the world with your ideas.*

Comments: After talking about the importance of world peace, the speaker calls for the audience to take actions by challenging them to change the world from themselves.

2) Echo Close

Focus on one word in a quotation and emphasize that word to echo your final point.

Example: *More than 450 years before the birth of Christ, Confucius said: "What I hear, I forget; what I see, I remember; what I do, I understand." Let's do it together. We've heard what we have to do. We've seen what we need to do. Now is the time to do it, and, together, we can do it.*

Comments: As a typical echo close, this piece uses a quote from Confucius and analyzes it respectively, which highlights the theme as well as the purpose of the speech.

3) Repetitive Close

Find a phrase and structure it in a repetitive format that strikes the cadence of a drummer, building to a crescendo ending of a motivational speech:

Example: *So there's a clear message: whether you care about a fundamental, basic research of really interesting, bizarre, wonderful animals, or you want to build a search-and-rescue robot that can help you in an earthquake, or to save someone in a fire, or you care about medicine, we must preserve nature's designs. Otherwise, these secrets will be lost forever. Thank you.*

Comments: The speaker uses what has been mentioned in the speech to wrap it up. The pattern includes *whether ...or...*, which makes it catchy and easy to read.

4) Sing Song Close

Ask the audience to repeat a phrase that you used several times in your speech.

Example: *Let's say your phrase is: "Together, we can win." You repeat that phrase over and over again. Then just before your close, you say: "I know that all of you are talented, all of you are driven. I know that none of us can do this alone, but (pause) Together (pause) we can (pause until the audience responds).*

5) Tieback Close

Usually your opening attention-getter and closing statement are related in some way. A strong tieback will instill that same sense of familiarity as well as a sense of closure at the end of a speech. You could tie back your message to something you've mentioned previously in the speech.

Example: *So happiness is the most popular word we have heard through the past two years. happiness is not only related to personal experiences and personal values, but also, it's about the environment. People are thinking about the following questions: are we going to sacrifice our environment further to produce higher GDP? How are we going to perform our social and political reform to keep pace with economic growth, to keep sustainability and stability? And also, how capable is the system of self-correctness to keep more people content with all sorts of friction going on at the same time? I guess these are the questions people are going to answer. And our younger generations are going to transform this country while at the same time being transformed themselves.*

Comments: Happiness is mentioned in the introductory part of the speech, and towards the ending, it was mentioned again. By asking different questions related to happiness, the speaker heightens the theme and emphasizes it again.

6) Quotation Close

Use a famous quotation to harness the audience's attention, much like turning on a spotlight.

Example: *Speaking of Gandhi, he was a recovering lawyer, as I've heard the term, and he was called to a greater cause, something that mattered to him, he couldn't do. And he has this quote that I absolutely live by. "First they ignore you, then they laugh at you, then they fight you, then you win".*

Comments: Different from other endings, quotation close is comparatively easier but more powerful. The point is that a quotation which is closely connected to the key message should be found, or it will do harm to the ending with its loose bond to the theme.

4.2.3 Some DO's and DON'Ts for Conclusions

1) DO's

(1) Use summarized statements.

During your conclusion, you need to summarize what you've said during your speech. A quick overview of your main points is all it really takes.

(2) Leave enough time in your speech for a solid conclusion.

Take your time and don't rush through the conclusion. This applies to both the writing and the delivery of the conclusion.

(3) Be brief. Don't make the conclusion too long.

It's supposed to wrap everything up and signal the end of your speech. Usually it takes about 5 to 10% of the entire talk.

(4) Develop different conclusions and select the one that works best.

Come up with a wide range of conclusions and choose one that leaves the audience thinking.

(5) Write your conclusion out entirely.

Just as with the introduction, write out the conclusion word for word and then practice delivering it to make it come out smoothly and sound convincing.

2) DON'Ts

(1) Don't end with an apology.

Avoid saying "I guess I've rambled on long enough…" "I don't know if I've made this clear…". You need to wrap up everything confidently.

(2) Don't introduce a whole new idea in your conclusion.

The body of your speech is the place for new ideas. A conclusion should simply review what you've said and give your last opinions.

(3) Don't use the phrases "in conclusion" or "in summary" in any part of the speech other than the actual conclusion. You will lose part of your audience while they reorient themselves to the fact that the speech is continuing even though they thought it was winding down.

Key Takeaways of This Chapter

★ Linking the attention-getter to the speech topic is essential so that the relevance of the attention-getter is clear to your audience.

★ Establishing how your speech topic is relevant and important shows the audience why they should listen to your speech.

★ To be an effective speaker, you should convey all three components of credibility, competence, trustworthiness, and caring/goodwill, by the content and delivery of your introduction.

★ An effective conclusion contains three basic parts: a restatement of the speech's thesis; a review of the main points discussed within the speech; and a concluding device that helps create a lasting image in audiences' minds.

Part II

Exercises

I. Discuss the following questions.

1. What are the functions served by the introduction of a speech? Use a sample speech to illustrate an effective/ineffective beginning of that speech.
2. How can you establish your credibility with an audience to speak on a topic?
3. What are the functions of a speech conclusion? Use a sample speech to illustrate an effective/ineffective ending of that speech.
4. How would you like to begin and end your speech on the topic "College Romance"? Share your ideas with your classmates.

II. Choose the corrnect answer.

1. Which of the following is a function of a speech introduction?
    A. Establish the importance of your topic.
    B. State your topic.
    C. Get the attention of the audience.
    D. All of the above.
2. A good speech introduction will _____.
    A. state the information on the outline
    B. get the attention of the audience
    C. leave the introduction of the content to the body of the speech
    D. not be necessary with a captive audience
3. The attention-getter should be the _____.
    A. first sentence in the body of the speech   B. specific goal
    C. opening statement   D. thesis statement

4. Asking a question is a technique used to _____.
   A. get your listeners thinking about an idea
   B. entertain an audience
   C. startle an audience
   D. ridicule your audience's lack of knowledge on a subject

5. Which of the following is NOT a type of introduction?
   A. Rhetorical question.   B. Summary.
   C. Startling statement.   D. Personal reference.

6. "This morning, I will discuss the scientific, therapeutic, and physiological facts as well as myths about the effects and effectiveness of alternative medicine." Which function of a speech introduction does this example have?
   A. Establishing your credibility to speak on the topic.
   B. Previewing your key ideas.
   C. Getting your audience's attention.
   D. Establishing the importance of the topic.

7. A person began a speech with the words: "It's a pleasure for me to return to State University. As you know, I graduated from here—let's not talk about how many years ago. But in talking with students the last two days, State University still seems to have those same characteristics that have made it one of the leading universities in the country." You would know from this that the person was trying to begin the speech with _____.
   A. a startling statement   B. a quotation
   C. an example   D. a personal reference

8. One goal of your conclusion is to _____.
   A. put yourself at ease
   B. leave your audience with a memorable idea or suggestion
   C. make the structure of the speech obvious
   D. suggest to the audience that you have more to say

9. Which of these should a speech conclusion do?
   A. Summarize the main ideas.
   B. Stir guilt in the audience.
   C. Provide new material.
   D. Fade out gradually.

10. According to your textbook, a conclusion should be _____.
    A. the longest part of the speech
    B. twice as long as the introduction
    C. of minor concern
    D. no more than 5 percent of the speech

III. Decide whether the following statements are true or false. Write T/F in the brackets.

1. ( ) One goal of the introduction to your speech should be to convince the listeners that the topic is important to them.

2. ( ) Your introduction and conclusion provide your listeners with important first and final impressions of both you and your speech.

3. ( ) As a speaker, it is not your responsibility to provide your audience a reason to listen to you.

4. ( ) Startling an audience with the extent of a situation or problem invariably catches its members' attention but discourages them from listening further.

5. ( ) Referring to a recent event in the introduction of your speech decreases your credibility by showing that you are only knowledgeable about current events.

6. ( ) An effective conclusion only serves to summarize the speech and provide closure.

7. ( ) An excellent speech summary does more than just repeat your key ideas.

8. ( ) Saying, "that's it" or "that's my speech" is an appropriate closure.

9. ( ) Inspirational appeals or challenges have no place in an effective conclusion.

10. ( ) You are not supposed to rush to conclude, but design your conclusion wisely.

IV. Decide what type of attention-getters the following statements belong to?

1. How many of you have taken tests? Well, if you could reduce the number of tests your teacher gives, what would you think?

2. When I got off the plane this morning, I realized that I forgot my heels. So you'll remember me as the only professional public speaker who addressed you in flip-flops!

3. John F. Kennedy, former president of the United States, once said, "Ask not what your country can do for you. Ask what you can do for your country."

4. When asked what was their No.1 fear, most Americans said fear to give a speech in front of a group of people. No.2 was death.

5. One dark summer night in 1849, a young woman in her 20's left Bucktown, Maryland, and followed the North Star. What was her name? Harriet Tubman. She went back some 19 times to rescue her fellow slaves. Today I would like to introduce Harriet Tubman, an amazing woman, to you.

6. How would you feel if you were hungry but could find no restaurant? How would you feel if you wanted to sleep but could find no motel? How would you feel if you wanted to refresh yourself but could find no washroom? How would you feel if you wanted to be entertained but could find no theatre? How would you feel if you wanted respect, but could find none—anywhere?

7. A famous Chinese proverb states, "Tell me and I forget. Show me and I remember. Ask me to do and I understand." This proverb is true not only in school, but also in business. One company, Aspen Productions, has taken this motto to hear and dramatically increased their productivity.

8. "You know, in the last ten months, I've been called a lot of things, but nobody's called me a bishop yet. When I was about nine years old, my beloved and now departed grandmother, who was a very wise woman, looked at me and she said, "You know, I believe you could be a preacher if you were just a little better boy." (Bill Clinton)

9. Let me ask you this: On a scale of 1 to 10, how would you rate yourself as a listener? Most Chinese adults would rate themselves a 7.5. Unfortunately, according to the National Communication Association, if you're like most adults, you listen with just 25% efficiency!

10. How many people here have experienced regret in their lives? Would anyone care to share one of their biggest regrets?

V. Use the following worksheet to map out the introduction for your next speech.

1. What is your general purpose? (tick one)

☐ To inform	☐ To persuade	☐ To entertain

2. What is your specific purpose?

_____

3. Which attention-getting device do you plan on using?

_____

4. How will you link your attention-getting device to your actual topic?

_____

5. Why should your audience listen to your speech?

_____

6. How will you establish your credibility during speech?
1) Competence

_____

2) Trustworthiness

_____

3) Caring/goodwill

_____

4) What is your thesis statement?

_____

7. What are your three main body points?
   1) Body point 1

   _____

   2) Body point 2

   _____

   3) Body point 3

   _____

   4) Write a preview of your three main body points.

   _____

VI. The following conclusions are ineffective. What could be the problems of each? Discuss and rewrite them to include some essential elements of a good conclusion.

1. In conclusion, today, we talked about three tourist attractions in Beijing. Any questions?

2. So, have breakfast is important! Unfortunately, I am out of time, so I don't have any time left for questions. More information is given in your handouts.

3. Today I gave the definition of team building, and I gave some examples of team building, and I talked about the advantages of team building, and I ended with disadvantages of team building. I don't know if you have any questions for me.

4. To conclude, drugs are very harmful to us because they affect society by making people lose respect for authority and they affect people because people neglect to take care of themselves and they affect our bodies because we don't eat and sleep right, and they affect our children because we don't take care of them so well, and they affect our health too. That' all I have to say about it.

5. In conclusion, we have seen that there are definite problems with our medical care system. For example, some real poor people cannot get immediate treatment.

VII. Never neglect speaking ethical issues. Discuss the situation with your partner and provide your thoughts on the questions given.

Imagine that you are preparing a presentation on the benefits of a new drug, and you find a direct quotation that clearly establishes your argument. Unfortunately, you soon realize that the source of your quotation is actually a lobbyist who works for the pharmaceutical company that manufactures the drug. You really want to use this quotation as your attention-getter, but you realize that the source is clearly biased. Which of the following options do you think is the most ethical? Why?

(1) Disregard the quotation and find another way to start your speech.

(2) Use the quotation, but acknowledge that the source comes from a paid lobbyist of the pharmaceutical company who manufactures the drug.

(3) Use the quotation and just give the name of the source. If your audience is interested in your topic, they'll do their own research and make informed decisions for themselves.

Chapter **5**

Use of Language

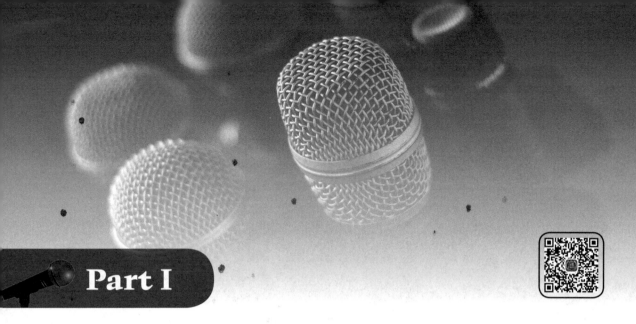

Part I

How to Use Language in a Speech

1. Without knowing the force of words, it is impossible to know men. (不知言，无以知人也。)

—*Confucius*

2. Your purpose is to make your audience see what you saw, hear what you heard, feel what you felt. Relevant detail, couched in concrete, colorful language, is the best way to recreate the incident as it happened and to picture it for the audience.

—*Dale Carnegie*

 5.1 The Power of Language

Language is central to our experience of being human, and the languages we speak deeply shape the way we think, the way we see the world, and the way we live our lives. Through language we share experiences, formulate values, exchange ideas, transmit knowledge, and sustain culture. Language is one of the most influential and powerful aspects of our daily lives and yet very few people pay attention to it in their interpersonal and public communication. The power of language cannot be overemphasized since language constructs, reflects, and maintains our social realities, or what we believe to be "true" with regard to the world around us. To understand the power of language, we need to differentiate between communication and language. Communication occurs when we try to transfer what is in our minds to the minds of our audience. Whether speaking to inform, persuade, or entertain, the main goal of a speaker is to effectively communicate his or her thoughts to audience members. Language, on the other hand, is the means by which we communicate—a system of symbols we use to form messages. When language is used wisely, it can evoke very deep feelings in others, motivate others to action and construe the nature of our relationships.

Should a public speaker use very basic language because the audience is unfamiliar with his/her topic? Or more technical language with many acronyms, abbreviations, and jargon because the audience has expertise in the topic? Or academic language with abstract vocabulary, or flowery, poetic language with lots of metaphors? Perhaps you have never thought about those questions, but they are ones that influence both the clarity of the message as well as the credibility a speaker will gain during the speech. In this chapter, we will examine how language functions in communication and how one can become more proficient in using language in public speaking.

5.2 Spoken Language vs. Written Language

When we use the word "language", we refer to the words we choose to use in our speech, i.e., spoken language. Spoken language exists prior to written language. There are many differences between spoken and written language. Spoken language involves speaking and listening skills whereas written language involves reading and writing skills. The following graph demonstrates the differences between spoken and written language.

Spoken Language	vs.	Written Language
Spoken language involves speaking and listening skills		Written language involves reading and writing skills
Older than written language		Not as old as spoken
More informal and simple		More formal and complex
Mostly used between people who are in the same place		Promotes communication across space and time
Can use tone, pitch, volume, etc.		Can use heading, punctuation, layouts, etc.
Temporary since there are no records.		Permanent since there are records.
Contains repetitions, incomplete sentences, interruptions, corrections, etc.		Often grammatically correct, and may contain long sentences in complex tenses.

1) Spoken Language

Spoken language is the language we speak. It is often spontaneous and transient. Spoken language is used for interactions; the two participants of the communication, that is, the listener and the speaker are often in the same place. Thus, they can correct any mistake they make and change their utterances as they go along. Except for scripted speeches, spoken language tends to be full of incomplete sentences, repetitions, interruptions, and corrections. Speakers also use gestures, tone, pitch, volume, etc. to create additional meaning in spoken language. Unless the conversation is recorded, there is no record of the spoken language conversation that took place. Some forms and informal grammatical structures are also specific to spoken language. For example, words and phrases used in spoken language such as "my bad", "you know", "ain't", or "gonna" are rarely used in written language.

2) Written Language

Written language is the language we use to write. The two main language skills used in written language are reading and writing skills. Written language is not transient like spoken language; it tends to be permanent since there are written records of it. Once we have written something, it is not very easy to change it. Another interesting aspect of written language is that the reader and writer usually communicate across time and space, unlike in spoken language. Written language is typically more formal, complex and intricate than spoken language. It may contain longer sentences in complex tenses. However, some forms of written language such as instant messages and informal letters are closer to spoken language. Written language can make use of features like punctuation, headings, layouts, and colors, etc. to make a message clearer. Since written language does not receive immediate feedback, it should be very clear and unambiguous.

Speeches should have oral characteristics. American poet Eliot once said, "If we spoke as we write, no one would listen; and if we wrote as we speak, no one would read". Public speaking is a type of oral communication and therefore different from written communication to some extent. Oral language is intended basically for the ear while written language is intended for the eye.

Written language and spoken language are distinct from each other. However, they are interchangeable. "All written languages may be spoken." There is no doubt that public speaking can be considered as a written passage delivered by voice. As a result, **the language of public speaking possesses some features of oral language and some characteristics of written language.** In public speaking, the speaker and listeners communicate through talking and listening, hardly with any repeated interaction. Most of the public speaking is delivered based on scripts written in advance. In public speaking most of the sentences used are complete and have the tendency toward complexity to enhance credibility, but they do not try to obscure listeners. Languages of public speaking are of both the features of spoken language and written language.

Audiences for public speeches do not have the benefit of being able to go back and reread sentences, and they cannot look at a page and see section headings. Thus, public audiences have a more limited capacity to comprehend complicated ideas and to take in long sentences and difficult or dense language. Public speakers have to compensate for these limits by using the principles of repetition of content, clarity of structure, and simplicity of language.

5.3 Meaning of Words

"The difference between the almost right word and the right word is really a large matter", wrote American author and humorist Mark Twain in 1888. Word choice affects the meaning and tone that an audience perceives in a speech. To be most effective, communicators select their words with care so that an audience is more likely to comprehend intended meanings.

One of the first components necessary for understanding language is to understand how we assign meaning to words. Words consist of sounds (oral) and shapes (written) that have agreed-upon meanings embedded in concepts, ideas, and memories. When we write the word "blue", we may refer to a portion of the visual spectrum dominated by energy with a wavelength of roughly 440–490 nanometers. We could also say that this color is an equal mixture of both red and green light. While both of these are technically correct ways to interpret the word "blue", we're pretty sure that neither of these definitions is how we think about the word. When hearing the word "blue", we may have thought of our favorite color, the color of the sky on a spring day, or the color of a really fancy car we saw in the parking lot. When we think about language, there are two different types of meanings that we should be aware of: denotative and connotative.

A denotation is the precise and exact definition of a word. Denotative meaning is precise, literal, and objective. It simply describes the object, person, place, idea, or event to which the word refers. One way to think of a word's denotative meaning is its dictionary definition. A connotation is the secondary or implied meaning of a word, stemming from the common feeling associated with the word. Connotative meaning is more variable, figurative, and subjective. Simply put, it is what the word suggests or implies. Connotations can vary based on geography and culture, and may change over time. Connotation describes the images and feelings called up by a particular word, rather than its strict definition. For example, in addition to referring to a color, the word "blue" can evoke many other ideas, such as *state of depression* (feeling blue), *indication of winning* (a blue ribbon), *side during the Civil War* (blues vs. grays), *sudden event* (out of the blue). Likewise, the adjectives "mad" and "furious" both denote that someone is angry. "Furious", however, evokes an image of a much stronger, more intense feeling. This is connotation. Another example would be to compare the words "work" and "toil". Both denote exerting oneself. To say that a man works, however, could mean that he expends great effort or simply that he has a job. To say that a man toils conjures up an impression of someone who labors very hard, probably in a physical job, and possibly in a very difficult situation.

Understanding both the denotation and connotation of words can help convey meanings more clearly. Writers often use connotation to great effect in books, songs and plays. For example, rather than saying that a night was dark, a writer who wants to create a feeling of foreboding might instead say that the night was pitch black. Choosing words skillfully for the denotative and connotative meanings is a crucial part of speaking art.

5.4 Guidelines for Using Effective Language in a Speech

5.4.1 Use Simple Language

Simplicity in language is crucial to conveying information effectively. Oral discourses differ from written ones in its use of language. The first person pronoun such as "I" and "we" is often employed in oral discourse for such language gives the speech a sense of immediacy and helps the speaker to connect with the audience. The simplicity of expression will make sure the audience understands us. When choosing between two synonyms, choose the simpler one. Furthermore, oral language needs to be less dense and jargon-laden than written language. When academic papers are read out loud, they seldom make effective speeches. A common mistake that can be identified from speeches delivered by inexperienced speakers is to rely heavily on a thesaurus, searching for bigger, more impressive words. Using a long word when a short one will do inhibits your ability to communicate clearly. Your goal as a speaker should be as clear as you possibly can. Using complex language that makes it difficult for the audience to understand can negatively impact your ability to get a clear message across to your audience. If your audience can't understand your vocabulary, they can't understand your message. This can also affect delivery, as speakers are more likely to stumble over unfamiliar words. In a speech, instead of using "expeditious", "convene", "forfeit", and "notify", the words "fast", "meet", "lose" and "tell" are suggested. When writing your speech, you are also advised to avoid technical jargon, slang, clichés, and euphemisms. This type of language is difficult to understand and tends to exert low impact. For instance, it is the usual case to use scientific jargon when making a public speaking to the audience of scientists. However, that would be ineffective for the audience of college students. It is among the professionals the same case that terminology of drugs is useful for communicating with people in drug industry, but it would not be effective among the common people who are unfamiliar with the terminology.

Compare the **Low Impact** language column with the **High Impact** column below to see how simple language can be more powerful.

Low Impact	High Impact
Under the present circumstances	Currently
At the present time	Now
Are in agreement with	Agree
Due to the fact that	Because
Is fully operational	Works
In close proximity to	Near
Of sufficient magnitude	Big enough
In the event of	If
Each and every one	Each
In the course of	During

5.4.2   Use Clear Language

The speaker should be aware that the most important thing he/she should do is to make himself/herself understood via clarity of the expression. Therefore, a speaker should try to articulate clearly and pronounce correctly so as to avoid unclear utterances which will obstruct the audience's reception and the speaker should use some appropriate body language to ensure clarity. In order to catch the audience's attention, some syntactic means such as repetition or paraphrasing can be used.

1) Use Short Sentences

Sentences in public speaking must always be concise. As a rule, use fewer words rather than more words to express your thoughts. As you work on and edit your speech draft, bear in mind that easy-to-pronounce words and shorter words are more easily understood. A sentence that is beautifully written for the page can be impossible to decipher by the listening audience, no matter how awesome your presentation skills are. For example, in a Memorial Day speech President Clinton gave at the Vietnam Veteran's Memorial, he could have said:

"These men and women, who were known to all of us—there is not one person here who did not know someone on the wall—fought for freedom, brought honor to their communities, loved, and died for their country."

Instead, he said:

"These men and women fought for freedom, brought honor to their communities, loved their country, and died for it. They were known to all of us. There's not a person in this crowd today who did not know someone on this wall."

By keeping each idea a separate sentence, Clinton made his speech easier to follow. For more examples of how sentences differ in oral versus written communication, you may read the news from the news APP, and then listen to the same news via TV. You could notice that the sentences used in oral communication are shorter.

2) Use Concrete Words

Concrete words are mainly objects that can be named through seeing, hearing, touching, tasting, or smelling. Abstract words are names for qualities, attributes, or concepts. Enough has shown that listeners retain concrete nouns and verbs more easily. Each time listeners hear an abstract word, they try to find a concrete reference for it, and if you haven't provided one, they will search for their own experience for it. In speaking classes, the often overused abstractions in student speeches are: old, thing, bad, big, a lot, long, short, new, good, and late. For example,

> *Abstract: The big police officer was mean to us.*
> *Concrete: The police officer, who must have weighed 350 pounds, shouted to us.*
> *Abstract: His office is fully equipped.*
> *Concrete: His office is equipped with a PC Mac, a laser printer and a new fax machine.*

We can assume that the audience has good knowledge of concrete words. When we use concrete language, we actually help our audiences see specific realities or actual instances instead of abstract theories and ideas. The goal of concreteness is to help us, as speakers, show the audience something instead of just telling them. Concrete words will enable listeners to instantly see what we mean, instead of having to translate the word into an image. In other words, we should appeal to listeners' senses by using concrete and descriptive language.

In what follows, some tips regarding how to reinforce the concrete nature of our statements are presented.

(1) Avoid abstractions in the nouns and verbs.

As for nouns, specificity should be prioritized. Instead of using "cars," say "Ford" and instead of using "breakfast", say "bread and eggs". In addition, use fewer passive verbs and more action verbs. For example, say, "Ask me anything" instead of, "I was hoping you'd have questions." Overall, using fewer adjectives and adverbs but sticking to concrete nouns and verbs will boost your credibility.

(2) Avoid ambiguity.

Ambiguity generally emanates from poor word choice. If care is not used when selecting words or if the sentences are not properly constructed, the results can often be confusing for listeners. For example, in the sentence, *"The professor said on Monday he would give an exam"*, it could mean either that it was on Monday that the professor told the class about the exam or that the exam would be given on Monday. Thus, reading your lines aloud to a friend will help you determine the words that will make the audience pause and think through confusing terms.

(3) Add illustrations.

Suppose you've decided to give a speech on the importance of freedom. You could easily stand up and talk about the philosophical work of Rudolf Steiner, who divided the ideas of freedom into freedom of thought and freedom of action. If you're like us, even reading that sentence can make you want to go to sleep. Instead of defining what those terms mean and discussing the philosophical merits of Steiner, you could use real examples where people's freedom to think or freedom to behave has been stifled. For example, you could talk about how Afghani women under Taliban rule have been denied access to education, and how those seeking education have risked public flogging and even execution. You could further illustrate how Afghani women under the Taliban are forced to adhere to rigid interpretations of the Islamic law that functionally limit their behavior. As illustrations of the two freedoms discussed by Steiner, these examples make things more concrete for audience members and thus easier to remember. Ultimately, the goal of concreteness is to show an audience something instead of talking about it abstractly.

5.4.3 Use Accurate Language

Using language accurately is as vital to a speaker as using numbers accurately is to an accountant. However, we all commit subtle errors, especially using one word when another will capture our ideas more precisely. Every word has shades of meaning that distinguish it from the other word. If you have serious aspirations as a speaker, you should work out a systematic plan to improve your vocabulary. The purpose of this is to learn how to use the proper word at the proper time. Don't leave room for misinterpretation. If you use the wrong words, it will distort your intended message. When you feel it is necessary, use a dictionary to clear up any misunderstandings you may have. As you prepare your speeches, ask yourself constantly, "What do I really want to say? What do I really mean?" Choose words that are precise and accurate. Misuse of words and phrases can cause difficulty in comprehension. Look at the following examples:

- *Inaccurate: Speaking ability in English can be achieved through a lot of practice.*
  More accurate: Speaking ability in English can be acquired through a lot of practice.
- *Inaccurate: When I took the little girl's temperature, it was degrees above average.*
  More accurate: When I took the little girl's temperature, it was degrees above normal.
- *Inaccurate: His scores in the exam were good enough to satisfy him for a graduate program.*
  More accurate: His scores in the exam were good enough to qualify him for a graduate program.

5.4.4 Use Appropriate Language

Another important concept a speaker needs to think about regarding language use is appropriateness. Appropriate language is another decisive quality in effective speeches. Public speakers always seek appropriateness in the process of adapting their language to the subject, audience, occasion and themselves. For example, when talking on a political subject in a quite formal situation, you are naturally expected not to use informal, conversational language. And if you imitate too much of the language style of a well-known speaker, you will probably lose appropriateness, too.

1) Appropriateness for the Speaker

One of the questions to ask yourself is whether the language you plan to use in a speech fits with your own speaking pattern. Not all language choices are appropriate for all speakers. The language you select should be suitable for you, not for someone else. If you're a first-year college student, there's no need to force yourself to sound like an astrophysicist even if you are giving a speech on new planets. One of the biggest mistakes novice speakers make is thinking that they have to use million-dollar words because it makes them sound smarter. Actually, million-dollar words don't tend to function well in oral communication, so using them will probably make you uncomfortable as a speaker. What's more, it may be difficult for you or the audience to understand the nuances of meaning when you use such words. In other words, using them can increase the risk of denotative or connotative misunderstandings.

2) Appropriateness for the Audience

The second aspect of appropriateness concerns with whether the language you are choosing is appropriate for your specific audience. Suppose you're an engineering student giving a presentation in an engineering class, you can use language that other engineering students can understand. On the other hand, if you use that engineering vocabulary in a public speaking class composed of listeners from various departments, many audience members may not understand your message. Similarly, if you are speaking about space explorations to an audience of young adults, you can't assume they will know the meaning of terms like "linear (as opposed to rotation-based) artificial-gravity system" which would be familiar to an expert in the field. Audience analysis is a key factor in choosing the language in a speech.

3) Appropriateness for the Context

The next question about appropriateness is whether the language you use is suitable or fitting for the context itself. The language you employ to address a student assembly in a high school auditorium will differ from the language you would use at a business meeting in a hotel ballroom. If you're giving a speech at an outdoor rally, you cannot use the same language you would use in a classroom. The speaking context includes the occasion, the time of day, the mood of the audience, and other factors in addition to the physical location. You are expected to take the entire speaking context into consideration when you make the language choices for your speech.

4) Appropriateness for the Topic

The final question about the appropriateness of language involves whether the language is appropriate for your specific topic. If you are speaking about the early years of The Walt Disney Company, would you want to refer to Walt Disney as a "thaumaturgic" individual (i.e., one who works wonders or miracles)? While the word "thaumaturgic" may be accurate, is it the most appropriate for the topic at hand? As another example, if your speech topic is the dual residence model of string theory, it makes sense to expect that you will use more sophisticated language than if your topic was a basic introduction to the physics of sound or light waves.

5.4.5 Use Vivid Language

Just as you can be accurate without being clear, you can be both accurate and clear without being interesting. If you want to move people with your speech, use moving language. Dull, dreary words make for dull, dreary speeches. Bring your speech to life by using vivid, animated language. Vivid language helps your listeners create strong, distinct, clear, and memorable mental images. A good choice of vivid language helps an audience member truly understand and imagine what a speaker is saying. The art of using language to persuade an audience is called rhetoric. There are many rhetorical devices the speaker can choose from to enhance the effectiveness of a speech.

1) Imagery

Imagery is the use of language to represent objects, actions, or ideas. The goal of imagery is to help an audience create a mental picture of what a speaker is conveying. A speaker who uses imagery successfully will tap into one or more of the audience's five basic senses (hearing, taste, touch, smell, and sight). In order to harness that power, you have to create word pictures. By delivering powerful images, you narrow the distance between you and your listeners; you enable your listeners to think your thoughts and feel your feelings. You put your listeners in your shoes and enable them to take the same steps that you have taken. Once your listeners are in your shoes, they are more likely to believe what you believe and do what you want them to do. Usually, powerful images are used to transfer emotion and make others feel like they are standing next to you, experiencing the same moment that you are experiencing.

Here's an example:

At the end of his career, General Douglas MacArthur returned to West Point to address the cadets. He spoke as a soldier of one era to the soldiers of another...

"The shadows are lengthening for me. The twilight is here. My days of old have vanished—tone and tints. They have gone glimmering through the dreams of things that were. Their memory is one of wondrous beauty, watered by tears and coaxed and caressed by the smiles of yesterday. I listen, then, but with thirsty ear, for the witching melody of faint bugles blowing reveille, of far drums beating the long roll."

This is a great example because it uses two senses. We see the "wondrous beauty watered by tears...", and we also hear the "faint bugles blowing reveille...". If you read that and you aren't moved... check your pulse!

Three common tools of imagery are concreteness, simile, and metaphor.

(1) Concreteness

As we have discussed earlier in this chapter, choosing concrete words over abstract ones is one way to bring your speech to the maximum effect. Concrete words are also the key to creating imagery.

For example, in your speech, you'd better:

use "chimpanzee" instead of "monkey"

use "$1,000,000" instead of "a large sum of money"

use "raising the minimum wage" instead of "economic policies"

use "camping" instead of "outdoor activities"

(2) Simile

The second form of imagery is simile. It is a figure of speech involving the comparison of one thing with another thing of a different kind (specifically using the terms "like" or "as") to make a description more emphatic or vivid.

Some examples:

The thunderous applause was like a party among the gods.

After the revelation, she was as angry as a raccoon caught in a cage.

Life is like a stage where we have different roles to play.

Speakers use similes to help an audience understand a specific characteristic being described within the speech. In the first example, we are connecting the type of applause being heard to something supernatural, so we can imagine that the applause was huge and enormous.

To effectively use similes within your speech, first look for instances where you may already be finding yourself using the words "like" or "as", for example, "his breath smelled like a fishing boat on a hot summer day". Second, when you find situations where you are comparing two things using "like" or "as", examine what it is that you are actually comparing. For example, maybe you're comparing someone's breath to the odor of a fishing vessel. Finally, once you see what two ideas you are comparing, check the mental picture for yourself. Are you getting the kind of mental image you desire? Is the image too strong? Is the image too weak? You can always alter the image to make it stronger or weaker depending on what your aim is.

(3) Metaphor

Metaphor is another stylistic device that uses language in effective ways. Metaphors make the connection of a new idea to an object the audience already knows. Metaphors enliven language by making a comparison between two items to make a point.

Some examples:

- *Love is a battlefield.*

- *Upon hearing the charges, the accused clammed up and refused to speak without a lawyer.*

- *Every year a new crop of activists are born.*

In the first one, the word "like" is omitted; instead of being like a battlefield, the metaphor states that love is a battlefield. In the second example, the accused "clams up", which means that the accused refused to talk in the same way a clam's shell is closed. In the third example, we refer to activists as "crops" that arise anew with each growing season, and we use "born" figuratively to indicate that they come into being. For rhetorical purposes, metaphors are considered stronger, but both simile and metaphor can help you achieve clearer language if chosen wisely. To think about how metaphor is stronger than simile, think of the difference between "love is a battlefield"and "love is like a battlefield".

To use a metaphor effectively, first determine what you are trying to describe. For example, maybe you are talking about a college catalog that offers a wide variety of courses. Second, identify what it is that you want to say about the object you are trying to describe. Depending on whether you want your audience to think of the catalog as good or bad, you'll use different words to describe it. Finally, identify the other object you want to compare the first one to, which should mirror the intentions in the second step.

Let's look at two possible metaphors:

- *Students groped their way through the maze of courses in the catalog.*

- *Students feasted on the abundance of courses in the catalog.*

While both examples evoke comparisons with the course catalog, with the first one being clearly more negative and the second more positive. One mistake people often make in using metaphors is to make two incompatible comparisons in the same sentence or line of thought. Here is an example:

"That's awfully thin gruel for the right-wing to hang their hats on."

This is known as a mixed metaphor, and it often has an incongruous or even hilarious effect. Unless you are aiming to entertain your audience with fractured use of language, be careful to avoid mixed metaphors.

2) Analogy

Analogy is a kind of extended metaphor or long simile in which a comparison is made between two things in order to develop a line of reasoning. While it is similar to simile, similes are generally more artistic and brief, while an analogy is longer and explains a thought process, which helps to engage audiences and help them better understand a complex policy or procedure. Analogies compare something that your audience knows and understands with something new and different. For your speech, you can use an analogy to show a connection between your speech topic (something new and different for the audience) and something that is known by your audience. Use an analogy whenever you need to explain a new process or new procedure particularly to a general audience. To create an analogy, find an object that your audience is already familiar with. Then look for characteristics in that object that could be compared to traits or various aspects of your process.

Here's an example of an analogy that links specific processes of a stove and stomach to encourage people to eat breakfast.

"Think of your body as an old-fashioned steam engine. You need to feed the fire with coal. When there is no coal available, the stoker slows down so that all the available fuel is not consumed. Likewise, your metabolism slows down for the rest of the day when you don't eat breakfast."

3) Allusion

Allusion is a short reference to a familiar person, place, thing, or an event. It is also important because allusion explains or enhances the subject under discussion without sidetracking the listener. For speakers, the purpose would need to be simpler and more obvious to a wider group, providing resonance with a well-known aspect of culture.

Consider the allusions used by Martin Luther King Jr in *"I have a dream"* speech:

"Five score years ago…" refers to Lincoln's famous Gettysburg Address speech, which began with *"Four score and seven years ago…"* This allusion is particularly poignant given that King was speaking in front of the Lincoln Memorial. The purpose was to suggest a parallel cross-road for the nation in these two struggles, the Civil War and the movement for civil rights for African Americans.

"Life, Liberty, and the Pursuit of Happiness" is a reference to the Declaration of Independence.

Numerous Biblical allusions provide the moral basis for King's arguments:

"It came as a joyous daybreak to end the long night of their captivity." This alludes to Psalms (From Old Testament of Bible) *"For his anger is but for a moment; his favor is for a lifetime. Weeping may linger for the night, but joy comes with the morning."*

"Let us not seek to satisfy our thirst for freedom by drinking from the cup of bitterness and hatred." evokes Jeremiah (From Old Testament of Bible) *"…for my people have committed two evils: They have forsaken me, the fountain of living water, and dug out cisterns for themselves, cracked cisterns that can hold no water"*.

4) Personification

Personification is another commonly used literary device. Writers may take a non-human object, animal, or idea and give it human characteristics, thus giving it life. Audiences can then relate better to these objects or animals. A frequent example of personification is "winking stars", in which non-human objects (stars) are given human characteristics (the ability to wink).

More examples:

Many voices are heard as we face a great decision. Comfort says, "Tarry a while." Opportunism says, "This is a good spot." Timidity asks, "How difficult is the road ahead?"

—Franklin D. Roosevelt

Fed upon such food, what will the mind of a nation be?

— Goldwin Smith

In the long march across public speaking history, style has walked a road which rises and falls between high peaks of precision and deep valleys of neglect. Unfortunately, in contemporary American speaking, style has been forced to build her home in the valley, ignored, if not forgotten.

— Carl Wayne Hensley

5) Climax

Climax is the arrangement of words or phrases in order of increasing importance or emphasis. It is often used with parallelism because it offers a sense of continuity, order, and movement—up the ladder of importance.

Some examples:

And from the crew of Apollo 8, we close with good night, good luck, a merry Christmas, and God bless all of you, all of you on the good earth.

—Frank Borman, Apollo 8 astronaut

And now I ask you, ladies and gentlemen, brothers and sisters, for the good of all of us, for the love of this great nation, for the family of America, for the love of God; please make this nation remember how futures are built.

—Mario Cuomo, Governor of New York

The world watches. The world listens. The world waits to see what we will do.

—Richard Nixon

4) *We want peace. We want freedom. We want a better life.*

—Ronald Reagan

6) Rhythm

Another guideline for effective language in a speech is to use rhythm. When most people think of rhythm, they immediately think about music. What they may not realize is that language is inherently musical; at least it can be. Rhythm refers to the patterned, recurring variance of elements of sound or speech. Whether someone is striking a drum with a stick or standing in front of a group speaking, rhythm is an important aspect of human communication. If you analyze your favorite public speaker's speaking pattern, you'll notice that there is a certain cadence to the speech. While much of this cadence is a result of the nonverbal components of speaking, some of the cadence comes from the language that is chosen as well. Let's examine four types of rhythmic language: parallelism, repetition, alliteration, and antithesis.

(1) Parallelism

It is the linkage of similar words or ideas in a balanced construction that repeatedly uses the same grammatical form to convey parallel or coordinated ideas. When listing items in a sequence, audiences will respond more strongly when those ideas are presented in a grammatically parallel fashion, which is referred to as parallelism. For example, look at the following two examples and determine which one sounds better to you:

"Give me liberty or I'd rather die."

"Give me liberty or give me death."

Technically, you're saying the same thing in both, but the second one has better rhythm, and this rhythm comes from the parallel construction of "give me". The lack of parallelism in the first example makes the sentence sound disjointed and ineffective.

More examples:

Let every nation know, whether it wishes us well or ill, that we shall pay any price, bear any burden, meet any hardship, support any friend, oppose any foe to assure the survival and the success of liberty.

—John F. Kennedy

We have seen the state of our Union in the endurance of rescuers, working past exhaustion. We've seen the unfurling of flags, the lighting of candles, the giving of blood, the saying of prayers in English, Hebrew, and Arabic.

—George W. Bush

Tell me and I forget. Teach me and I may remember. Involve me and I will learn.

—Benjamin Franklin

Interwoven into the warp and woof of this human complexity is the moving story of men and women of nearly every race and color in their progress from slavery to freedom, from poverty to wealth, from weakness to power, from ignorance to intelligence.

—Booker T. Washington

We shall fight him by land; we shall fight him by sea; we shall fight him in the air, until, with God's help, we have rid the earth of his shadow and liberated its people from his yoke.

—Winston Churchill

(2) Repetition

The most effective speech is one the audience remembers. Stylistically, there are many things a speaker can do to add emphasis to their spoken language. Repetition as a linguistic device is designed to help audiences become familiar with a short piece of the speech as they hear it over and over again. By repeating a phrase during a speech, you create a specific rhythm. Repetition is common, especially in persuasive speaking. Repetition shouldn't be redundant or boring, but instead add a sense of importance to the repeated phrase, word, or idea. Repetition with variation is a basic speech-writing tool used by many of the greatest speakers to emphasize key elements while avoiding monotony. Martin Luther King's "I Have a Dream" speech repeats the rhetorical effect "I have a dream." President Obama also uses repetition in his victory speech in November 2008. The line "but tonight, because of what we did on **this** day, in **this** election, at **this** defining moment, change has come to America" illustrates how the repetition of a single word ("this") can work well in a speech.

More examples:

We cannot dedicate, we cannot consecrate, we cannot hallow this ground, ...

—Abraham Lincoln

We shall fight in France and on the seas and oceans, we shall fight with growing confidence and growing strength in the air. We shall defend our island whatever the cost may be; we shall fight on the beaches and landing grounds, in fields, in streets and on the hills, ... we shall never surrender.

—Winston Churchill

We need to lead a global effort against nuclear proliferation to keep the most dangerous weapons in the world out of the most dangerous hands in the world.

—John Kerry

May we pursue the right without self-righteousness.

May we know unity without conformity.

May we grow in strength without pride in self.

May we, in our dealings with all peoples of the earth, ever speak truth and serve justice.

—Dwight D. Eisenhower

(3) Alliteration

Another type of rhythmic language is alliteration, or repeating two or more words in series that begin with the same consonant.

Some examples:

Somewhere at this very moment, a child is being born in America. Let it be our cause to give that child a happy home, a healthy family, and a hopeful future.

—Bill Clinton

Let us go forth to lead the land we love...

—J. F. Kennedy

My style is public negotiations for parity, rather than private negotiations for position ...

—Jesse Jackson

...a place where destiny was not a destination, but a journey to be shared and shaped...

—Barack Obama

(4) Antithesis

It is a common form of parallel structure comparing and contrasting dissimilar elements. It is a figure of balance in which two contrasting ideas are deliberately used in consecutive phrases or sentences. Antithesis allows you to use contrasting statements in order to make a rhetorical point.

Some examples:

We must learn to live together as brothers or perish together as fools.

—Martin Luther King, Jr.

Reasonable men adapt to the world. Unreasonable men adapt the world to themselves. That's why all progress depends on unreasonable men.

—George Bernard Shaw

Again, you can't connect the dots looking forward; you can only connect them looking backward.

—Steve Jobs

That's one small step for a man, one giant leap for mankind.

—Neil Armstrong

Ask not what your country can do for you, ask what you can do for your country; let us never negotiate out of fear. But let us never fear to negotiate.

—John F. Kennedy

5.4.6 Use Inclusive Language

Language can either inspire your listeners or turn them off very quickly. One of the fastest ways to alienate an audience is to use non-inclusive language. Different from non-inclusive language, inclusive language aims to ensure that all members of society are treated with equal respect and that no individual or group is overlooked. Inclusive language avoids terms that might be considered offensive or which stereotype some people by needlessly concentrating on how they differ from others. For example, language that makes assumptions about individuals on the basis of their race, disability, sexuality or gender could not be considered inclusive. The purpose of inclusive language is to establish and demonstrate that all are equal citizens. This means inclusive language is particularly important in any official documents or statements from public bodies, such as schools, hospitals or government agencies. To escape any impression of bias, for instance, a police chief might speak of "police officers" rather than "policemen". Let's look at some common problem areas related to language about gender, ethnicity, sexual orientation, and disabilities.

1) Gender-specific language

The first common form of non-inclusive language is the language that privileges one of the sexes over the other. There are three common problem areas that speakers run into while speaking: using "he" as generic, using "man" to mean all humans and gender typing jobs.

(1) Generic "he"

The generic "he" happens when a speaker labels all people within a group as "he" when in reality there is a mixed-sex group involved. Consider the statement, *"Every morning when an officer of the law puts on his badge, he risks his life to serve and protect his fellow citizens."* In this case, we have a police officer who is labeled as male four different times in one sentence. Obviously, both male and female police officers risk their lives when they put on their badges. A better way to word the sentence would be, *"Every morning when officers of the law put on their badges, they risk their lives to serve and protect their fellow citizens."* Notice that in the second sentence, we made the subject plural ("officers") and used neutral pronouns ("they" and "their") to avoid the generic "he".

(2) Use of "man"

Traditionally, speakers of English have used terms like "man", "mankind", and (in casual contexts) "guys" when referring to both females and males. In the second half of the twentieth century, as society became more aware of gender bias in language, organizations like the National Council of Teachers of English developed guidelines for nonsexist language. For example, instead of using the word "man", you could refer to the "human race." Instead of saying, "hey, guys," you could say, "Hi, everyone." By using gender-fair language you will be able to convey your meaning just as well, and you won't risk alienating half of your audience.

(3) Gender-typed jobs

The last common area where speakers get into trouble with gender and language has to do with job titles. It is not unusual for people to assume, for example, that doctors are male and nurses are female. As a result, they may say "she is a woman doctor" or "he is a male nurse" when mentioning someone's occupation, perhaps not realizing that the statements "she is a doctor" and "he is a nurse" already inform the listener about the sex of the person holding that job. Speakers sometimes also use a gender-specific pronoun to refer to an occupation that has both males and females.

Exclusive Language	Inclusive Language
Policeman	Police officer
Businessman	Businessperson
Fireman	Firefighter
Stewardess	Flight attendant
Waiters	Wait staff/servers
Mailman	postal worker

2) Ethnic identity

Another type of inclusive language relates to the categories used to highlight an individual's ethnic identity. Ethnic identity refers to a group with which an individual identifies based on a common culture. If you want to be safe, the best thing you can do is to ask a couple of people who belong to an ethnic group how they prefer to label themselves.

3) Sexual orientation

Another area that can cause some problems is referred to as heterosexism. Heterosexism occurs when a speaker presumes that everyone in an audience is heterosexual or that opposite-sex relationships are the only norm. For example, a speaker might begin a speech by saying, *"I am going to talk about the legal obligations you will have with your future husband or wife."* While this speech starts with the notion that everyone plans to get married, which might not be the case, it also assumes that everyone will label their significant others as either "husbands" or "wives". Although some members of the gay, lesbian, bisexual, and transgender/transsexual community will use these terms, others prefer more gender-neutral terms like "spouse" and "partner". Moreover, legal obligations for same-sex couples may be very different from those for heterosexual couples. Notice also that we have used the phrase "members of the gay, lesbian, bisexual, and transgender/transsexual community" instead of the more clinical-sounding term "homosexual".

4) Disability

The last category of exclusive versus inclusive language that causes problems for some speakers relates to individuals with physical or mental disabilities. See the following Table "Inclusive Language for Disabilities" which provides some examples of exclusive versus inclusive language.

Exclusive Language	Inclusive Language
Handicapped People	People with disabilities
Person in a wheelchair	Person who uses a wheelchair
Crippled	Person with a physical disability
Mentally retarded	Person with an intellectual disability
Special needs program	Accessible needs program

Key Takeaways of This Chapter

★ Oral language is designed to be listened to and to sound conversational, which means that word choice must be simpler, more informal, and more repetitive. Written language uses a larger vocabulary and is more formal.

★ Denotative definitions are the agreed-upon meanings of words that are often found in dictionaries, whereas connotative definitions involve individual perceptions of words.

★ Using simple and familiar language is important for a speaker because this kind of language is a factor of attention and draws in the audience.

★ Using appropriate language means that a speaker's language is suitable or fitting for themselves as the speakers, the audience, the speaking context, and the speech itself.

★ Vivid language helps listeners create mental images. It involves both imagery (e.g., concreteness, simile, and metaphor) and rhythm (e.g., parallelism, repetition, alliteration, and assonance).

★ Using Inclusive language avoids placing any one group of people above or below other groups while speaking. As such, speakers need to think about how they refer to various groups within society.

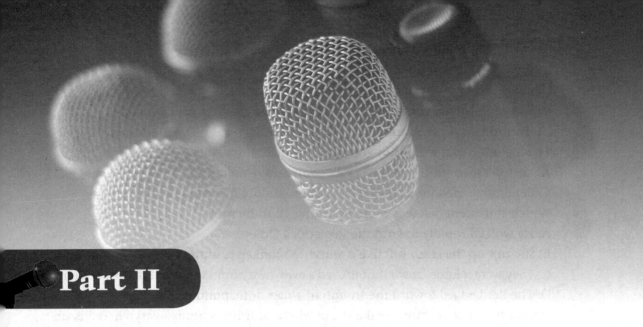

Part II

Exercises

I. Disscuss the following questions.

1. What is the difference between denotative and connotative meanings? Why/ when might you choose one over the other?
2. What are the basic criteria for the effective use of language in public speaking?
3. Give some examples regarding the use of rhetorical devices in speech and explain how that rhetoric functions to communicate a specific idea more clearly.
4. Watch a presidential press conference or a political speech via accessible websites. Identify the uses of imagery and rhythm. How did the imagery and rhythm enhance the effect of the speech?
5. Why is inclusive language important? Write down the various groups you belong to in life; how would you want these groups to be referred to by a speaker? Share your list with your classmates and see if that person reaches the similar conclusions with you. If there are differences in your perceptions, why do you think those differences are present?

II. Choose the correct answer.

1. Which of the following is NOT a guideline for using language appropriately?
    A. Using language appropriately for the topic.
    B. Using language appropriately for the speaker.
    C. Using language appropriately for the audience.
    D. Using language appropriately for the medium.

2. Which of the given words or phrases is the most concrete and specific?

    A. Performer.   B. Actress.   C. Movie star.   D. Entertainer.

3. The meaning of a word that you find in a dictionary is its _____.

    A. abstract meaning   B. connotative meaning

    C. denotative meaning   D. approximate meaning

4. Which statement below is more figurative than literal?

    A. He walked rapidly toward the Registrar's Office.

    B. She ran up the steep hill like a starving monkey running to a ripe banana.

    C. They were a large crowd that moved slowly away from the scene of the accident.

    D. The herd edged toward the trough in eager anticipation.

5. "Freedom is like a drum; strike it anywhere and it resounds everywhere" is an example of _____.

    A. metaphor   B. repetition

    C. antithesis   D. simile

6. In his speech on the importance of regular exercise, David stated, "Taking the first step toward a healthier lifestyle requires three commitments: discipline, determination, and desire." In this statement, David used _____.

    A. metaphor   B. alliteration

    C. antithesis   D. repetition

7. Your textbook recommends using repetition and parallelism to enhance the _____ of your speeches.

    A. rhythm   B. credibility

    C. emotional appeal   D. appropriateness

8. "Let us never negotiate out of fear. But let us never fear to negotiate" is an example of _____.

    A. imagery   B. repetition

    C. antithesis   D. metaphor

9. "A voter without a ballot is like a soldier without a bullet" is an example of _____.

    A. simile and parallelism   B. metaphor and parallelism

    C. personification and parallelism D. antithesis and simile

10. Which of the following is not an example of inclusive language?

    A. Person with disability.   B. Flight attendant.

    C. Lesbian woman.   D. Businessman.

Ⅲ. Decide whether the following statements are true or false. Write T/F in the brackets.

1. ( ) As your textbook explains, if you want to sound eloquent, you should use words that are unfamiliar to the audience.

2. (   ) A speech dominated by abstract words will always be clearer than one dominated by concrete words.
3. (   ) The more abstract a word, the more ambiguous it will be.
4. (   ) A public speaker needs to use big words to impress the audience.
5. (   ) In dealing with technical topics, a speaker has little choice but to use technical language.
6. (   ) Using metaphor is an excellent way to enhance the imagery of a speech.
7. (   ) Antithesis and alliteration are excellent ways to enhance the rhythm of a speech.
8. (   ) Denotative meanings are ideas suggested by a word.
9. (   ) Saying a Wolf is "a man who aggressively pursues women" is a denotative meaning.
10. (   ) A speaker would be more likely to use shorter sentences than a writer.
11. (   ) Inaccurate use of language can harm a speaker's credibility.
12. (   ) An excellent way to improve your credibility as a speaker is to use fancy, complicated words rather than familiar words.
13. (   ) Language that is appropriate for some occasions may not be appropriate for others.
14. (   ) Using inclusive language is an important part of being an audience-centered public speaker.
15. (   ) Using inclusive language is important in public speaking both as a matter of audience adaptation and as a matter of accuracy in language.

IV. Modify the language used in the given written text and make it suitable for a speech.

Why you should call instead of texting?

So many things can keep you from seeing your loved ones in person, from busy schedules to long distances to a rather unexpected pandemic. Fortunately, thanks to modern technology, the people we miss are often only a phone call or text message away. But if you're someone who is more prone to type out messages than verbal ones, you may want to reconsider. According to science, if you want to feel more connected to the people you're talking to, you should call them instead of texting.

A new study, published in the *Journal of Experimental Psychology*, found that communication interactions that included voice, like a phone call or video chat, created stronger social bonds than communication through typing, like text messaging or email.

In the study, researchers used various experiments to gauge connectedness.

In one, they asked 200 people to make predictions about what it would be like to reconnect with an old friend by email or by phone and then assigned people at random to do one or the other. Although people anticipated that a phone call would be more awkward, hearing someone's voice actually made the experience better.

"People reported they did form a significantly stronger bond with their old friend on the phone versus email, and they did not feel more awkward", study co-author Amit Kumar, an assistant professor of marketing at the McCombs School of Business, said in a statement.

In another experiment, the researchers had strangers connect by either texting, talking over video chat, or talking using only audio. They found that both forms of voice communication—whether video or audio only—made the strangers feel significantly more connected than when they communicated via text.

Sabrina Romanoff, a Harvard trained clinical psychologist based in New York City, says people tend to text or email instead of calling because of convenience, as they see it as a controlled form of communication where they can "correspond information exactly in the way they intend without unexpected additions by the other person".

Romanoff says that in reality, texting can make it hard to determine the true meaning behind a conversation. "A phone call is actually more convenient when considering the net effects of the message", she explains. "Each party is more present, and therefore, able to gauge the meaning behind the content without ruminating on the endless possible meanings behind words and punctuation."

V. Explore a number of rhetorical figures at "Glossary of Rhetorical Terms" by scaning the code. As you look through them, which ones do you find interesting and helpful? Which ones have you heard speakers use more frequently?

VI. Speech Practice.

You are asked to write and deliver a 3-minute speech on one of the following topics:

(1) Cultural Symbols of China;

(2) Two Cheers for "made in China;

(3) My Big Story in 2049;

(4) _____ is a Challenge to All.

Try to integrate at least 3 examples from these rhetorical devices discussed in the textbook. You are also expected to avoid any of the non-inclusive language discussed in the textbook.

Ⅶ. Never neglect speaking ethical issues. Discuss the situation with your partner and provide your thoughts on the questions given.

Jonathan knows he hasn't really prepared for his speech very well. Instead of going to the library, he went to a party over the weekend. Instead of finding supporting evidence, he went to the movies with his best friend. Two days before he's going to give his speech, Jonathan decides that he won't even bother with the library. Instead, he opts to just write out a quick speech and fill it with lots of "flowery" language. He creates a number of interesting similes and metaphors. He makes sure that his speech has a fun rhythm to it and has some great instances of alliteration. Upon finishing his preparation, Jonathan thinks to himself; well, the speech may have no content, but no one will really notice.

(1) Is it ever ethical to be devoid of content and opt instead for colorful language?

(2) Should language ever be a substitute for strong arguments?

(3) If you were a friend of Jonathan's, how would you explain to him that his behavior was unethical?

Chapter 6

Delivery

Part I

Understanding Delivery

1. A gentleman remains composed and being polite to others. (君子不失色于人，不失口于人。)

—*Book of Rites* (《礼记》)

2. Without effective delivery, a speech of the highest mental capacity can be held in no esteem. With effective delivery, even one with moderate abilities may surpass those of the highest talent.

—*Cicero*

In the context of public speaking, delivery refers to the presentation of the speech you have researched, organized, outlined, and practiced. Delivery is of great importance because it is what is most immediate to the audience.

Delivery can communicate confidence and preparedness to our audience. Effective delivery shows the audience that we have researched our topic and understood what we are speaking about. However, delivery is not everything in public speaking. A good delivery cannot compensate for a poorly prepared message, or one lacking in substance. The delivery isn't more essential than what we have to say, but without good delivery, our listeners may never hear what we have to say.

In public speaking, we should dismiss the myth that public speaking is just reading and talking at the same time. Speaking in public has more formality than talking. During a speech, we should present ourselves professionally. This doesn't necessarily mean we must wear a suit or "dress up", but it does mean making ourselves presentable by being well groomed and wearing clean, appropriate clothes. It also means being prepared to use language correctly and appropriately for the audience and the topic, to make eye contact with our audience, and to look like we know your topic very well. While speaking has more formality than talking, it has less formality than reading. Speaking allows for flexibility, meaningful pauses, eye contact, small changes in word order, and vocal emphasis. Reading is a more or less exact replication of words on paper without the use of any nonverbal interpretation. Speaking, as we will realize if we think about excellent speakers we have seen and heard, provides a more animated message.

 # 6.1   Four Modes of Delivery

There are four types of delivery that most speakers utilize in a speech: **Speaking from memory**, **Reading from manuscript**, **Speaking impromptu** and **Speaking extemporaneously**. Each term refers to the method used by the speaker in delivering a speech.

1) Speaking from memory

The memorized style of speaking refers to when the manuscript is committed to memory and recited to the audience verbatim (word for word). Actors, of course, recite from memory whenever they perform from a script in a stage play, television program, or movie scene. When it comes to speeches, memorization can be useful when the message needs to be exact and the speaker doesn't want to be confined by notes.

The advantage of memorization is that it enables the speaker to maintain eye contact with the audience throughout the speech. Being free of notes means that you can move freely around the stage and use your hands to make gestures. If your speech uses visual aids, this freedom is even more of an advantage. However, there are some real and potential costs. First, unless you also plan and memorize every vocal cue (the subtle but meaningful variations in speech delivery, which can include the use of pitch, tone, volume, and pace), gesture, and facial expression, your presentation will be flat and uninteresting, and even the most fascinating topic will suffer. You might end up speaking in a monotone or a sing-song repetitive delivery pattern. Second, if you lose your place and start trying to *ad lib* (Latin, deliver spontaneously), the contrast in your style of delivery will alert your audience that something is wrong. More frighteningly, if you go completely blank during the presentation, it will be extremely difficult to find your place and keep going.

2) Reading from manuscript

Manuscript speaking is the word-for-word iteration of a written message. In a manuscript speech, the speaker maintains his or her attention on the printed page except when using visual aids. This is not the best way to deliver a speech in front of an audience but certainly, there are instances when this mode of delivery is necessary as with statements where no mistakes must be made. One illustrative example would be a person in a position of great responsibility such as a head of state delivering a state-of-the-nation address. Another instance would be when strict limits are placed on a speech, for example, when delivering on radio or on television, or when the occasion is a solemn or historic one, the read speech is the most appropriate.

Reading a manuscript of a speech gives the speaker the advantage of not omitting vital information and staying focused, but it takes away from other important aspects, such as eye contact. A manuscript speech may be appropriate at a more formal affair (like a business report to shareholders) when the speech must be delivered exactly as written in order to convey the proper emotion or decorum the situation deserves. However, there are costs involved in manuscript presentations. First, it's typically an uninteresting way to present. Unless the presenter has rehearsed the reading as a complete performance animated with vocal expression and gestures, the speech tends to be dull. Keeping one's eyes glued to the script prevents eye contact with the audience. For this kind of "straight" manuscript presentation to hold the audience attention, the audience must be already interested in the message and speaker before the delivery begins.

It is worth noting that professional speakers, actors, news reporters, and politicians often read from an autocue device, commonly called a teleprompter, especially when appearing on television, where eye contact with the camera is crucial. With practice, a presenter can achieve a conversational tone and give the impression of speaking extemporaneously and maintaining eye contact while using an autocue device. However, success in this medium depends on two factors. First, the presenter is already an accomplished public speaker who has learned to use a conversational tone while delivering a prepared script. Second, the presentation is written in a style that sounds conversational.

3) Speaking impromptu

Impromptu speeches are ones that are delivered without notes or a plan, and without any formal preparation. In other words, they are very spontaneously delivered. This is one of the most nerve wracking situations for most speakers because there isn't a plan or agenda to follow—they just have to get up and speak without any "thinking" time. Oftentimes, ceremonial toasts, grace before meals, an acknowledgement, an introduction, offering thanks and so on, fall into this category. The advantage of this kind of speaking is that it's spontaneous and responsive in an animated context. The disadvantage is that the speaker is given little or no time to contemplate the central theme of his/her message. As a result, the message may be disorganized and difficult for listeners to follow.

Actually, this kind of "on the spot" speech is the core of everyday conversation. So if someone turns to you and asks for your thoughts, don't panic. Take a deep breath and think through a logical beginning, middle and ending progression. Keep the audience on track by stressing key words such as: *The first point I'd like to cover..." "Next you will see..." "And finally I would like to add..."* Organizing a speech and breaking it down into parts is a quick way to mentally prepare a speech.

Here is a step-by-step guide that may be useful if you are called upon to give an impromptu speech in public.

> - Take a moment to collect your thoughts and plan the main points you want to make.
> - Thank the person for inviting you to speak. Avoid making comments about being unprepared, called upon at the last moment, or feeling uneasy.
> - Deliver your message, making your main point as briefly as you can while still covering it adequately and at a pace your listeners can follow.
> - Thank the person again for the opportunity to speak.
> - Stop talking (it is easy to "ramble on" when you don't have something prepared).

As you can see, impromptu speeches are generally most successful when they are brief and focus on a single point.

When you are organizing your points in impromptu speeches, you can refer to the three frequently used structures of an impromptu speech:

(1) **PREP (Point, Reason, Example, Point)**—Start off by clearly stating your point. Share the primary reason (or reasons, if you have more time). Then, share an example where your main point or reason is supported. Finally, conclude by summarizing your central point again. This prep pattern could be applied and adapted easily on many occasions.

(2) **IPCC: Issue, Pros vs. Cons, Conclusions**—Start off by framing the issue. Talk about the benefits, and then talk about the drawbacks. Conclude with your recommendation. For example, you want to talk about online shopping, you may start with describing its popularity, continue with its blessings and curses, and then conclude with your suggestions. As a matter of fact, any controversial topic which covers more than one aspect could follow this pattern.

(3) **5W**—In this pattern, approach your topic by addressing Who, What, When, Where, and Why elements. For example, if you are asked to talk about your traveling experience, you could talk about: with whom you travelled; where and when did you go; what activities did you enjoy? why did you choose that place? This pattern sounds like a story!

4) Speaking extemporaneously

Extemporaneous speaking is the presentation of a carefully planned and rehearsed speech, spoken in a conversational manner using brief notes. By using notes rather than a full manuscript, the extemporaneous speaker can establish and maintain eye contact with the audience and assess how well they are understanding the speech as it progresses. The opportunity to assess is also an opportunity to restate more clearly any idea or concept that the audience seems to have trouble grasping. For instance, suppose you are speaking about workplace safety and you use the term "sleep deprivation". If you notice your audience's eyes glazing over, this might not be a result of their own sleep deprivation, but rather an indication of their uncertainty about what you mean. If this happens, you can add a short explanation; for example, "sleep deprivation is sleep loss serious enough to threaten one's cognition, hand-to-eye coordination, judgment, and emotional health." You might also (or instead) provide a concrete example to illustrate the idea. Then you can resume your message after having clarified an important concept.

Speaking extemporaneously has some advantages. It promotes the likelihood that you, the speaker, will be perceived as knowledgeable and credible. In addition, your audience is likely to pay better attention to the message because it is engaging both verbally and nonverbally. The disadvantage of extemporaneous speaking is that it requires a great deal of preparation for both the verbal and the nonverbal components of the speech. Adequate preparation cannot be achieved the day before you're scheduled to speak. The extemporaneous style is the method most often recommended (and often required) in today's public speaking occasions, and is generally the best method in other settings as well. While it is not the only method of delivering a speech, it is the mostly desired for presentations in other courses, in the business world and in pursuing future careers.

To sum up, the speech delivery method you choose will depend on many factors, such as how formal or informal the presentation is, how well you know your subject, who the audience is, and your own comfort level. When you take the time to analyze these factors and educate yourself about your choices, you can make the best decision about what method to use and give a great speech.

6.2 Practicing Speech Delivery

When giving a speech or presentation, the "how" is as important as the "what". The subject alone may not be enough to hold the interest of an audience. As a matter of fact, there are many potentially interesting and entertaining topics that are made boring because the speaker has not learned how to deliver his/her information appropriately.

The elements of delivery can be divided into vocal delivery (i.e. volume, pace, pitch, pronunciation, enunciation and articulation) and physical delivery (i.e. appearance, stance, gestures and eye contact). It also includes the use of aids and timing. In what follows, these elements of speech delivery will be discussed.

6.2.1 Vocal Aspects of Speech Delivery

Vocalics, also known as paralanguage, is the subfield of nonverbal communication that examines how we use our voices to communicate orally. For all speakers, good vocalic technique could be best achieved by facing the audience with our chin up and our eyes away from the notecards and by setting our voice at a moderate speed. Effective use of vocalics also means that we make use of appropriate pitch, pauses, vocal variety, and correct pronunciation.

1) Volume

Volume refers to the loudness or softness of a speaker's voice. As mentioned, public speakers need to speak loudly enough to be heard. In addition, volume is often needed to overcome ambient noise, such as the hum of an air conditioner or the dull roar of traffic passing by. In addition, we can use volume strategically to emphasize the most important points in the speech. In other words, increasing public speaking volume on certain key words in the speech can create a dramatic effect as it seeks to underscore certain key points we are driving at. For example, if we want to say:

"While last year's report shows a dip in profits in the first quarter, our team has managed to drive up profits in the same period through intensive marketing efforts."

The dramatic effect immediately shoots up when we increase the speaking volume by a notch at the keywords *"drive up"*, as it demonstrates that the team has helped the organization to increase profits. Our objective is to say that profits have increased, right? So, emphasize that!

Furthermore, using slightly increased public speaking volume at the beginning of the presentation definitely gives the impression of a confident, credible speaker. However, if we want to indicate something negative, sad, add a sense of mystery, or elicit a sense of sympathy, the volume may drop a notch and trail away (but we must be audible!). For example:

"The Tsunami which hit Indonesia in 2004, has claimed lives in the thousands, and even more were made homeless. This morning, many lives were again claimed by the forces of nature in Indonesia…"

Do remember to adjust the volume to the physical setting of the presentation. If we are in a large auditorium and the audience is several yards away, we will need to speak louder. Conversely, if we speak in a smaller space, with the audience a few feet away, we want to avoid overwhelming the audience with shouting or speaking too loudly.

2) Rate

Rate is the speed at which a person speaks. A common problem of nervous public speakers is speaking too quickly or feeling like the speaker is rushing through a speech. Rate is an important tool in enhancing the meanings of the speech. A rapid, lively rate can communicate such meanings as enthusiasm, urgency, or humor while a slower, moderate rate can convey respect, seriousness, or careful reasoning. By varying rapid and slower rates within a single speech, we can emphasize the main points and keep our audience interested.

How to calculate the speaking rate?

The most common way to express one's speaking rate is in words per minute (wpm). To calculate this, simply take the total number of words spoken and divide by the number of minutes it took you to speak them.

Speaking Rate (wpm) = Total words / # of minutes

Another way to measure speaking rate is in syllables per minute (spm):

Speaking Rate (spm) = Total syllables / # of minutes

Why syllables per minute? Not all words are equal. Consider these two sentences:

"Modern readability tests are designed to indicate comprehension difficulty when reading a passage of contemporary academic English." (17 words; 41 syllables)

"Ask not what your country can do for you; ask what you can do for your country." (17 words; 19 syllables)

If you were to speak these two sentences at the same rate in words per minute, the second sentence would seem considerably faster with fewer syllables. Despite the sensibility of using syllables/minute, the words/minute measure is more commonly used, because it is generally easier to calculate.

How to determine your speaking rate?

A really quick estimate of your speaking rate can be obtained by timing yourself while reading a selection of text with a known word count. Then, simply calculate using the method above. But, this is not really your speaking rate. It's your reading rate. Even if you read something out loud, it's not the same thing as a speaking rate. The best way to determine your speaking rate is to time yourself delivering a real speech with a real audience. (Video helps—you can count your words from it too.) Most professional speakers speak at approximately 145-160 words per minute (wpm), while many sources state that an average American English speaker engaged in a friendly conversation speaks at a rate of approximately 110-150 wpm. One single-spaced, 12-point font page would normally last about 3-5 minutes (approximately 500 words).

A general rule of thumb is that the larger the audience is, the slower should be the delivery. In a face-to-face conversation, it is relatively easy to tell if your listener is hearing and understanding you; however, with a large audience you need to allow for the fact that some listeners will think and react slower than others. This is also true if you are using a microphone. You need to speak in a more measured tone in order to counter the effects of amplification. This does not, of course, mean that you should speak so slowly that people are in danger of falling asleep waiting for your next word.

3) Pitch/intonation

Pitch refers to the highness or lowness of a speaker's voice. All languages use pitch pragmatically as intonation to communicate different meanings, for example, to emphasize, to convey surprise or irony, or to pose a question. Generally speaking, there are four types of pitch changes as follows:

Rising Intonation means the pitch of the voice rises over time [↗];

Falling Intonation means that the pitch falls with time [↘];

Dipping Intonation falls and then rises [↘ ↗];

Peaking Intonation rises and then falls [↗ ↘].

Consciously or unconsciously, the speaker will use the different patterns of pitch to convey different meanings to the listeners. The following table demonstrates the use of pitch changes and the associated meanings in different categories.

> **Informational**: for example, "I saw a ↘ man in the garden" answers "Who did you see?" or "What happened?", while "I ↘ saw a man in the garden" answers "Did you hear a man in the garden?"
>
> **Grammatical**: for example, a rising pitch turns a statement into a yes-no question, as in "He's going ↗ home?"
>
> **Illocution**: the intentional meaning is signaled by the pitch pattern, for example, "Why ↘ don't you move to California?" (a question) versus "Why don't you ↗ move to California?" (a suggestion).
>
> **Attitudinal**: high declining pitch signals more excitement than does low declining pitch, as in "Good ↗ morn ↘ ing" versus "Good morn ↘ ing."
>
> **Textual**: information not in the sentence is signaled by the absence of a statement-ending decline in pitch, as in "The lecture was canceled" (high pitch on both syllables of "canceled", indicating continuation); versus "The lecture was can ↘ celed." (high pitch on the first syllable of "canceled", but declining pitch on the second syllable, indicating the end of the first thought).

There are some speakers who don't change their pitch at all while speaking, which is called **monotone**. One way to ascertain whether you sound monotone is to record your voice and see how you sound. If you notice that your voice doesn't fluctuate very much, you need to alter your pitch to ensure that the emphasis of your speech isn't completely lost on your audience. In a nutshell, the effective use of pitch is one of the keys to an interesting delivery that will hold your audience's attention.

4) Pause

Pauses are brief breaks in a speaker's delivery that can show emphasis and enhance the clarity of a message. A pause is also a good way of signaling that something important is coming up, thus, building up tension. In printed texts of any sort, punctuation is used to separate words. The varying punctuation marks give information about how we should read and comprehend them. They arrange the words in parcels, separating one unit from the next, so we can easily unwrap or decode them one at a time. In a speech, punctuation marks are implied in the way we deliver our words. Well-timed pauses create suspense; they add emphasis; they provide a dramatic way of expressing our feelings more forcefully than words.

A pause in the right place at the right time gives YOU:

—time to breathe

—time to consider what it is you're going to say next

—time to receive, and digest the feedback you're getting from your audience

A pause in the right place at the right time gives YOUR AUDIENCE:

—time to breathe

—time to let the images or ideas you've given them "flower" in their minds

—time to summarize what's been said

—time to prepare for what may be coming next

When to Use Pauses?

The occasions when silent pauses are useful, or even essential, are:

(1) Just before we begin the speech

When we are called upon to give our speech, we should walk up to the lectern confidently, arrange our notes, look up at the audience, and pause for a moment before speaking the first few words. We have all seen speakers uttering their first few words while looking down and arranging their notes. This does not come across very well to the audience, nor project an image of a confident speaker.

(2) When moving from one main point to another

When we move from one main point to another, we should pause to signal to our audience that we are moving to a new point. This enhances the clarity of our speech structure and avoids possible confusion on the part of the audience. Here, a pause serves the same purpose as a new paragraph in written articles.

(3) When we want to emphasize a specific point

Pausing after we have made an important point in our speech helps to provide emphasis to the point that we have just made. It forces the audience to reflect on the importance of the point, instead of rushing to catch up with our speech if we had continued on. For example,

"But, Ladies and Gentlemen, in today's increasingly competitive economic environment, do you realize that one in every three of us in this room can expect to be retrenched within the next 5 years? ..."

Here, a pause after a startling statement has been made will add emphasis to the point, and allow the audience some time to reflect on the statement, and actually feel the significance of it.

(4) When posing the audience a series of rhetorical questions

If we ask the audience a series of rhetorical questions during the speech, our intention must be for the audience to answer these questions internally to themselves to lead them to the point we want to emphasize. It is therefore important that when we posed these questions, we should pause after each question to allow the audience some time to reflect on the questions. Not doing so will leave the audience frustrated or confused, and defeat the purpose of asking these questions. This mistake is common among some speakers who went on to ask a series of rhetorical questions in their speeches without pauses. For example,

"What is most important to you in life?... Suppose you were told by your doctor tomorrow that you have only three more months to live, is that project that you have been working on till late nights everyday for the past few months, while neglecting your family, still important to you? ... So, Ladies and Gentlemen, the next time your rush around, stop to ask yourself "What Am I Rushing For?"...

Here, the silent pause after each question will allow the audience some time to reflect on the questions asked, and lead them to the main message in your speech, which in this instance, is about being clear on our goals in life.

5) Pronunciation

Another important category related to vocalics is pronunciation, or the conventional patterns of speech used to form a word. Word pronunciation is important because mispronouncing a word the audience is familiar with will harm our credibility as speakers and can confuse and even misinform our audience. One important aspect of pronunciation is articulation, or the ability to clearly pronounce each of a succession of syllables used to make up a word. Some people have difficulty in articulating because of physiological problems that can be treated by trained speech therapists, but other people have articulation problems because they come from a cultural milieu where a dialect other than standard English is the norm. Another aspect of pronunciation in public speaking is avoiding the use of verbal surrogates or "filler" words used as placeholders for actual words (like *er, um, uh*, etc.). Do remember to get away with saying "um" as many as two or three times in your speech before it becomes distracting.

6.2.2 Bodily Aspects of Speech Delivery

In addition to using our voices effectively, a key to effective public speaking is physical manipulation, or the use of the body to emphasize meanings or convey meanings during a speech. A few basic aspects of physical manipulation are discussed here, including posture, body movement, facial expressions, eye contact and dress. These aspects add up to the overall physical dimension of the speech, which we call self-presentation.

1) Posture

"Stand up tall!" I'm sure we've all heard this statement from a parent or a teacher at some point in our lives. The fact is that, posture is actually quite important. When you stand up straight, you communicate to your audience, without saying a word, that you hold a position of power and take your position seriously. If however, you are slouching, hunched over, or leaning on something, you could be perceived as ill-prepared, anxious, lacking of credibility, or not serious about your responsibilities as a speaker. While speakers often assume a more casual posture as a presentation continues (especially if it is a long one, such as a ninety-minute class lecture), it is always wise to start by standing up straight. Remember, you only get one shot at making the first impression, and your body's orientation is one of the first pieces of information audiences use to form that impression. More importantly, good posture facilitates better voice projection, improved airflow and is better for your back. Standing up straight is always better than slouching!

Correct posture for public speaking INCLUDES:

- Keeping your shoulders back and down, not slumped forward. This causes your rib cage to rise slightly, and it makes you sound better.

- Keeping the core of your body tight. This helps you stand straighter and not slouch.

- Planting your feet flat on the ground about shoulder-width apart.

- Keeping your chest slightly raised. Again, it's important not to slouch! Raising your chest slightly opens your lungs and improves your voice projection.

- Holding your chin slightly up, You don't need to look at the ceiling, but avoid putting your head down! Lowering your head hinders airflow and diminishes voice projection.

When it comes to public speaking, AVOID:

- Standing with your hands behind your back or, worse, with your arms crossed in front of your chest

- Slouching (even slightly!)

- Lowering your head (even if you don't have your speech memorized, don't keep your head bent, reading off note cards the whole time)

---

2) Body movement

Unless you are stuck behind a podium because of the need to use a non-movable microphone, you should never stand in one place during a speech. However, movement during a speech should not resemble pacing. As speakers, we must be mindful of how we go about moving while speaking. One common method for easily integrating some movements into our speech is to take a few steps any time we transition from one idea to the next. By moving at transitional points, we help to draw the audience's attention to the transition from one idea to the next, and increase the nonverbal immediacy by getting closer to different segments of the audience as well. In addition, moving our body in a controlled, purposeful manner helps to support and reinforce what we say, attracts the audience's attention and burns up our nervous energy and relieves our physical tension.

> **Bear in mind the following types of body movement:**
>
> - Stepping forward during a speech suggests we are arriving at an important point.
>
> - Stepping backward indicates we've concluded an idea and want the audience to relax for a moment.
>
> - Lateral movement implies a transitional, indicating that we are leaving one thought and taking up another. For example, if we are ready to move on to our next point, move slowly sideways until we are standing next to the lectern.

Body movement also includes gestures. These should be neither over-dramatic nor subdued. At one extreme, arm-waving and fist-pounding will distract the audience from our message and reduce our credibility. At the other extreme, refraining from the use of gestures is the waste of an opportunity to suggest emphasis, enthusiasm, or other personal connection with our topic. There are many ways to use gestures. The most obvious are hand gestures, which should be used in moderation at carefully selected times in the speech. If we overuse gestures, they lose meaning. In other words, the well-placed use of simple, natural gestures to indicate emphasis, direction, size is usually effective. Normally, a gesture with one hand is enough. Rather than trying to have a gesture for every sentence, use just a few well-planned gestures. It is often more effective to make a gesture and hold it for a few moments than to begin waving your hands and arms around in a series of gestures.

3) Facial expressions

Faces are amazing things and convey so much information. As speakers, we must be acutely aware of what our face looks like while speaking. There are two extremes we need to avoid: no facial expressions and over-animated facial expressions. First, we do not want to have a completely blank face while speaking. Some people just do not show much emotion with their faces naturally, but this blankness is often increased when the speaker is nervous. Audiences will react negatively to the message of such a speaker because they will sense that something is amiss. If a speaker is talking about the joys of Disney World and his face doesn't show any excitement, the audience is going to be turned off by the speaker and his message. On the other extreme end is the speaker whose face looks like that of an exaggerated cartoon character. Instead, our goal is to show a variety of appropriate facial expressions while speaking.

Similar to vocalics and gestures, facial expressions can be used strategically to enhance meaning. Professional public speakers know how to give their audience a special look, a side-ways glance, or simply a raised eyebrow and they elicit laughter, meaning and rapport. Raised eyebrows indicate wonder or excitement, and concern or importance is perfectly illustrated by slightly furrowed brows. A smile or pleasant facial expression is generally appropriate at the beginning of a speech to indicate your wish for a good transaction with your audience. However, you should not smile throughout a speech on child abuse, poverty, or the COVID-19 pandemic. An inappropriate smile creates confusion about your meaning and may make your audience feel uncomfortable. On the other hand, a serious scowl might look hostile or threatening to audience members and become a distraction from the message. If you keep the meaning of your speech foremost in your mind, you will more readily find the balance in facial expression.

4) Eye contact

Eye contact is sustained, meaningful contact with the eyes of audience members. Making eye contact with each person is perhaps the most important way of developing rapport with an audience. Lack of eye contact creates a barrier between you and the audience; it makes you look untrustworthy or unsure of yourself. On the contrary, maintaining eye contact is key to building a relationship that is likely to continue even after your speech ends.

Benefits of great eye contact

- **To establish a connection**

Eye contact can communicate to the audience just how much you care about their thoughts. A sustained eye contact is an invitation to turn your talk into a conversation. It creates a bond between speaker and listener, i.e., a connection that is reassuring to both parties.

- **To project authority**

With eye contact comes authority. So if you don't look at people in the eye, you can't expect them to believe your words or agree with your views. The eyes can communicate confidence and conviction.

- **To facilitate engagement**

People will feel welcome to participate when they see you scanning the crowd. They'll be at a liberty to nod, frown, smile, and raise their brows. If you look at them long enough to create a bond, you'll find a spark of recognition in their eyes. In that precise moment, you can transform them from being passive receivers to active participants.

How can we give our audience the eye contact and personal attention they deserve?

(1) See the audience as individual listeners

Before speaking, take a moment to pause and scan the room for friendly faces. Connect with listeners who you think will engage with you and focus on one audience member at a time. You'll be more conversational and confident if you do so.

(2) Involve everyone in the conversation

The key here is to connect with as many people as possible. If you're dealing with a large crowd and it's impractical to make eye contact with everyone, divide the audience into sections and just choose one member from each group to connect with.

(3) Ensure eye contact as you deliver all critical lines

Nobody expects you to sustain eye contact for an entire 30-minute presentation. However, be sure to highlight key points with strong eye contact. This includes your opening, your closing, and all other critical lines throughout. If you combine this with expressing emotion, the impact of your words will be much stronger.

(4) Meet audience members before the presentation starts

Most speakers have poor eye contact at the beginning of their presentation, improving only as the audience begins to engage with the presentation. This is natural for humans since it's hard to connect immediately with total strangers. A good tip is to meet as many of them as possible before your presentation begins by greeting people at the entrance. By the time you start speaking, at least some of them will be on your side.

Note: Cultural Differences in Eye Contact

Keep in mind that the length of eye contact varies by culture. Some cultures use eye contact more than others. If you're giving a presentation in a culture other than your own, make sure you investigate the cultural norms and behaviour of the people in your audience. For example, lack of eye contact is usually perceived to be rude or inattentive in Western cultures. In Middle Eastern cultures, it's considered inappropriate for people of the opposite sex to look each other in the eye, as that can denote a romantic interest between them. In Asian cultures, however, eye contact is seen more as a sign of disrespect, especially when the contact is made by a subordinate to his or her superior. This is because most Asian countries are largely authoritarian.

---

5) Dress

While there are no clear-cut guidelines for how you should dress for every speech you'll give, dressing is still a very important part of how others will perceive you (again, it's all about the first impression). A simple rule is "dress to impress", which means what you wear can vary greatly with your audience.

One general rule you can use for determining dress is the "step-above rule", which states that you should dress one step above your audience. If your audience is going to be dressed casually in shorts and jeans, then wear nice casual clothing such as a pair of neatly pressed slacks and a collared shirt or blouse. If, however, your audience is going to be wearing "business casual" attire, then you should probably wear a dress, or a suit. The goal of the step-above rule is to establish yourself as someone to be taken seriously. On the other hand, if you dress two steps above your audience, you may put too much distance between yourself and your audience, coming across as overly formal or even arrogant.

6) Self-presentation

When you present your speech, you are also presenting yourself. Self-presentation, sometimes also referred to as poise or stage presence, is determined by how you look, how you stand, how you walk to the lectern, and how you use your voice and gestures. Your self-presentation can either enhance your message or detract from it. Worse, a poor self-presentation can turn a good, well-prepared speech into a forgettable waste of time. You want your self-presentation to support your credibility and improve the likelihood that the audience will listen with interest.

Your personal appearance should reflect the careful preparation of your speech. Your personal appearance is the first thing your audience will see, and from it, they will make inferences about the speech you're about to present.

Be cautious with humor

Many speakers like to use humor in their speeches to keep the audience engaged and the tone more lighthearted. While humor can be a very effective tool for keeping an audience engaged, it can also be problematic, especially when dealing with cultural issues. Here is a list of issues to consider when incorporating humor into a speech.

Some basic rules to remember

- Each culture has its own style of humor.
- Humor is very difficult to export.
- Humor often involves wordplay and very colloquial expressions.
- Humor requires exceptional knowledge of a language.
- Understanding humor requires an in-depth understanding of the culture.
- Ethnic-type humor, stereotyping, and sexist, off-color, cultural, or religious humor should generally be avoided.
- Political humor can be effective in certain circumstances.
- Knowing the type of humor your audience appreciates can guide you.
- When in doubt, the safest approach is to avoid humor.
- Americans in particular begin speeches with a joke. Not all cultures appreciate or respond to this approach.
- Laughing at yourself often diffuses tense situations.

6.2.3　Other Aspects of Speech Delivery

1) Time management

Do you regularly go overtime when you're delivering a presentation? If a time limit has been set for your presentation, then it's your responsibility to finish it within that time. Knowing how long to speak is an important aspect of the art of public speaking. The length of any speech should be guided not only by audience expectations and context, but by your content as well. In some instances, the guidelines are rather loose such as speeches at weddings and retirement celebrations. In other cases, the time limits are very strict, and you may be cut off before you finish. For example, a public speaking contest often faces strict time limits. In this case, you should respect and adhere to those time guidelines.

On the one hand, if your speech is significantly longer than expected, your audience may become restless, impatient, and even hostile. On the other hand, if your speech is significantly shorter than the time expected, your audience may leave feeling disappointed or shortchanged since they may have made a significant effort to be at your presentation. But with expectations remain unfulfilled. In addition, your speech may be part of a larger program, and the planners may be dependent on you to fill a particular time slot.

In classroom speech situations, you are often told how long to speak, for instance, for five minutes. In this situation, your audience actually expects you to speak for only five minutes and your instructor expects you to speak for no less than five minutes. One way to make sure you comply with time is to time yourself when you practice your speech. Doing this will ensure that you know how long your speech runs and whether you need to adjust it. If you have prepared, practiced, and timed your speech, you should have no problem meeting your time requirement. In non-classroom situations, the goal is to meet the time expectations of the audience. If others are also scheduled to speak, be sure that your speech is not too long. If you speak for much longer than expected, someone else may not have the opportunity to speak. Your long presentation could be perceived as inconsiderate of others.

How to Manage Timing?

If you are aware of how much time you need to speak, start to look at each section of your speech, i.e., the introduction, each main idea or example, and the conclusion to see where you must either cut or add to your speech. A very general guideline to follow is that your introduction should be 10 to 15%, your conclusion should also be about 5 to 10%, with your main ideas totaling about 75 to 85% of your time.

When practicing, most speakers find they have too much material. If you just talk faster, that would be a disaster. Bear the following in mind:

(1) Decide on your "talking time"

You can't keep to time unless you know beforehand how long you should be talking. Your "talking time" is different than the total time you've been given for your presentation because of a combination of factors. You might start a couple of minutes late, you might take longer to make a point, and there may be other interruptions that delay you. So if your presentation time is one hour, your talking time will be 40 minutes (15 minutes for questions and 5 minutes for interruptions and delays).

(2) Find out how long it takes to deliver your material

This is a prerequisite to being able to keep to time. If you don't know how long your talk takes, how can you hope to meet the time limit? Time yourself early on in your planning process. This will save you time and agony. If you leave timing your presentation till the end of your planning process, you're likely to find that you've prepared too much material which will mean you have to edit your presentation. In addition, editing can be agonizing when you've familiarized yourself with your material.

(3) Write up assertions so that you don't waffle

Waffling is one of the things that can make a live presentation go longer than the rehearsal. Here's what can happen: you make your point but the audience looks blank. So you elaborate on it some more, and then some more... and before you know it you're waffling. The antidote to this is proper planning. During your planning, write each point as a full sentence (not a bullet-point) which expresses what you want to get across. You may later reduce this to a keyword or phrase in your notes. It's much better to do your thinking before, rather than during, the presentation.

(4) Be ready to adapt

Despite all your preparations, you may still run out of time. The solution is not simply to talk faster! Work out ahead of time what segment you will drop if this should happen. Make a note on the previous slide before the dropped segment. By clicking on the note on that slide, you will jump straight to something you want to cover next. This is much more professional than clicking through your slides. Your audience does not need to know that you are editing on the fly.

2) Effective use of notes

Earlier in this chapter, we've mentioned that extemporaneous speaking provides the best opportunity for speaker-audience contact and speaking extemporaneously means speakers do not have a full manuscript. Instead, speakers will use notecards.

The cards should have notes, not the full text of the speech.

> **The Purpose of Speaker Notes**
>
> Using notes adds to your credibility as a speaker. If you depend on a full manuscript to get through your delivery, your listeners might believe you don't know the content of your speech. Second, the temptation to read the entire speech directly from a manuscript is nearly overwhelming even if you're only carrying it as a safety net. Third, well-prepared cards are more gracefully handled than sheets of paper, and they don't rattle if your hands tremble from nervousness. Finally, cards look better than sheets of paper. Carefully prepared cards, together with practice, will help you more than you might think.

How to use notes?

Plan on using just five cards, written on one side only. Get 4 × 6 (cm) cards. Use one card for the introduction, one card for each of your three main points, and one card for the conclusion.

The "trick" to selecting the words to write on your cards is to identify the keywords that will trigger a recall sequence. For instance, if the word "Fukushima" brings to mind the nuclear power plant meltdown that followed the earthquake and tsunami that hit Japan in 2011, then that one word on your notecard should propel you through a sizable sequence of points and details. Once you have delivered that material, perhaps you'll glance at your card again to remind yourself of the key word or phrase that comes next.

If you use as much care in developing your notecards as you do your speech, they should serve you well. If you lose your place or go blank during the speech, you will only need a few seconds to find where you were and get going again. In addition, the use of notecards allows you to depart from the exactly prepared wordings in your manuscript. In your recovery from losing your place, you can transpose a word or phrase to make your recovery graceful. It allows you to avoid feeling pressured to say every single word in your manuscript. Under no circumstances should you ever attempt to put your entire speech on cards in little tiny writing. You will end up reading words to your audience instead of telling them your meaning, and the visual aspect of your speech will be spoiled by your need to squint to read your cards.

3) Effective use of visual aids

Jane has to give a speech in her speaking class. She's going to talk to people about the importance of exercise. She knows what she wants to say, but she's wondering if she needs something beyond just her voice. Should she prepare a poster or something to help them visualize what she's talking about?

Visual aids, or supplemental materials for public speaking that incorporate visuals, like posters, charts, or graphs, are an important part of every speech. They help audience members remember, understand, and engage in what the speaker is saying.

Power of Visual Communication

- Make your speech more interesting
- Enhance your credibility as a speaker
- Serve as guides to transitions, helping the audience stay on track
- Communicate complex or intriguing information in a short period of time
- Reinforce your verbal message
- Help the audience use and retain the information

Your visual aids should meet the following criteria:

- Big. They should be legible for everyone, and should be "back row certified".
- Clear. Your audience should "get it" the first time they see it.
- Simple. They should serve to simplify the concepts they illustrate.
- Consistent. They should reinforce continuity by using the same visual style.

---

4) Handouts

Handouts may serve to communicate complex or detailed information to the audience, but do not give handouts to the audience at the beginning of your speech since that might divert and divide the audience's attention. People will listen to the words from the handout in their minds and tune you out. They will read at their own pace and have questions. If you need to use one, state at the beginning of the speech that you will provide one at the conclusion of your presentation. This will alleviate the audience's worry about capturing all your content by taking notes, and keep their attention focused on you while you speak.

5) Video clips

Video clips can also be effective visual aids. Remember to keep the clip short and make sure it reinforces the central message of your presentation. Be a good editor, introduce the clip and state what will happen out loud, point out a key aspect of it to the audience while it plays, and then make a clear transitional statement as you turn it off. Transitions are often the hardest part of any speech as the audience can get off track, and video clips are one of the most challenging visual aids you can choose because of their power to attract attention. Use that power wisely.

6) PowerPoint slides

PowerPoint or similar visual representation programs can be an effective tool to help audiences remember your message. You'll be able to import, or cut and paste, words from text files, images, or video clips to create slides to represent your ideas. You can even incorporate web links. When using any software program, it's always a good idea to experiment with it long before you intend to use it, explore its many options and functions, and see how it can be an effective tool for you.

Tips for Using PowerPoint Slides:

- Only use bullet points. Use short fragments or keywords to keep your presentation organized.

- Be aware of your font type. Script fonts are typically difficult to see when projected onto a large screen. Your font type should also align with the occasion. If you are giving a presentation for work, stick to a font that communicates professionalism.

- Be aware of your font size. Be sure that the audience will be able to read the font. This may require you to check on the size of the room in which you will be presenting.

- Be aware of your font color. Keep it simple. When projected onto a large screen, blue letters on a black background, for instance, can be difficult to see.

- Use Animations very carefully. It may look nice, but it can also be a distraction. Only use them if they play an essential role in your presentation.

- Show a slide when it's relevant. Use a black screen or a blank slide to hide slides you're not ready to show the audience. You can keep your audience's focus on you rather than on the slides.

- Have someone proofread your slides. Typos and misspellings do more than distract the audience; it makes the speaker look careless and unprepared!

Becoming proficient at using visual aids takes time and practice. The more you practice before your speech, the more comfortable you will be with your visual aids and the role they serve in illustrating your message. Speaking to a visual aid (or reading it to the audience) is not an effective strategy. Know your material well enough that you refer to your visual aids, not rely on them.

6.3 Practicing Your Speech

Once your speech is prepared and you have considered issues of delivery (anxiety, language, style, tone, visual aids, time limits, delivery methods, and persona), stand up somewhere private and speak as if you were in front of an audience. Accomplished public speakers advise that rehearsals are almost as important to a good oral presentation as the actual content of the talk. In order to develop your best speech delivery, you need to practice and use your practice time effectively. Practicing does not mean reading over your notes or mentally running through your speech. Instead, you need to practice with the goal of identifying the weaknesses in your delivery, improving upon them, and building up good speech delivery habits.

At times, most speakers read through the outline silently a few times and think they are all set for delivery. But there is a great difference between reading about how to deliver an effective speech and actually doing it. Feeling confident while speaking is one of the advantages of practicing. It is not enough to read through your talk a couple of times. Things that read well can sound awkward. Speaking aloud, preferably standing in front of some type of audience (e.g. spouse, a friend, classmate, or colleague) who will give you honest, constructive feedback will help you find the rough spots so you can smooth them out before you are on the podium. Rehearsals, with visual aids, are also utterly essential to timing your talk properly. Your goal is to achieve the comfortable, confident, conversational style without running overtime.

Here are **guidelines** when practicing your speech.

(1) First, read through your speech silently several times until you are ready to begin. However, doing this is not practicing speech delivery. It may help you check for problems of organization and may help you familiarize yourself with the material, but it won't help in any way with your vocal and visual delivery and will only help a little with your verbal delivery.

(2) Practice delivering your speech aloud with your notes and outline. Use your notes and visual aids, practice your gestures and eye contact, and speak aloud.

(3) Stand straight, if possible, before a full-length mirror placed at a distance where your audience would be.

(4) For the first rehearsal, use your outline until you are sure of your main points and their order.

(5) After the first rehearsal, pause and ask yourself: if the order you followed is the best order of ideas, if the material you gathered is enough, if the way you expressed your ideas is the best, and if your choice of words is appropriate.

(6) Divide the speech into different parts and practice major sections, such as the introduction, several times repeatedly.

(7) Repeat the practice session as many times as needed until you have gained self-confidence and self-assurance, taking note of the proper enunciation and pronunciation of your vowels and consonants, appropriate pausing and phrasing, stress, optimum pitch, and volume.

(8) Practice alone at first. Record (either audio or video) your speech and play it back in order to get feedback on your vocal delivery.

You may use the following form to help you to rehearse your speech.

Rehearsing Your Speech: Self-Evaluation Form

1. Find a place where you can be alone to practice and record your speech using your presentational aids.

2. After your first rehearsal, listen to and watch the recording. Review your outline as you watch and listen and then answer the following questions.

Are you satisfied with how well:

The introduction got attention and led into the speech? _____

Main points were clearly stated? _____

And well developed? _____

Material adapted to the audience? _____

Section transitions were used? _____

The conclusion summarized the main points? _____

Left the speech on a high note? _____

Presentational aids were used? _____

Ideas were expressed vividly? _____ And clearly? _____

Sounded conversational throughout? _____

Sounded animated? _____ Sounded intelligible? _____

Used natural gestures and movement? _____

Used effective eye contact? _____

Facial Expression? _____

Posture? _____

Appearance? _____

List the three most important changes you will make in your next practice session:

One: _____

Two: _____

Three: _____

3. Go through the speech again. Then assess: Did you achieve the goals you set for the second practice? _____

4. Reevaluate the speech using the checklist and continue to practice until you are satisfied with all parts of your presentation.

Key Takeaways of This Chapter

★ There are four main kinds of speech delivery: impromptu speaking, extemporaneous speaking, manuscript speaking, and memorized speaking.

★ Vocalics are the nonverbal components of the verbal message. These are the important vocalic components for a speaker to be aware of: volume (loudness or softness), pitch (highness or lowness), rate (fastness or slowness), pauses (use of breaks to add emphasis), vocal variety (use of a range of vocalic strategies), and pronunciation.

★ Eye contact helps capture and maintain an audience's interest while contributing to the speaker's credibility.

★ Physical manipulation is the use of one's body to add meaning and emphasis to a speech. As such, excessive or nonexistent physical manipulation can detract from a speaker's speech.

★ Good notecards keep the speaker from reading to the audience. Good notecards are carefully based on key words and phrases to promote recall.

★ Good delivery is a habit that is built through effective practice.

Part II

Exercises

I. Discuss the following questions.

1. How do you understand that delivery is an invisible part of speech?
2. What are the four types of delivery of public speaking? What are the features of each type?
3. What are the advantages and disadvantages of speaking extemporaneously compared with speaking from a manuscript?
4. Why should you pay attention to the time limit of a speech?
5. What are the guidelines for rehearsal? Name some of them that may work for you.
6. Create your own presentation of three to five slides with no less than three images and three words per slide. Share the slides with the class and invite their feedback.

II. Choose the correct answer.

1. _____ is based on a person's use of voice and body, rather than on the use of words.
    A. Informal communication   B. Subjective communication
    C. Nonverbal communication   D. Direct communication
2. In which situation would a speaker be most likely to read from a manuscript?
    A. A speech accepting an award at a company banquet.
    B. A speech in honor of a retiring employee.
    C. A speech of welcome to new members of the Rotary Club.
    D. A speech on international policy at the United Nations.

3. Eric is preparing a speech for his public speaking class. He goes to the library and does his research. He then prepares a basic outline and creates five notecards with basic ideas to use during his speech. What type of delivery is Eric using?
   A. Manuscript.   B. Memorized.
   C. Extemporaneous.   D. Impromptu.
4. When you answer a question in class, you are using which mode of delivery?
   A. Manuscript speech.   B. Impromptu speech.
   C. Extemporaneous speech.   D. Memorized speech.
5. Which of the following types of delivery has little or no preparation?
   A. Extemporaneous.   B. Impromptu.
   C. Manuscript.   D. Memorized.
6. A radio or television anchor typically uses a script to present the news. Which type of speech preparation mode is this?
   A. Mediated.   B. Extemporaneous.
   C. Memorized.   D. Manuscript.
7. Which of the following does your textbook mention as an advantage of extemporaneous delivery?
   A. It requires only a minimal amount of gesturing by the speaker.
   B. It reduces the likelihood of a speaker making vocalized pauses.
   C. It allows greater spontaneity than does speaking from a manuscript.
   D. It requires little or no preparation before the speech is delivered.
8. Your stance, or the way you hold yourself during a presentation, is referred to as

   _____.
   A. posture   B. gesture
   C. physical delivery   D. appearance
9. Which form of vocalics is concerned with the highness or lowness of someone's speech? _____.
   A. volume   B. pitch   C. rate   D. pauses
10. A public speaker who frequently says "uh," "er," or "um" is failing to make effective use of _____.
    A. vocal variety   B. pauses
    C. pitch   D. rate
11. Which of the following does pitch NOT do?
    A. Changing the meaning of a word or expression.
    B. Affecting what audiences perceive as good voices.
    C. Altering the way an audience will respond to words.
    D. Improving the audience's ability to remember the message.

12. Which of the following is a recommendation for creating and using notes during a speech?

    A. Including only key words to trigger your memory.

    B. Reading from your notes as much as possible.

    C. Never showing your notes to your audience.

    D. Writing in small letters on your notes so that your audience can't see them.

13. Which of the following is NOT a strategy for using presentational aids during a speech?

    A. Keeping your aid in view until the audience understands your point.

    B. Talking to your audience—not the aid.

    C. Revealing the aid only when you are ready for it.

    D. Placing the aid somewhere the audience can see.

14. When using computer graphics, such as PowerPoint slides, you should do all of the following except _____.

    A. maintain simplicity

    B. showcase the software

    C. maintain background and text contrast

    D. strive for clarity

15. When practicing your speech delivery, you should do all the following except _____.

    A. record the speech to see how you sound

    B. include delivery cues on your speaking outline

    C. try to learn your speech word for word

    D. practice in front of your friends or family

Ⅲ. Decide whether the following statements are true or false. Write T/F in the brackets.

1. ( ) Speaking from a manuscript allows for greater spontaneity and directness than does speaking extemporaneously.

2. ( ) Speaking from memory is less effective when a speaker wants to be very responsive to feedback from the audience.

3. ( ) Impromptu speaking gives more precise control over thought and language than extemporaneous speaking does.

4. ( ) When speaking impromptu, you should use "5W" organizational pattern to defend your viewpoints.

5. ( ) No two people have exactly the same vocal characteristics.

6. ( ) A faster rate of speech is usually called for since it shows the fluency of a speech.

7.   (   ) Varying your pitch is much desired when giving a speech.

8.   (   ) Appearance does not impact a speaker's credibility.

9.   (   ) It is not a problem if a speaker goes over her allotted time for presenting her speech.

10.   (   ) The primary rule of using gestures in a speech is to gesture frequently and emphatically so listeners notice what you are doing.

Ⅳ. Read the following story in an expressive way. Vary your rate, pitch and volume to achieve effective vocal variety.

The Story of Mulan

Many years ago, China was in the middle of a great war. The Emperor said that one man from each Chinese family must leave his family to join the army. Mulan, a teenage girl who lived in a faraway village in China, heard the news when she was outside washing clothes.

Mulan ran into the house. Her father was sitting in a chair, carving a piece of wood. "Father!" she said. "Did you hear what the Emperor says each family must do?"

"Yes," said her old father, "I heard about it in town. Well, I may as well go pack up." He put down his carving, stood up and walked very slowly to his room.

"Wait!" said Mulan, "Father, you have not been well. If I may say so, why at your age must you keep up with all those young men?"

"What else can be done?" said her father. "Your brother is a child. He cannot go."

"Of course that's true," said Mulan. "He is too little. But I have an idea." She poured her father a cup of tea and handed it to him. "Father, have some tea. Please sit a minute. I will be right back."

"Very well, dear," said the father.

Mulan went into her room. With her sword, she cut off her long, black hair. She put on her father's robe. Going back to her father, Mulan said, "Look at me. I am your son now. I will go in your place. I will do my part for China."

"No, my daughter!" said the old man. "You cannot do this!"

"Father, listen please," said Mulan. "For years, you trained me in Kung Fu. You showed me how to use a sword." Mulan swung the sword back and forth with might.

"Only so that you could stay safe!" said her father. "I never meant for you to go to war. If they find out you are a woman, you know as well as I do that you will die!"

"No one will find out, Father," said Mulan. She picked up her sword.

"Mulan!" said the Father. He tried to get up but had to hold on to his chair.

The daughter kissed him goodbye. "I love you, Father," she said. "Take care of yourself. Tell my brother I said goodbye." She climbed on a family horse. And off she went to join the Emperor's army.

In the army, Mulan proved to be a brave soldier. In time, she was put in charge of other soldiers. Her battles went so well that she was put in charge of more soldiers. Her battles kept on going well. After a few years Mulan was given the top job—she would be General of the entire army.

Not long after that, a very bad fever swept through the army. Many soldiers were sick. And Mulan became sick, too, the General of the army.

When the doctor came out of Mulan's tent, he knew the truth.

"The General is a woman?" yelled the soldiers. "How can this be?" Some called out, "She tricked us!" and "We will not fight for a woman!" They said, "Punish her! Make her pay! The cost is for her to die!" But others called out, in voices just as loud, "With Mulan, we win every battle!" They said, "Stay away from our General!"

Just then, a soldier ran up. "Everyone!" he called. "A surprise attack is coming!"

Mulan heard this from inside her tent. She got dressed and went outside. She was not yet strong, but stood tall. She told the soldiers where they must go to hide so they could attack when the enemy came. But they must get there fast! The soldiers, even those who did not like that their General was a woman, could tell that Mulan knew what she was talking about.

It worked! The battle was won. It was such a big victory that the enemy gave up, at last. The war was over, and China was saved! You can be sure that after that last battle, no one cared anymore that Mulan was a woman.

She told the soldiers where they must goo hide so they could attack when the enemy came.

The Emperor was so glad that Mulan had ended the long war, he set aside the rule about being a woman. "Mulan, stay with me in the palace," he said. "Someone as smart as you would be a fine royal adviser."

Mulan bowed deeply. "You are too kind, Sire," she said. "But if you please,what I wish most of all is to return home to my family."

"Then at least take these fine gifts," said the Emperor. "So everyone at your home village will know how much the Emperor of China thinks of you."

Mulan returned to her village with six fine horses and six fine swords. Everyone cheered that she was safe. The person who had saved China was their very own Mulan!

V. Practice your delivery skills with the following activities.

1. Share one interesting story happened in your life to the whole class using facial expressions and body movements to emphasize key messages. When you speak, try to be as expressive as possible and ask your classmates to give your feedback on your performance to see if your delivery is a success.

2. Ask a friend to record you while you are having a typical conversation with another friend. Watch the video and observe your movements and gestures. What would you do differently if you were making a presentation? Discuss your thoughts with your classmates.

3. Divide the entire class into small groups. Play "Lie to Me," a game in which each person creates three statements (one is a lie) and tells all three statements to the group. The listeners have to guess which statement is a lie by observing the possible hints revealed from the facial expressions.

VI. Search on the TED website and find a presentation you are interested in. Watch closely the presenter's delivery and consider what you might emulate for this presentation. Give your comments on the delivery and share them with the entire class.

VII. Never neglect speaking ethical issues. Discuss the situation with your partner and provide your thoughts on the questions given.

Janet knew that her argument was really weak. She kept looking at the data trying to find a way around the weakness. Finally, it hit her. She realized that she could hide the weakest part of her argument in a really complex presentation aid. If the people can't understand it, they can't use it against me, she thought to herself.

While she was nervous during her presentation, she was confident that no one would notice what she did. Thankfully, at the end of her presentation, everyone applauded. During the question and answer period that followed, no one questioned the weak information. In fact, no one seemed to even remember the presentation aid at all.

(1) Is hiding weak information in a complex presentation aid ethical?

(2) Are complex aids that don't lead to audience understanding ever ethical?

(3) Do you think she was an unethical person or just a good, albeit manipulative, speaker?

Chapter **7**

Major Types of Speech

Part I

Informative Speech and Persuasive Speech

1. If you wish to understand a matter profoundly, you must gain it by personal practice; because you will only be able to learn the surface of the matter by only reading books. (纸上得来终觉浅，绝知此事要躬行。)

   —*Lu You*

2. A great man once said it is necessary to drill as much as possible, and the more you apply it in real situations, the more natural it will become.

   —*Robert Hutchins*

 ## 7.1 Informative Speech

Informative speaking is a means for the delivery of knowledge. Even if the audience does have some general knowledge of the topic, an informative speech will give them new knowledge or more in-depth information relevant. This kind of speech is frequently employed by teachers, professors, tour guides and journalists.

Some examples of an informative speech:

A teacher telling students how to give effective presentations

A student telling people about his/her research

A tour guide telling people about the Bell Tower in Xi'an in China

A computer programmer telling people about a new software

7.1.1   Characteristics of Informative Speeches

As a speech to teach the audience about a specific topic, an informative speech has the following characteristics.

1) Topic

The topic of an informative speech should be useful, unique and interesting. Under the guidance of this sole purpose, the speaker will try all means to create interest and uniqueness in some way.

2) Purpose

The main purpose of an informative speech is to give your audience a clear and concise picture of a topic without inserting your personal views and opinions on the matter. As a speaker, you should serve as an unbiased presenter who aims to explain the facts in a fair and equal manner.

3) Structure

Informative speeches begin with an introduction that explains the topic in a captivating manner. The body of the speech is next; it provides greater details about the subject. The last section is the conclusion, which is designed to summarize the subject and tie all of the loose ends together.

4) Organization

When the speaker writes an informative speech, he/she should research the topic thoroughly and organize the information in a clear, logical manner. List each goal or point of the speech topic in order and determine ways to move from one point to the next.

5) Presentation

Address your audience in a clear and loud voice when you are presenting your informative speech. Stimulate the thinking ability of your target audience by using visual aids or other tactics to help the audience hear, see and even feel what you are trying to share. Because the purpose of this speech is to teach your audience something new, allow a period of time at the end of your speech for questions and comments.

7.1.2   Establishing Credibility in an Informative Speech

It seems common that we do not listen to speakers who do not know what they are talking about, who cannot relate to us, or who give the impression of being dishonest. Thus, establishing credibility takes a large part of making the speech successful, particularly in informative speaking in which knowledge sharing is desired. There are at least three ways to boost your credibility as a speaker: establishing your expertise, helping your audience identify with you, and showing you are telling the truth.

Boost Your Credibility

Establish Expertise	• Cite reputable sources • Make sure your facts are accurate • Cover your points in enough detail to demonstrate your knowledge • Reveal your personal expertise with the topic
Help The Audience Identify with You	• Wear appropriate and attractive clothing • Mention what you have in common • Be friendly and enthusiastic • Relate to listeners' situation, feelin gs and motives
Show You Are Telling the Truth	• Present both sides of an issue • Share what motivated you to select your topic • Have open, natural non-verbals that correspond to what you say • Approach the speech with ethics and positive intentions

7.1.3 General Types of Informative Speeches

1) Speeches about objects

Speeches about objects focus on things like people, places, animals, or products. These types of informative speeches are about things in our sensory and physical world—things we can see, hear, smell, feel and taste.

Because we are usually speaking under time constraints, we cannot discuss any topic in its entirety. Therefore, we should limit our speech to a focused discussion of some aspects of the topic. A speech on a country, an important person, a plant, an animal, buildings, etc would all be a speech about objects.

Here is a sample informative speech about objects:

Topic: The Terra-cotta Warriors

Organizational Pattern: Topical

General Purpose: To inform

Specific Purpose: To inform my audience of some basic information of the Terra-cotta Warriors.

Introduction

Attention Getter:

Are you impressed by the magnificent scene? (A picture in the slide) Seeing it for the first time, I was holding back my breath and asking in my mind: "Who had ever made it? And why is it?"

Credibility Statement:

After searching all the relevant information online, talking to historians and even visiting it time and again, I started thinking about telling it to more people. What a splendid wonder in the world! The Terracotta Army in China!

Body

The Terracotta Army or Terracotta Warriors and Horses is a collection of 8,099 life-size Terracotta figures of warriors and horses located in the Mausoleum of the First Qin Emperor. The figures were discovered in 1974 near Xi'an, Shaanxi province, The terracotta figures were buried with the First Emperor of Qin in 210-209 BC. Consequently, they are also sometimes referred to as "Qin's Army."

The tomb of Qin Shi Huang is near an earthen pyramid 76 meters tall and nearly 350 meters square. The tomb presently remains unopened. There are plans to seal off the area around the tomb with a special tent-type structure to prevent corrosion from exposure to the outside air. However, there is at present only one company in the world that makes these tents, and their largest model will not cover the site as needed.

Qin Shi Huang's necropolis complex was constructed to serve as an imperial compound or palace. It is comprised of several offices, halls and other structures and is surrounded by a wall with gateway entrances. The remains of the craftsmen working in the tomb may also be found within its confines, as it is believed they were sealed inside alive to keep them from divulging any secrets about its riches or entrance. It was only fitting, therefore, to have this compound protected for eternity by the massive terracotta army interred nearby.

Conclusion

In 1987, the Terracotta Warriors was included in the World Heritage List by The United Nations. Today, the Terracotta Warriors is a tourist scenery of history. As one of the greatest archeological discoveries in the world, it fully demonstrates the extraordinary wisdom and superb creativity of the ancient Chinese people.

2) Speeches about processes

Speeches about processes focus on explaining a process in broader terms. Some examples of this type include: how the fingerprint lock works, how to prepare a good meal, how to tune a guitar, how to do research on your topic, etc.

Here is a sample informative speech about the process.

Topic: How to organize headphones

Organizational Pattern: Chronological

General Purpose: To inform my audience

Specific Purpose: To inform my audience of the 3 steps on how to organize headphones

Introduction

Attention Getter:

Have you ever met this situation, when you want to enjoy the music with your iPod or cellphones, but your headphones are such a mess? You have to spend a lot of time on unfastening these headphones?

Importance:

Today I'm going to tell you how to make your life easier, or save your time. After this speech you will learn how to organize your headphones.

Credibility Statement:

My friends and I love to find some tips and share them; we have found more than a hundred tips for life tips.

Body

First of all, you need to make a circle on the top of your iPod. The first step is always important.

You do not have to care how big the circle is and you do not have to measure how long the headphones are. Next, make sure you leave the plug outside. Remember this is also important for the final step. In addition, you do not have to measure how long you have to leave.

Transition:

Now that I have discussed how to make a circle, then I will now talk about making more circles.

The second step is to make more circles with your iPod player. Make sure your finger keeps pressing on the first circle. This is important because if you do not press it, you cannot complete the final step. Remember that you do not have to press it too hard. One more note: make sure you are twisting the circles in the same direction.

Transition:

Now that I have talked about how to make more circles, next, also the final step is to pull.

When you found that you do not have much line left, you need to put the left line under the first circle, and then you pull the plug we left during the first step. Make sure you do not use the headphones under the first circle, just the lines. This prepares for the situation that when you want to use them, the lines will become straight because you just pull the headphones. Remember that you do not have to care about how long the lines are and just make sure you pull the plug gently. If you pull it too hard, the circles you made before will loose. Got it? It is really a miracle, isn't it?

Conclusion

In conclusion, you have been informed how to organize headphones and it just very 3 easy steps, they are making a circle, make more circles and pull. You can try it after class. You will know how useful it is. I am sure you are going to love it and you may tell your friends who are still annoyed to spend time on unfastening the headphones.

3) Speeches about events

Speeches about events focus on things that happened, are happening, or will happen. When speaking about an event, remember to relate the topic to your audience. A speech chronicling history is informative, but you should adapt the information to your audience and provide them with some way to use the information. You should limit your focus to those aspects of an event that can be adequately discussed within the time limit. Examples of speeches about events include the Chinese Anti-Japanese War, Online Banking, the Special Olympic Games, and the 2020 US Presidential Elections.

Here is a sample informative speech about events.

Topic: The Titanic

General Purpose: To Inform

Specific Purpose: To inform my audience about one of the most famous tragedies in history, the Titanic.

Introduction

Attention Getter:

An American writer named Morgan Robertson once wrote a book called *The Wreck of the Titan*. The book was about an "unsinkable" ship called the Titan that set sail from England to New York with many rich and famous passengers on board. On its journey, the Titan hit an iceberg in the North Atlantic and sunk. Many lives were lost because there were not enough lifeboats. So, what is so strange about this? Well, *the Wreck of the Titanic* was written 14 years before the Titanic sank.

Reason to Listen:

The sinking of the Titanic was one of the largest non-war related disasters in history, and it is important to be knowledgeable about the past.

Credibility Statement:

I have been fascinated by the history of the Titanic for as long as I can remember. I have read and studied my collection of books about the Titanic many times, and have done research on the Internet.

Preview of Main Points:

First, I will discuss the Titanic itself. Second, I will discuss the sinking of the ship. Finally, I will discuss the movie that was made about the Titanic.

Body

The sinking of the Titanic remains one of the most famous tragedies in history. As known to all, the Titanic was thought to be the largest, safest, most luxurious ship ever built. At the time of her launch, she was the biggest existing ship and the largest moveable object ever built. According to Geoff Tibbals, in his 1997 book *The Titanic: the Extraordinary Story of the "Unsinkable" Ship*, the Titanic was 882 feet long and weighed about 46,000 tons. This was 100 feet longer and 15,000 tons heavier than the world's current largest ships. It could accommodate around 2,345 passengers and 860 crewmembers.

According to a quotation from *Shipbuilders* magazine, "Everything has been done in regard to the furniture and fittings to make the first class accommodation more than equal to that provided in the finest hotels onshore". Fine parlor suites located on the ship consisted of a sitting room, two bedrooms, two wardrobe rooms, a private bath, and a lavatory. The first-class dining room was the largest on any liner; it could serve 500 passengers at one sitting. Other first-class accommodations included a squash court, swimming pool, library, barber's shop, Turkish baths, and a photographer's darkroom.

Tibbals, as previously cited, described the Titanic as having an outer layer that shielded an inner layer—a "double bottom" —that was created to keep water out of the ship if the outer layer was pierced. The bottom of the ship was divided into 16 watertight compartments equipped with automatic watertight doors. The doors could be closed immediately if water were to enter into the compartments. Because of these safety features, the Titanic was deemed unsinkable and very safe.

Transition:

Now that I've discussed the Titanic itself, I will now discuss the tragedy that occurred on its maiden voyage.

The beginning of the maiden voyage was mostly uneventful. Tibbals stated that the ship departed from Queenstown in Ireland at 1:30 pm on April 10th, 1912, destined for New York. The weather was perfect for sailing—there was blue sky, light winds, and a calm ocean. According to Walter Lord in *A Night to Remember* from 1955, the Atlantic Ocean was like polished plate glass on the night of April.

The journey took a horrible turn when the ship struck an iceberg and began to sink. In the book *Titanic: an Illustrated History from 1992*, Lynch explains that the collision occurred at 11:40 pm on Sunday, April. According to Robert Ballard's 1988 book *Exploring the Titanic*, the largest part of the iceberg was under water. Some of the ship's watertight compartments had been punctured and the first five compartments rapidly filled with water. Tibbals wrote that distress rockets were fired and distress signals were sent out, but there were no ships close enough to arrive in time.

Thresh in 1992 stated that there were only 20 lifeboats on the ship. This was only enough for about half of the 2,200 people who were on board. The lifeboats were filled quickly with women and children loaded first. The ship eventually disappeared from sight. Tibbals in 1997 explains that at 2:20 am on Monday, the ship broke in half and slowly slipped under the water. At 4:10 am, the Carpathia answered Titanic's distress call and arrived to rescue those floating in the lifeboats. It was reported that in the end, 1,522 lives were lost.

Transition:

Now that we have learned about the history of the Titanic, I will discuss the movie that was made about it.

A movie depicting the Titanic and a group of fictional characters was made. The movie was written, produced, and directed by James Cameron. According to Marsh in James Cameron's Titanic from 1997, Cameron set out to write a film that would bring the event of the Titanic to life. Cameron conducted six months of research to compile a highly detailed timeline so that the film would be realistic. Cameron spent more time on the Titanic than the ships' original passengers because he made 12 trips to the wreck site that lasted between ten and twelve hours each.

Making Titanic was extremely expensive and involved much hard work. According to a 1998 article from the *Historical Journal of Films, Radio, and Television*, Kramer stated that the film had a 250 million dollar budget. A full-sized replica of the ship was constructed in Baja California, Mexico in a 17 million gallon oceanfront tank. Cameron assembled an expedition to dive to the wreck on the ocean floor to film footage that was later used in the opening scenes of the movie. Marsh in 1997 further explained that the smallest details were attended to, including imprinting the thousands of pieces of china, crystal, and silver cutlery used in the dining room scenes with White Star's emblem and pattern.

The movie was extremely successful. Kramer in 1998 reported that Titanic made approximately 600 million dollars in the United States, making it the number one movie of all time. It made approximately 1.8 billion dollars worldwide and is also the number one movie of all time worldwide. Titanic was nominated for a record eight *Golden Globe Awards* only a few weeks after its release and won four. It was also nominated for a record of fourteen *Academy Awards*, and it won eleven.

Conclusion

Review of Main Points:

Today I first discussed the Titanic itself. Second, I discussed the sinking of the ship. Finally, I discussed the movie that was made about the Titanic. The sinking of the Titanic remains one of the most famous tragedies in history.

Closure:

In conclusion, remember *the Wreck of the Titanic*, the story written fourteen years before the Titanic sank. It now seems as if it was a sheer prophecy, or a case of life imitating art. Whatever the case, the loss of lives on the Titanic was tremendous, and it is something that should never be forgotten.

4) Speech about concepts

Speeches about concepts are about beliefs, ideas, and theories. Because concepts can be vague and involved, you should limit your speech to aspects that can be readily explained and understood within the time limit. Some examples of topics for concept speeches include Taoism, Calligraphy, Principles of Feminism, the Philosophy of Non-violent Protest, Globalization, Tea Culture and Legal Requirements of Advertising.

Here is a sample informative speech about concepts.

Topic: Euthanasia

Organizational Pattern: Topical

General Purpose: To Inform

Specific Purpose: To inform my audience about its history and debates on euthanasia

Introduction

Attention Getter:

Imagine you are unable to get out of bed, to eat, unassisted, needing another person to clothe and bathe you day in and day out. Is that living? When it's your time to go, would that be dying with dignity? Let's say you have a chronic illness and you are in extreme physical pain. Wouldn't you want the right to ask your doctor to end your suffering? Welcome to the debate on euthanasia.

Statement of the General Topic and Purpose:

Today I will discuss the history and argumentation of assisted suicide.

Importance of the Topic:

Assisted suicide, also known as euthanasia, is a hot-button issue that was brought into the light by Dr. Jack Kevorkian. Dr. Kevorkian was a controversial activist who tried to legalize assisted suicide under the argument that everyone deserves a humane death. There had been much debate on the issue, and our legislatures have explored what the practice entails and the moral implications of assisted suicide. However, it is still illegal in all of the United States. But Physician Aid in Dying or PAD is legal in Washington, Oregon, and Montana. The difference is that euthanasia involves a third party administering the dose, whereas PAD leaves it up to the patient to take it.

Preview of the Main Points:

In this presentation, I will focus solely on euthanasia, including the role of Dr. Kevorkian and the moral implications of legalizing assisted suicide.

Body

The concept of choosing a time to die with the help of a physician was first medically explored by Dr. Jack Kevorkian. Born in Royal Oak, Michigan, he attended the University of Michigan. There, he saw patients suffering. Especially in cases where there was no cure available, he wanted to end their suffering in a humane way. In his own words, Dr. Kevorkian stated, "I'm going to do it right." That was published in the *New York Times* in 2007. According to a 2011 *New York Times* article, in 1990, Kevorkian helped 130 people die using his machine titled the *Thanatron*, which is Greek for "death machine". A 2011 *Washington Post* article described his infamous death machine, which is said to have been made from scraps for just $30.

Other methods Kevorkian employed were carbon monoxide masking and overdose by injection. His practice earned him the nickname Doctor Death. Due to the contentious nature of the procedures, Dr. Kevorkian had to perform them in secrecy; as I stated, this was not an open practice. No church or hospital would host his practice. This forced Dr. Kevorkian to perform assisted suicides in his Volkswagen van. However, Dr. Kevorkian grew tired of doing everything in secrecy, and the demand was high. So, he brought his practice out into the public sphere.

Transition between two Main Points:

By publicizing his work, writing about the need for assisted suicide and the humanness of dying with dignity, he started a great debate in the United States in a more elaborate and graphic attempt to draw public attention.

Dr. Kevorkian taped filming of an assisted suicide by a man who had Lou Gehrig's disease. The taping was shown on 60 Minutes in order to draw the attention of the courts. The courts decided that the taping of his assisted suicide was considered first-degree murder. In 1999. NPR stated that the court sentenced Dr. Kevorkian to 10 to 25 years in prison for this, but he only served 8. He was released on parole on June 1, 2007, on the condition that he would not offer advice on suicide to anyone. He died four years later of natural causes. Before he died, however, Kevorkian stated, "Dying is not a crime." And ever since he called attention to the idea and practice of assisted suicide, people have been debating the "how" of that quote.

Indeed it is how one enters death that stems all the debate. The moral implications alone are enough to prompt the nation's most notable academics and doctors to take a look at assisted suicide, also known as death counseling and euthanasia. According to an article released by the *New York Times* in 2011, 60% of Kevorkian's patients who chose to be euthanized were not terminally ill. In addition, the biggest critique of the method was the lack of psychiatric analysis and counseling before the procedure. According to another 2011 *New York Times* article, in at least 19 cases, persons chose to die within 24 hours of meeting Dr. Kevorkian. The *Economist* stated, "Studies of those who sought Dr. Kevorkian's help suggest that though many had a worsening illness, it was not usually terminal. Autopsies show that five people had no disease at all. A little over a third were in pain. Some presumably suffered from no more than hypochondria or depression. In response to this, Kevorkian stated on CNN on June 14, 2010, "What difference does it make if someone is terminal? We are all terminal." You see, for Kevorkian, a patient didn't necessarily need to be terminal, just suffering. "While there are heavy critiques against the procedure, Kevorkian's work can be credited for stimulating the debate and improving end-of-life care in the United States." That was printed in the *Detroit Free Press* in 2011.

Conclusion

Transitions to the Conclusion:

Today I have discussed the difficult and loaded topic of assisted suicide.

Closure with Referring Back to the Attention Getter:

Its history is synonymous with the name Dr. Jack Kevorkian. Kevorkian, while his work was controversial, did make public the topic of extreme patient suffering and a doctor's role in addressing it. Whether you support or oppose Dr. Kevorkian's work, remember that there is only one absolute rule in life, that is, it will end one day. When your time comes, I hope you are able to go with as much dignity as you lived.

7.1.4 Tips for Developing Informative Speaking

Informative speaking is about more than just informing people about a specific topic. Audiences must be kept fully engaged and interested in what is being said. Fortunately, there are easy and subtle techniques that can greatly improve your informative speaking prowess.

1) Making information clear and interesting for the audience

A clear and interesting speech can make use of description, causal analysis, or categories. With description, you use words to create a picture in the minds of your audience. You can describe physical realities, social realities, emotional experiences, sequences, consequences, or contexts. For example, in speaking about health care costs, you could explain how a serious illness can put even a well-insured family into bankruptcy. You can also use categories to group things together. For instance, you could say that there are three categories of investment for the future: liquid savings, avoiding debt, and acquiring properties that will increase in value.

2) Adjusting complexity to the audience

If your speech is too complex or too simplistic, it will not hold the interest of your listeners. How can you determine the right level of complexity? Your audience analysis is one important way to do this. Will your listeners belong to a given age group, or are they more diverse? Are some of your listeners international students? Are they all students majoring in communication studies, or is there a mixture of majors in your audience? The answers to these and other audience analysis questions will help you gauge what they know and what they are curious about.

Never assume that just because your audience is made up of students, they all share your knowledge set. If you base your speech on an assumption of similar knowledge, you might not make sense to everyone. If, for instance, you're an intercultural communication student discussing multiple identities, the psychology students in your audience will most likely reject your message. Similarly, the term "viral" has very different meanings depending on whether it is used with respect to human disease, popular response to a website, or population theory. In using the word "viral", you absolutely must explain specifically what you mean. You should not hurry your explanation of a term that's vulnerable to misinterpretation. Make certain your listeners know what you mean before continuing your speech. You should define terms to help listeners understand them the way you mean them to, give explanations that are consistent with your definitions, and show how those ideas apply to your speech topic. In this way, you can avoid many misunderstandings.

3) Keeping information limited

When you developed your speech, you should carefully narrow down your topic in order to keep information limited yet complete and coherent. If you carefully adhere to your own narrowing, you can keep from going off the track or confusing your audience. If you overload your audience with information, they will be unable to follow your narrative. Use the definitions, descriptions, explanations, and examples you need in order to make your meanings clear, but resist the temptation to add tangential information merely because you find it interesting.

4) Linking current knowledge to new knowledge

Certain sets of knowledge are common to many people in your classroom audience. For instance, most of them know what Wikipedia is. Many have found it a useful and convenient source of information about topics related to their coursework. Because many Wikipedia entries are lengthy, greatly annotated, and followed by substantial lists of authoritative sources, many students have relied on information acquired from Wikipedia in writing papers to fulfill course requirements. This is the information that virtually every classroom listener is likely to know. This is the current knowledge of your audience.

Because your listeners are already familiar with Wikipedia, you can link important new knowledge to their already-existing knowledge. Wikipedia is an "open source", meaning that anyone can supplement, edit, correct, distort, or otherwise alter the information in Wikipedia. In addition to your listeners' knowledge that a great deal of good information can be found in Wikipedia, they must now know that it isn't authoritative. Some of your listeners may not enjoy hearing this message, so you must find a way to make it acceptable.

One way to make the message acceptable to your listeners is to show what Wikipedia does well. For example, some Wikipedia entries contain many good references at the end. Most of those references are likely to be authoritative, having been written by scholars. In searching for information on a topic, a student can look up one or more of those references in full-text databases or in the library. In this way, Wikipedia can be helpful in steering a student toward the authoritative information they need.

5) Demonstrating your interest in the subject matter

Enthusiasm shows. If a speaker is interested and fully engaged in the issue he/she is speaking about, he/she will demonstrate that to the audience. The best way to get an audience to pay attention to a less-than-stellar topic is to show the audience why they should care about the issue. Successful informative speakers demonstrate to their audience that their topic is the one worth their time and attention.

Informative Speaking Preparation Model for Reference

Introduction	
Attention-Getting Opener	**Things to consider**
	Make sure you consider the background and the needs of your audience as you prepare your speech.
Relevance/Reason to Listen	
	Include visual aids and gestures to make a greater impact on your audience
Credibility	
Thesis Statement	Decide how you want to organize the body of your speech.
Preview of the key points of your speech	Here are some possible organizational patterns:
	Spatial/Sequential/Categorical/Comparative/Causation/Temporal
Transition to your Body	

(to be continued)

(continued)

Body
Main Point 1
    Supporting Point A
    Supporting Point B
Transition to your next point
Main Point 2
    Supporting Point A
    Supporting Point B
Transition to your next point
Main Point 3
    Supporting Point A
    Supporting Point B
	You should have 2-5 well-developed main points.
	
	Define any special terms that you might use.
	
	Personalize your speech to make it more interesting. You can tell personal stories, or anecdotes that reflect the experiences of the audience.
	Make your speech authoritative by including references to credible sources.
	Provide internal previews and summaries for each of the main points
	Use detailed and concrete examples in your body.

Conclusion Summary Concluding Remarks	Make your endings memorable.

7.2   Persuasive Speech

We are bombarded by persuasive messages in today's world, so thinking about how to create persuasive messages effectively is very important for modern public speakers. In persuasive speeches, you provide your own opinions and attempt to persuade the audience to accept that. The best persuasive speech marries factual information with reason and logic to convince the audience that they should reevaluate their thinking. If the logic of the persuasive argument is sound, it can then persuade the listener to go one step further and make changes to his/her own beliefs.

Persuasive speaking can involve everything from arguing about politics to talking about what to eat for dinner. It should be informative but isn't as reliable or complete as thorough facts. Like informative speeches, persuasive speeches should be delivered creatively to capture the audience's attention, but it must go one step further and allow listeners to reconsider their views or beliefs.

Some examples of a persuasive speech:

- A salesclerk trying to persuade customers to buy a new product

- A politician asking people to vote for him/her
- A student trying to get a friend to lend him some money
- An environmentalist trying to get people to start thinking about the environment

7.2.1 Characteristics of Persuasive Speeches

1) Content

One of the major characteristics of a persuasive speech is its content. The speech will typically identify a need or address a problem. Once the problem is identified, the speaker will then work to explain or prove a practical solution. The speech content will contain proof that supports these ideas to validate a point.

2) Speaking manner

The person giving the persuasive speech will speak at a rate that does not cause the audience to view him as a "fast talker." Clear, deliberate speech allows the speaker to appear as an authority on the subject matter.

3) Anticipation

A persuasive speech will also anticipate any kind of doubts, hesitations or reservations the audience may have. The persuasive speaker should be equipped with a rebuttal and a claim for each point a doubtful member of the audience might address.

7.2.2 How to Establish Credibility in a Persuasive Speech

Successful persuasive speaking involves appeals to emotions, logical arguments and the establishment of credibility. Credibility, in this context, can be defined as the power to elicit belief in what the speaker is saying and trust in the speaker himself.

1) Discuss your experience

You will be a much more credible speaker if you can demonstrate significant experience with the particular topic or subject matter of your discussion. If possible, explain why you are speaking to the audience. Did someone ask you to speak based on your experience? Did you recently complete a research project related to the speech? Whatever the reason, share it with the audience if it will contribute to your legitimacy.

2) Use authorities and cite your factual statements.

Whenever you are making a factual assertion, particularly one that is central to your argument, make sure to cite reliable, authoritative sources for that information.

3) Be specific

When making assertions to your audience, whether as the ultimate issue of your speech or as a supporting element, you should be as specific as you can. For example, it is much more credible to say *"35 out of every 1,000 children on campus are subject to bullying, which can bring great physical and psychological harms to the kids who are bullied"* than it is to say *"lots of children on campus are subject to bullying, which can make the kids who are bullied suffer a lot"*. Specificity tells the audience you have done your homework and know exactly what you are talking about.

7.2.3　General Types of Persuasive speeches

1) Questions of fact

Facts are very hard to prove. Typically, persuasive speeches of fact occur when the speaker argues that something did or did not happen. Whenever there is a question about the occurrence or existence of something, then we see a persuasive message regarding a **question of fact**. For example, you may want to persuade your audience that violence in video games causes real-world violence or stocks will continue to rise.

2) Questions of value

People place value on almost everything. We value money, time, freedom, choice, family, friendship, and a whole host of other things, but when people try to get us to value something more than something else, or to value it more than we already do, they are providing an argument in response to a **question of value**. A question about the worth, rightness, or morality of an idea or action all demands value judgments. For example, you may want to persuade the audience that it is wrong to drive over the speed limit or we should value more on our health than the money we can earn.

3) Questions of policy

Questions of policy advocate a question about whether a specific course of action should or should not be taken. These types of speeches question what should be done, such as where money should be allocated. Policy claims are probably the most common form of persuasive speaking because we live in a society surrounded by problems and people who have ideas care about how to fix these problems. For example, you may want to persuade the audience that TV talent shows should be banned or the government needs to invest more in preventing poverty at home and less in feeding the starving around the world.

Three basic issues when discussing a question of policy:

- Need—Is there a serious problem or need that requires a change from the current policy? The speaker must prove that a change from the current policy is needed.

- Plan—If there is a problem with the current policy, the speaker must have a plan to solve the problem.
- Practicality—The speaker's plan should be able to solve the problem, rather than create new and more serious problems. The speaker should show that the solution is workable.

7.2.4 Rhetorical Triangle of Persuasion

2300 years ago in his work called *On Rhetoric*, Aristotle, one of ancient Greece's greatest minds, wrote down the secret to being a persuasive speaker. They are referred to as the three pillars of persuasion: ethos, pathos and logos. Knowing how to present ethos, pathos and logos in your persuasive speech is one of the keys to making an effective argument. What are ethos, pathos and logos?

Ethos, pathos and logos are modes of persuasion used to convince and appeal to an audience. You need these qualities for your audience to accept your messages.

Ethos: your credibility and character

Pathos: emotional bond with your listeners

Logos: logical and rational arguments

1) Ethos

Ethos pertains to convincing your audience that you have good character and you are credible therefore your words can be trusted. Ethos must be established from the start of your talk or the audience will not fully accept what you will say.

Ethos appeals are based on ethics and reputation. In a speech, this could include endorsements from key people, building your own personal credibility, and citing expert testimony. To build your credibility, you have to persuade others that you are of good character, that you are trustworthy, and you are an authority on the topic of your talk. The audience's perception of you as a speaker is influential in determining whether or not they will choose to accept your proposition.

Actually, what you wear and how you behave, even before opening your mouth, can go far in shaping your ethos. Thus, you should dress appropriately for the occasion and try to appear confident, but not arrogant, and be sure to maintain enthusiasm about your topic throughout the speech. Particularly, you are suggested to give great attention to the crafting of your opening sentences because they will set the tone for what your audience should expect of your personality as you proceed.

Four main characteristics of ethos	Trustworthiness and respect
	Similarity to the audience
	Authority
	Expertise and reputation/history

2) Pathos

Pathos concerns with persuasion by appealing to the audience's emotions. As the speaker, you want the audience to feel the same emotions you feel about something, you want to emotionally connect with them and influence them. If you have low pathos, the audience is likely to try to find flaws in your arguments.

Pathos appeals are based on emotion. In a persuasive speech, you could use pathos in two ways: either to attract people towards what they want to happen or frighten them away from what they don't want to happen. Today, pathos appeals are sometimes called "pull" arguments because they persuade people by locking into what they need and then offering some resolution of these needs. Speaking with pathos means using empathy and emotion to connect with the audience. As humans, our feelings can often influence our decisions. Moreover, we are moved by our emotions—hitting the heart and the gut. Not everyone is moved by the same things, however. Some people are motivated by money; others by prestige or power. The better you know the people who you want to persuade (their demographics, job levels, reasons for being there, etc.), the better you can use examples that will move them. Overall, a speaker's goal is to create a need—driven by the positives that the people will achieve by doing what the presenter suggests or the pain they will experience by not doing it.

For example, to persuade someone to stop smoking, you might tell them a personal story about a family member who died of lung cancer and all the grief that you're suffering because of this person's fatal addiction to cigarettes. You could also allude to all the suffering that this person's smoking causes to loved ones in his life. You might also mention the discomfort that this person suffered due to chemotherapy and show pictures of lungs and other organs infected with cancer from smoking.

3) Logos

Logos mean rational appeal. Logos appeals are based on logic and include statistics, facts and evidence in support of a case. Aristotle thought it was the most important of the three appeals. Today, "logos" appeals are sometimes called "push" arguments because they persuade people by the force of the evidence. A good persuasive talk will have a good amount of logical evidence that convinces an audience that your proposition makes sense and is the best and most reasonable course to adopt. The information must make sense—it needs to be organized logically so people can follow along. Sometimes we come to believe something or to act upon something simply because someone gave us what we considered to be a "good reason". Here is where we consider evidence and reasoning as parts of the persuasive process. The key is to couch your argument or opinion in such a way that it seems to be the most rational path to take. When you use this strategy most effectively, those who disagree with you should almost seem irrational or lack common sense.

For example, when convincing someone to quit smoking, you might simply ask them a question along the lines of "Why do you engage in a habit that puts your health in extreme harm, infects your hair and clothes with a foul odor, stains your teeth and drains your wallet?" Alternatively, to appeal to the logic of reason, show the smoker how much money he is spending each year on cigarettes and talk about other things that money could go for something that would more positively benefit his life, such as a vacation, or a new computer.

7.3 Speaking on Special Occasions / Ceremonial Speeches

Special occasion speeches are different from the typical public speeches. They are more unstructured and can be either informative or persuasive or even both.

Special occasion speeches are usually shorter than informative or persuasive speeches, demonstrating that their purpose is different than other types of speeches delivered at a conference or political rally. Depending on the context, the purpose of a special occasion speech may be to remember, to praise or to humorously tease. They may contain the use of pathos that aims to convince the audience to be happy, possibly by being comedic. However, they may use pathos intended to make the audience reflective, as in a speech given at a memorial service.

7.3.1 Speeches of Introduction

1) Introducing yourself

First impressions have a big impact on how others perceive you, so how you introduce yourself to others is extremely important. Many people call an introductory speech an elevator speech because it should be succinct enough that you could introduce yourself and tell someone about your goals or interests in the time it takes to ride an elevator. It may also be called an "icebreaker" speech, as it breaks the ice and lets others get to know you. Consider your words carefully when you write a speech introducing yourself. Crafting a good self-introduction can either build or enhance your credibility.

In your preparation, you could follow the tips:

Tips	Illustrations
Make an outline of your speech.	1. State your name in the very first sentence of your speech. 2. If the introduction is work-related, mention your interests and your career goals together in the same sentence. 3. You may want to mention your education or professional training background, if it is relevant and appropriate.
Mention hobbies or outside interests.	Try writing one draft with your experience/hobbies and one without, and run both versions by an objective listener who can give you feedback before your speech.
Sell yourself.	1. If you are trying to make a good first impression in a professional context, it's important that your speech conveys your capabilities and skills. 2. Highlight the qualities, skills and experience you have which are most relevant for the audience and occasion. 3. Try to present yourself as a professional while making a strong and lasting impression.

While it is difficult to give a template, there are many examples that you can refer to, while framing your speech. Given below is an example of introducing oneself, given by a guest speaker at the graduation ceremony of a college.

One Four One One! That is the number of tigers left in the Indian subcontinent. And for the past five years, those are the numbers I have been trying to better. Needless to say, I am a tiger conservationist and after a lifetime of chasing money, success and to extent fame, I am devoting my life to chasing poachers.

No, I did not take a page out of the life of characters in best-selling books, though the parallels drawn are inevitable. I did this because this is what my life's aim was when I was, let us say, younger and naive. It took me 10 years to realize that my naivety had more individuality in it than my success did. After behaving like a groupie of Ansel Adams for years, I was more than content being just another face in the crowd. By the way, for those of you who are too young (or not worldly-wise) to have heard of Adams, he was an environmentalist and photographer, who took brilliant photographs of the Yosemite National Park in America.

You may wonder why, while addressing a batch of graduates from one of the most prestigious journalism colleges in the world, I am reminiscing about my own life. Well, introducing myself, with all my faults and mistakes, is the one way I have of explaining to you how important it is to pursue your dreams. Do not let the big bad world outside (and it is big and bad), affect that idealism you have in your heart. Follow your dreams, however stupid and impractical, someone else tells you, they are. For a few weeks after you start your jobs, you will remember my words and fight the corruption of your soul but then you will give in. It is inevitable. But try and fight it as long as you can. Channel Dylan Thomas and remember, "Do Not Go Softly Into That Good Night."

2) Introducing another speaker

Introductions can make or break a speech. Guest speakers depend on you to give them an enthusiastic welcome that prompts the audience to pay attention. A good introduction requires researching the speaker's credentials. Write your speech to explain what the audience stands to gain from listening. By memorizing the introduction and giving it with enthusiasm, you can make any guest speaker sound amazing.

Researching your speaker may be the most important thing you should do in your preparation.

- Master pronouncing the speaker's name and check for any special titles the speaker has.
- Ask the speaker what they'd like you to say. Avoid using sensitive or embarrassing information without approval.
- Find out what subject the speaker will cover and other speeches the speaker has given.
- Look up biographical information on the speaker and include a surprising detail if it fits in your introduction.
- Keep it brief and simple; your audience wants to hear your guest and not you.

Examples may vary depending on the person who is being introduced. Given below is an example of an introduction speech for a new colleague.

I'd like to take a few moments to introduce our new warehouse manager. Although he's new to the company and the area, he has a fantastic background:

He has worked for over 20 years in warehouse management and I know this experience will benefit us all. His knowledge of warehouse systems and his ability to instigate improvements will be essential for us to move forward as a business.

So I'd like to finish by saying welcome Jim Hedrix and now you have the floor.

7.3.2 Speeches of Acceptance

When you win an award or honor, it's traditional to share a few words. Writing an acceptance speech can be challenging, so it helps to brainstorm and prepare in advance. You should open your speech with a brief introduction of gratitude, move on to thanking your benefactors, and conclude your speech with some inspiration and optimism. This is your time to shine, but showing humility will leave your audience feeling truly pleased for you and your success.

In your preparation, you could follow the tips:

- Make a list of reasons you're thankful for receiving the award or honor.
- Make a list of people you want to thank in your speech.
- Read other acceptance speeches for inspiration.

Here's an excerpt of a speech of acceptance delivered by Mo Yan in his Nobel Literature Prize in 2012.

Your Majesties, Your Royal Highnesses, Ladies and Gentlemen,

For me, a farm boy from Gaomi's Northeast Township in far-away China, standing here in this world-famous hall after having received the Nobel Prize in Literature feels like a fairy tale, but of course it is true.

My experiences during the months since the announcement have made me aware of the enormous impact of the Nobel Prize and the unquestionable respect it enjoys. I have tried to view what has happened during this period in a cool, detached way. It has been a golden opportunity for me to learn about the world and, even more so, an opportunity for me to learn about myself.

I am well aware that there are many writers in the world who would be more worthy Laureates than I. I am convinced that if they only continue to write, if they only believe that literature is the ornament of humanity and a God-given right, "She will give you a garland to grace your head and present you with a glorious crown."

I am also well aware that literature only has a minimal influence on political disputes or economic crises in the world, but its significance to human beings is ancient. When literature exists, perhaps we do not notice how important it is, but when it does not exist, our lives become coarsened and brutal. For this reason, I am proud of my profession, but also aware of its importance.

I want to take this opportunity to express my admiration for the members of the Swedish Academy, who stick firmly to their own convictions. I am confident that you will not let yourselves be affected by anything other than literature.

I also want to express my respect for the translators from various countries who have translated my work. Without you, there would be no world literature. Your work is a bridge that helps people to understand and respect each other. Nor, at this moment, can I forget my family and friends, who have given me their support and help. Their wisdom and friendship shine through my work.

Finally, I wish to extend special thanks to my older relatives and compatriots at home in Gaomi, Shandong, China. I was, am and always will be one of you. I also thank the fertile soil that gave birth to me and nurtured me. It is often said that a person is shaped by the place where he grows up. I am a storyteller, who has found nourishment in your humid soil. Everything that I have done, I have done to thank you!

My sincere thanks to all of you!

7.3.3　Speeches of Graduation / Commencement Speeches

If you've earned the prestigious honor of delivering the class graduation speech, that means you'll be the voice of your graduating class. It's a huge responsibility, but also a great fortune. To deliver a graduation speech, you are expected to work on writing something both memorable and meaningful, practice beforehand, memorize the bulk of your speech, use engaging body language, and speak at a slow yet natural pace. The truth is that when you've written an awesome graduation speech, delivering it in front of your peers, parents, and teachers is an experience that you'll never forget and hopefully, neither will they.

You could follow these tips for preparing a graduation speech.

Tips	Illustrations
Brainstorm about what your experience in school has meant to you.	Ask yourself several questions: What has this studying experience taught me, or others, about life, about success, and about growing up along the way?
Start to develop a theme.	There should be a theme in your speech, which can be very specific or very broad, but you want a theme to tie everything together.
Start the introduction with something catchy.	It can be an interesting quote, fact, story or even a good joke about your school or class.
Use your conclusion to draw a lesson.	Take your theme and ask the question *So what?* What can we learn from the theme? This will be your lesson.

The following is an example of a graduation speech.

Principal Brown, members of the School Board, teachers, parents, friends, and fellow graduates, it is an honor to speak to all of you today.

A little over 12 years ago I was 6, and I remember my first day of school. I was excited with my new Power Rangers lunchbox. My parents were there with their cameras, snapping pictures and wishing me well. And I met a cool kid named James. In some ways, not much has changed in 12 years.

Here I am today. OK, so I didn't bring my Power Rangers lunchbox but, my parents are here with their camera, snapping pictures and wishing me well. My best friend James is here, and he's still a really cool kid. And, I am excited.

But this is how things are different. Twelve years ago I was excited, but I had no idea about the implications of the journey I was about to begin. I had no idea that after 1st grade, there would be 2nd grade and 3rd grade and so on. I was just excited to be in first grade.

Today, I know that I am standing on the brink of my future—the first day of the rest of my life. As a "computer geek", I am inspired by the words of one of our greatest American computer scientists, Alan Kay. He said, "The greatest way to predict the future is to invent it."

Some of us here today, including our parents, are wondering how our lives are going to turn out. It is OK to wonder but, I also think it is important to realize that our future is not just something that happens to us. It is up to us to create.

So, fellow graduates, I urge you today to embrace the opportunity before you. Take what you have learned throughout the last 12 years and put it to good use.

Leave behind what isn't helpful (I'm leaving my Power Rangers lunchbox) and bring forward with you the lessons that will be the working parts of your greatest invention ever, YOUR LIFE! Congratulations!

7.3.4 Toasts

Offering a toast is a sincere and public way to pay tribute to someone special. The toast may be directed at a guest of honor, wedded couple and group of people or a specific special occasion. A proper toast will unite the room in their mutual respect for whomever or whatever is being toasted.

Different people are asked to give toasts on different occasions. Family members may toast an honored birthday guest, parents and attendants toast the bride and groom at both the rehearsal dinner and wedding reception, coworkers toast retiring employees, and parents toast graduating children.

In developing your toast, consider the following hints:

- Keep it brief, sincere and to the point; choose simple but substantial words to convey your feelings. Some of the best toasts are just a single sentence or two. Make it short or brief and meaningful.

- Focus attention on the person or persons you're toasting, not on yourself. Remember that when giving a toast, it's not about you. Yes, you have a moment in the spotlight, but your moment in the spotlight is there to shine the light on the subject of the occasion.

- Maintain eye contact. The first and last person you should look at should be the person/people you are giving your toast to and the entire speech should be to everyone. One of your tasks is to make sure that everyone in the room feels included in the celebration at that moment.

- Be appropriate. If you are debating whether a remark or story would be humorous or offensive, leave it out. If you think something is funny but aren't sure that the humor will be appreciated by the honoree and guests, leave it unsaid.

1) Speeches of wedding ceremony

For most people, their wedding day will be among the most important days of their lives. In the West, the roster of wedding speeches typically begins with the father of the bride, followed by a few words from the groom and finally a comedic showstopper courtesy of his best man. However, in recent years a trend has developed where the bride/groom also says a few words, especially in China. Regardless of who is doing the speaking, the purpose of a wedding speech is to thank everyone in attendance, pay tribute to those who made the day happen, offer a brief insight into the lives of the newlyweds, and entertain the audience.

Preparation tips are for your reference.

- Note down all the hobbies and interests of the person you are speaking about.

- Ask the family/friends for some amusing incidents in the life of the person.

- Order your speech into a clear pattern and decide in what order your points will flow best for each part.

- Pick out specific areas to make them feel special, such as dress, hairstyle, tones, etc. Be upbeat and positive, avoid jokes and embarrassing remarks.

Here are speech samples made by one best man and a bride's father.

Best man's speech:

For those of you who don't know me, my name is Jason, and I am the best man. That's official by the way. You see, (Groom) has many great friends, and he couldn't choose the best one out of all of us, so he put it to a vote. I won, but only because everyone voted for me as a joke to avoid helping a rival. But the joke's on you now boys. This is post-Brexit territory. We don't do second referenda.

Bride's father speech:

Honestly, it feels strange to be giving my little girl away today. If you want to make time fly, have a daughter. It seems like only yesterday I was holding a newborn nine-and-a-half pound baby girl with wisps of blonde streaky hair in my arms, the proudest moment of any father's life, until today. One only has to glance her way to see the radiance she gives off. Well, she did until I mentioned her baby weight, she still swears those scales were faulty.

2) Speeches of retirement

When someone retires, it is a very special occasion—the culmination of a career. It is often very difficult to know what exactly to say, particularly since retirement speeches are typically given at a party and shouldn't be too long. A successful retirement speech finds a balance between humor and sincerity. A round of retirement speeches ends with a toast to the retiree.

Here is one example:

It is hard to believe this day has finally come. I have to say that I have mixed feelings today. It's wonderful to look forward to a future of more leisure and to getting around to many of the things that I always said I would do "someday". But I also feel sadness at leaving behind me what has been such an important part of my life.

This company feels like a family. Although I know that I will see many of you around town, leaving today feels like moving away from home. It has great promise and yet the thought of no longer seeing my "family members" every day is hard to imagine.

I won't see Tim every day as I walk into the building, there at the front desk. I won't see Margaret at the desk beside my office door. I won't see all the rest of you in the hallways or the lunchroom and we won't be having those daily chats about the Red Sox and the Patriots and when the winter is going to be over. I will truly miss ALL of you—and ALL of those conversations.

But it is time to move on. I have enjoyed my time here at Parker International, and I'm proud of the things we've achieved.

Bob Johnson, I thank you for making this a great place to work and for all the support you have given me over the years.

This company is great, and I know that the growth and innovation that has been the hallmark of this organization will continue. I hope all of you feel as fortunate to work here as I have.

On a personal note, I'd like to thank Margaret for her tireless work on my behalf. And, my wife, Louise thanks you too because she knows that without you I would have been home so late every night that she and the kids would never have seen me! Thanks for helping me and also for so often pushing me out the door when I thought there was just "one more thing" that needed to get done.

And thank you to Louise for your tireless support of me over these years. I love you, honey, and I look forward to finally doing all the things we have planned.

Thank you all for being here today and for giving me this wonderful party. I feel richly blessed. Be well, and I will see you around.

7.3.5 Speeches of Funeral (Eulogy)

Eulogizing someone can be a very difficult thing to do. You want to talk with affection about someone you've lost, but you don't want to fall apart. You may fall apart a little, but you'll see in the end that it's okay to let the other people present know how much this person meant to you.

A eulogy should basically include a brief introduction of yourself and where you fit into the person's life; personal stories: anecdotes, songs, poetry or anything that speaks true.

Here is one example of how a eulogy from a friend might read.

Amanda and I met on the first day of kindergarten. I was crying, because, as many of you know, I don't do well with change. Amanda marched right up to me and took my hand. "Don't worry," she said. "I'll take care of you." That's the kind of person she was. She was always the kind of person who would step up and take care of someone sad or hurt or afraid.

That's why none of us were surprised when she became a firefighter. On the worst day of people's lives, she was there. She was willing to put herself on the line to protect people and their families. In the end, she died saving people and she wouldn't have had any regrets about that, so I can't either. I'm still sad about it though. I still don't do well with change. And I wish she was here to hold my hand and get me through.

Here are some well-known Funeral Quotes:

One life on this earth is all that we get, whether it is enough or not enough, and the obvious conclusion would seem to be that at the very least we are fools if we do not live it as fully and bravely and beautifully as we can.

—Frederick Buechner

As I love nature, as I love singing birds, and flowing rivers, and morning and evening, and summer, I love thee my friend.

—Thoreau

Many people will walk in and out of your life, but only true friends will leave footprints in your heart.

—Eleanor Roosevelt

Life itself is the most wonderful fairy tale.

—Hans Anderson

On life's journey faith is nourishment, virtuous deeds are a shelter, wisdom is the light by day and right mindfulness is the protection by night. If a man lives a pure life, nothing can destroy him.

—Buddha

All men will die, but death could be weightier than Mountain Tai, or lighter than a feather.

—The Grand Scribe's Records（《史记》）

Key Takeaways of This Chapter

★ Establishing credibility is very important both in informative speech and persuasive speech.

★ A variety of different topic categories are available for informative speaking. One way to develop your informative speech topic is to focus on areas that might be confusing to the audience. If the audience is likely to be confused about language or a concept, an elucidating explanation might be helpful.

★ Strategies to make information clear and interesting to an audience include adjusting the complexity of your information to the audience, limiting information only to what is most relevant, linking information to what the audience already knows, and making information memorable through language.

★ The three main types of persuasive speeches are questions of facts, value and policy. Factual claims argue the truth or falsity about an assertion being made. value claims argue a judgment about something (e.g., it's good or bad, it's right or wrong, it's beautiful or ugly, moral or immoral). Policy claims argue the nature of a problem and the solution that should be taken.

★ There are different forms of ceremonial speaking. For example, speeches of introduction are designed to introduce a speaker. Speeches of acceptance are delivered by the person receiving an award or honor. The commencement speech is usually given during a ceremony in which an academic degree or diploma is conferred. Toasts are given to acknowledge and honor someone on a special occasion (e.g., wedding, birthday, retirement). Eulogies are given during funerals and memorial services. Finally, speeches of farewell are delivered by an individual who is leaving a job, community, or organization and wants to acknowledge how much the group has meant.

Part II

Exercises

I. Choose the correct answer.

1. What is the essence of informative speaking?
   A. Establishing a community.
   B. Connecting with an audience.
   C. Disputing controversial ideas.
   D. Sharing knowledge.

2. Which of the following is an instance of persuasive speaking?
   A. A United States President praising World War II veterans.
   B. A marketing manager explaining a new product to the company's salesman.
   C. A judge explaining the rules of evidence during a criminal trial.
   D. A developer urging the city council to build a new convention center.

3. Toby is putting his speech together about the rising costs of textbooks on campus. Here is his preview statement: "Today, I am first going to detail the situation with the cost of our textbook, then, I will provide you with a reason, and finally, I will note a way to alleviate the costs of our books." What organization pattern is Toby going to use?
   A. Cause-effect.
   B. Problem-solution.
   C. Problem-cause-solution.
   D. Monroe's Motivated Sequence.

4. The three types of questions that give rise to persuasive speeches are questions of _____.
   A. opinion, fact, and policy
   B. problem, cause, and solution
   C. fact, value, and policy
   D. opinion, attitude, and value

5. To establish, maintain and sustain your credibility as a speaker, what quality must you convey?
   A. Dynamism.
   B. Trustworthiness.

C. Competence.   D. All of these.

6. "To persuade my audience that long-term exposure to electromagnetic fields can cause serious health problems" is a specific purpose statement for a persuasive speech on a question of _____ .

    A. value   B. fact   C. attitude   D. policy

7. Persuasive speeches on questions of _____ argue for or against particular courses of action.

    A. need   B. value   C. policy   D. fact

8. A brief, accurate speech where the goals are to provide information and build another speaker's credibility is _____ .

    A. a speech of introduction   B. a toast

    C. a commemorative address   D. an award presentation

9. The first step in an acceptance speech is usually to _____ .

    A. thank those who bestowed the award

    B. compliment the competition

    C. advocate for your favorite cause

    D. thank those who helped you attain the award

10. When offering a brief salute to a special occasion or person, you are giving _____ .

    A. an introduction   B. a eulogy

    C. a keynote address   D. a toast

II. Decide whether the following statements are true or false. Write T/F in the brackets.

1. ( ) When you inform someone, you assume the role of a teacher.

2. ( ) Persuasion is often defined as the process of influencing another person's values, beliefs, attitudes, or behaviors.

3. ( ) "To persuade my audience that downloading music from the Internet for personal use is ethically wrong" is a specific purpose statement for a persuasive speech on a question of fact.

4. ( ) "To persuade my audience that genetically-altered crops pose serious hazards to human health" is a specific purpose statement for a persuasive speech on a question of value.

5. ( ) Questions of policy deal with whether something should or should not be done.

6. ( ) "To persuade my audience that the federal government should ban all advertising for tobacco products" is a specific purpose statement for a persuasive speech on a question of policy.

7. ( ) Motivated sequence is most appropriate for speeches that try to persuade

listeners to take immediate action.

8. ( ) Regardless of whether a persuasive speaker uses the emotional appeal, she or he should always build the speech on a firm foundation of facts and logic.

9. ( ) There are no topics that could be considered inappropriate use of humor.

10. ( ) A large part of making the speech successful is first establishing credibility between the speaker and the audience.

Ⅲ. Use this guide to determine the direction of your speech.

1. What is my goal in this speech?
   - Inform my audience (go to Question 2)
   - Persuade my audience (go to Question 3)
   - Teach my audience some skills (go to Question 4)
   - Commemorate a special event (go to Question 5)

2. What facts do I want them to know? What will I need (visual aids, etc.) to convey those facts? (After filling in this information, go to Question 6.)

3. What opinion do I want to prove? What points of evidence will I provide? How will that evidence prove my thesis? (After filling in this information, go to Question 6.)

4. How exactly is this skill performed or learned? What steps are taken to accomplish it? What visual aids will I need to teach those steps? (After filling in this information, go to Question 6.)

5. Who or what is the reason my audience will be gathering? What facts do I want to discuss concerning that person or event? What anecdotes will I include?

6. What research is needed? What information do I not know?

Ⅳ. Below is a list of possible informative/persuasive speech topics. Choose three of them and explain what method of organization you prefer to use in structuring a speech.

Informative speech topics:

1. _____ is my biggest concern for the future.

2. The evolution history of Han Costume.

3. What has our society learned from the COVID-19 pandemic?

4. How do different cultures celebrate our Qi Xi festival?

5. What would I do if I were the President of our university?

---

6. A great scientist/movie/statesman/invention that greatly inspires our times.

7. Which book that has been published today would stand as classic literature in the future?

8. What does the selfie culture inform us?

9. Social media and its impact on mental health.

10. The future of AI(artificial intelligence)/VR(virtual reality)

Persuasive speech topics:

1. Newspapers and social media are no longer reliable and true.

2. Cities should offer free bike-sharing programs.

3. Fashion is an expression of the character.

4. It's wrong for the media to promote a certain beauty standard.

5. Should people agree to the use of identity chips?

6. Is machine learning a massive threat to jobs?

7. Cyberbullying should be recognized as a criminal offense.

8. Google and other search engines will lead to the death of libraries.

9. Recycling should be mandatory.

10. Does technology help connect people or isolate them?

V. Never neglect speaking ethical issues. Discuss the situation with your partner and provide your thoughts on the questions given.

Doreen is delivering a speech on the topic of donating money to help feed the children of AIDS victims in Africa. She set up her speech using Monroe's motivated sequence. She sails through attention, need, and satisfaction. She starts delivering her visualization step, and she goes a little crazy. She claims that if more people would donate to this cause, the world would be devoid of hunger, children in Africa could all get an education, and we could establish world peace. She then makes claims that not feeding the children of AIDS victims in Africa could lead to world chaos and nuclear war.

(1) Is it ethical to create unrealistic expectations during the visualization step?

(2) Should you try to exaggerate the visualization stage if you know, realistically, that the possible outcomes are not that impressive?

(3) If Doreen was your friend, how would you respond to this section of her speech? Should you point out that her argument is unethical?

Chapter 8

Debate: Some Basics

Part I

Fundamental Issues on Debating

1. One's word carries enormous weight and one's three-inch tongue is mightier than strong troops. (一言之辩重于九鼎，三寸之舌强于百万雄师。)

—*Records on the Warring States Period* (《战国策》)

2. The unexamined life is not worth living.

—*Socrates*

8.1 What Is Debate?

A debate is a process or an activity that involves presenting relevant arguments in support of a viewpoint. Debating and the principles that it teaches, such as logical thought construction, the selection and presentation of key arguments, and the appropriate use of data and statistics to support an argument, are becoming increasingly important in the modern world. The process of debate allows participants to analyze the similarities and differences between differing viewpoints, so that the audience can understand where opinions diverge and why.

Debate is, above all, a way for those who hold opposing views to discuss controversial issues without descending to insult, emotional appeals or personal bias. A key trademark of debate is that it rarely ends in agreement, but rather allows for a robust analysis of the question at hand. Perhaps this is what French philosopher Joseph Joubert meant when he said: "It is better to debate a question without settling it than to settle a question without debating it."

In daily communication, people's viewpoints on a topic are more likely to be divergent. For example, we may hold different beliefs on *the* **use of social media** in the digital age.

Pros of the use of social media	Cons of the use of social media
Social media allow us to connect with others and share information instantly.	Social media can be a drain on time and use up hours that we can't get back.
Social media allow for quick diffusion of information, especially public health and safety information during crisis events.	Social media can exacerbate feelings of disconnection and put youth at higher risk for anxiety, depression, or eating disorders.
Social media can help disarm social stigmas like anxiety or depression.	Social media use decreases face-to-face communication skills.
Social media sites like LinkedIn can help publicize job openings, source candidates and verify background information. ...	Using social media platforms opens the door to hacks, viruses and privacy breaches. ...

8.2   The Benefits of Debate

Debate provides transformational experiences that are conducive to life-changing, cognitive, and presentational skills for participants. Through debate, debaters can acquire unique educational benefits as they acquire and polish skills far beyond what can be learned in any other setting. To start with, participants can reap significant intellectual benefits and reward academic skills such as quick thinking, sound argument, and confident speaking. In addition, debating helps participants to see the power of deploying rational, reasoned arguments and compelling evidence in action. It enables them to elucidate their standpoint by utilizing rhetorical eloquence. Moreover, it instills in debaters a great sense of poise and confidence in public speaking. Finally, it teaches them the skills of researching, organizing, and presenting information in a compelling fashion. Therefore, the benefits that accrue as a result of engaging in the debate are numerous.

1) Critical thinking skills

Perhaps the most important skill debaters can learn is the ability to think rigorously and critically. A number of studies have reported that participation in debate increases debaters' critical thinking, promotes problem solving and helps to build links between words and ideas to make concepts more meaningful.

2) Public speaking skills

Debating provides a nonthreatening environment to practice public speaking skills so that debaters build confidence speaking in public and expressing their ideas eloquently. The comfort of speaking in front of others is helpful on a variety of occasions, from school presentations, discussions in college seminars and job interviews.

3) Research & analytical skills

In preparation for a debate, debaters must thoroughly research and examine the topic using reasoning, logic, and analysis to formulate opinions. Moreover, they have to engage in constructive work to unify their position and eliminate redundancy. This mechanism allows for taking on a position, the expression of opinions/arguments while maintaining composure during analytical rebuttals.

4) Teamwork

Debate encourages teamwork. Debaters could build friendships with teammates who enjoy similar interests.

In a nutshell, debate-related skills help one get ahead and stay there. The power to persuade is highly respected in society and there is no better way to master this art than through debate.

8.3 What Do We Debate?

There are three types of statements that are suitable for argumentation.

1) Proposition of fact   *Is/Is not*

Debates of this sort propose whether something is/isn't true or false; this type of proposition tries to establish a cause and effect relationship and draws on logical inferences. For example,

- Converting to solar energy can save homeowners money.

- The government is withholding information on UFOs.

- Obesity causes health problems.

2) Proposition of value   *Good/Bad*

The second type of statement is the proposition of value, which takes a more evaluative position. It judges whether something is good/bad, right/wrong, just/unjust, ethical/non-ethical, etc. For example,

- Private high schools are better than public high schools.

- Smith would make a better governor than Jones.

- College academic work is more important than college sports.

As the governorship example shows, value propositions appear frequently in politics. Value debate or Lincoln-Douglas debate is very common in high schools in Western countries for discussing value propositions. It's worthwhile to note that value propositions usually have factual propositions buried within them. For example, the proposition *Art education is more important than science education* will encourage the debaters to weigh the effectiveness of each type of education and to define the boundaries of Art and Science. These factual issues will then give support to the value arguments.

3) Proposition of policy   *Should/Should not*

Propositions of policy concern with what a society ought to do. For example,

- Chinese government should ban all genetically modified foods.

- Chinese government should require manufacturers to use significantly more recycled materials.

- The tobacco industry should be required to pay 100 percent of the medical bills for individuals dying of smoking-related cancers.

8.4 Debate Format

Different styles of debate offer their own distinct format and focus. The most widely used format at the university level is Parliamentary Debate, although certain regions of the world have their own, slightly different version of it. The International Debate Education Association (IDEA) predominantly employs the Karl Popper Debate format with secondary school students and the Parliamentary format with secondary and university students.

1) Karl Popper Debate

The Karl-Popper format focuses on relevant and often deeply divisive propositions, emphasizing the development of critical thinking skills and tolerance for different viewpoints. Debaters work together in teams of three and must research both sides of each issue. Each team is given the opportunity to offer arguments and direct questions to the opposing team. Judges then offer constructive feedback, commenting on logical flaws, insufficient evidence or arguments that debaters may have overlooked. This format was developed for use in secondary school programs and competitions. It is popular in Central and Eastern Europe and in Russia. In

Africa, it is becoming increasingly popular in Uganda, Kenya, Rwanda, Zimbabwe, Liberia and Nigeria. It is the format employed at the annual IDEA Youth Forum, a two-week debate event for secondary school students from all over the world.

The distinguishing feature of the format is cross-examination in which four of the six debaters ask their opponents questions. This format emphasizes teamwork and is much preferred by beginner debaters because each speaker speaks only once and members of the team need to communicate with each other during the designated preparation time.

2) Parliamentary Debate

Many formats of debate are described as "parliamentary". This is really a catch-all term which simply means that they are loosely modeled on the practices of the British parliamentary system and other parliaments around the world that adopted those practices. The motion (the idea to be discussed) always stands in the name of the Government (also called "the Proposition") and it is the job of the Opposition to demonstrate that the motion is either impractical or immoral.

The distinguishing factor of parliamentary formats is the use of Points of Information (POIs). These points allow debaters to interrupt a speaker by asking a question or offering information that favors their side of the debate. Both Proposition and Opposition speakers can offer POIs, but only to the other side. It is not compulsory to accept a POI, but in competitive debate, speakers are penalized if they fail to take any. Usually the first and last sections of a speech are "protected time" during which POIs are not allowed to offer.

In many parliamentary formats, the terminology of the House of Commons has also been adopted with the first proposition speaker being referred to as the Prime Minister and the first opposition speaker being known as the Leader of Opposition. The chair or presiding adjudicator is usually referred to as Mister or Madam Speaker and all remarks are addressed to them not the other debaters.

3) British Parliamentary (BP)

This is the name of the format used for the World Universities Debating Championship and has, as a result, become the default format for many universities across the globe. Debates comprise eight speakers with four speaking in favor of a motion and four against. Each side is made up of two teams of two individuals. They debate on a motion which is usually framed with the wording *This House Believes (THB)... or This House Would (THW)...*. For example, if the motion is *THW support assisted suicide*, it is the role of the Proposition (or "Government") speakers to explain why assisted suicide is a good idea and the Opposition should demonstrate that it is not. As a form of parliamentary debate, the government should propose a course of action and support it with philosophical, practical and consequential arguments. The burden of proof is on the government, but the opposition must also demonstrate the strength of the arguments.

Typically in BP, a motion is announced 15 minutes before the debate starts. Speeches are seven minutes in length, with the first and last minute protected (Points of Information cannot be offered in "protected" time). The first proposition speaker is required to present a definition of the motion that places an idea in a real-world setting. Once a motion has been defined, all speakers are required to address the definition, not some other variant that might be easier for them.

Note:

- Style of debating is different.

The form or style of parliamentary debating is flexible and is set and followed in different ways in different countries. There are differences in the number of teams on each side, in the number of people in each team, in the preparation and speaking times allowed, in the names given to the sides competing and in the roles designated to each speaker as well as the rules about rebuttals, motions and definitions.

For example, the standard American style has two teams of two contestants making a total of six speeches because one speaker will speak twice by giving a "reply" speech. The standard British style, however, brings a greater level of complexity by having four competing teams, two teams on each side, comprising of two people and making a total of eight speeches. Each team has a specific role to play depending on their order of speaking. For example, the summing up for the whole side is done by the last speakers of the second team.

- Adjudication is different.

In the UK, judges can bring a reasonable level of knowledge to their assessment of the debate contents, so that in theory, it is possible for teams to win by providing the best argument. If a judge knows that a side has made an incorrect statement, he/she can mark down for that. Marks will be given for strong arguments, effective rebuttals and speakers who fulfill their roles correctly.

In the USA, judges have to be told everything within the debate. For example, if a debater says that Canada should join NATO, it is up to the opposing side to say that Canada is already a member; otherwise, the judge must give the point to the affirmative, even if it is a relevant but an incorrect argument. This means that the affirmative side will usually win unless the negative side destroys every point of its argument.

The British style is most common at the World Championships, except when it takes place in America.

---

4) Legislative Debate

Legislative Debate is based upon the notion of asking representative student leaders to consider some of the problems that actually confront lawmakers. In doing so, the Legislative Debate provides unparalleled insights into the way legislation is drafted and establishes leadership and deliberation skills crucial to effective participation in democratic processes. The Legislative Debate also offers a vehicle for teaching parliamentary procedures and helps students internalize the value of decision-making processes that draw on consensus building and majority rule.

5) Lincoln-Douglas Debate

In Lincoln-Douglas Debate, the motion is a statement, phrased as a sentence that focuses on an issue of philosophical or political concern and which will be analyzed from a moral perspective. the Lincoln-Douglas Debate places primacy on the ability of debaters to make original, coherent and philosophically persuasive arguments on issues of ethics. Debaters should present a persuasive moral position that they can defend against criticism and use to argue against an opposing case, without falling into self-contradiction or denying the complexity of the issues at stake. Students should familiarize themselves with the work of major ethical philosophers and should inform their cases with real-world examples and analysis.

6) Cross-Examination (Policy) Debate

Like other forms of debate, The Cross-Examination Debate focuses on the core elements of a controversial issue. It is distinct from other formats (with the exception of the two-team Parliamentary Debate) in its use of a two-person team, along with an emphasis on cross-examination between constructive speeches. While specific practices vary, Cross-Examination Debate typically rewards intensive use of evidence and is more focused on content than delivery.

8.5 Basic Concepts in Debating

8.5.1 Motion

1) What is a motion?

A motion, also known as a proposition or resolution in other formats, is a statement that usually sets the topic for the given debate. Usually, this is an unambiguously worded statement which is quite general in order to be understood by not only the debaters themselves but also by the audience. Motions can also be called topics, subjects, resolutions, proposals, propositions or issues. Motions are usually worded as *This House believes that...* or *This House would...*

The House refers to the group of people taking part in and watching the debate.

The affirmative side proposes the motion and the negative side opposes it. The audience is expected to watch and listen critically. They assess the persuasiveness of the arguments and come to a conclusion regarding which argument is the strongest and whether the affirmative side has proved their case.

Some motions are quite self-evident such as the following ones:

Peer pressure is beneficial to individuals.

Euthanasia should be legalized.

All schools should make it a requirement to teach arts and music to their students.

Standardized testing is the enemy of learning.

However, some motions seem to be more philosophical. It is essential to identify what the motion is really about, that is, to find out the true theory behind it.

A woman needs a man like fish needs a bicycle. (feminism)

Experience is the best teacher. (nature vs. nurture)

Life is too hectic to be happy. (modernization)

Reward is the best stimulus. (motivation)

2) Defining a motion

In parliamentary style debating, the motion identifies a problem or situation that could be changed. The purpose of the debate is to test whether the proposed change offered by the affirmative side in their definition of the motion is workable and reasonable.

For a debate to proceed, both teams need a clear understanding of what the motion means. This requires the motion to be "defined" so that everyone (audience and adjudicators included) knows what is being debated. Problems arise if the two teams present different understandings of the meaning of the motion. This can result in a "definition debate", where the focus of the debate becomes the meaning of the words in the motion, rather than the motion itself. Interaction and clash between the two teams concentrate on whose definition is correct, rather than the issues raised by the motion. Definition debates should be avoided wherever possible.

The Proposition (affirmative) must present a reasonable definition of the motion. This means:

(1) Upon receiving a motion, both teams should ask: "What is the issue that the two teams are expected to debate? What would an ordinary intelligent person reading the motion think about?" For example: "Murder is indefensible." This would be impossible to argue against.

(2) If the motion poses a clear issue for debate (i.e. it has an obvious meaning),

the Proposition must define the motion accordingly. When the motion has an obvious meaning (one that the ordinary intelligent person would realize), any other definition would not be reasonable.

(3) If there is no obvious meaning to the motion, the range of possible meanings is limited to those that allow for a reasonable debate. Choosing a meaning that does not allow the Opposition room for debate would not be a reasonable definition.

How to Define a Motion?

(1) Define the subject.

Example: This House believes a carrot is better than a stick.

Do not define carrot and stick! Think about the issue—incentive and reward versus fear and punishment as a method of motivation.

(2) Set the scope.

Example: All schools should make it a requirement to teach arts and music to their students.

If "school" is in the motion, define the types of school: primary, middle, high, private, training, or universities.

(3) Define words by using commonly accepted definitions.

Try to keep away from dictionary definitions and certainly don't get into a "my dictionary is better than yours" argument. Don't list all the possible meanings of the word, and just say which meaning you will use.

Example: The nation's current welfare reform should be implemented.

Welfare could mean: food stamps, farms, subsidies, education, healthcare, pensions or unemployment benefits. Reform could mean: change (if so, how), abolish, reduce or expand. Therefore, an example of a definition of welfare reform could be: "By 'welfare reform', we mean specific changes to the healthcare. The changes we propose are (1) yearly free consultations with a qualified doctor for everyone over 60 and (2) a standard charge of no more than 50 Yuan for all medicines prescribed by a doctor."

Note:

(1) Terms in common usage should not be used in a way to confuse the opposition.

Example: "The Greens" are widely known to be environmentalists, not Martians from outer space.

(2) Any comparative expressions, such as "bigger, better, smaller" or expressions such as "we should" may require an explanation of how they can be evaluated.

Example: Does "we" refer to us here in this room, in China, in the world? How should we do it? Shall that be accomplished through legislation, a nationwide public awareness campaign or individually?

(3) There are no rules about expanding or narrowing the definition, but it is generally better to go into detail rather than to look at generalizations that can be difficult to prove.

The affirmative side should have a responsibility to provide a definition that will allow the negative side to debate. They should not define a motion in obscure terms. If the negative team accepts the definition, that definition must stand. The negative must adjust their case to that definition. If the negative side challenges the definition, their justification for doing so must be clearly stated. But unless the definition is clearly unreasonable, they should agree to debate the definition given by the affirmative. The negative side's best strategy is to look at the wider context and use the more general arguments to argue against the given definition.

For example:

The motion, "This House would not smoke"defined in terms of the issue about drug abuse is acceptable. However, if the affirmative side's case is that the motion should stand because drug abuse increases the spread of Aids and that drunkenness leads to violence, the negative side can reasonably object since injecting drugs and drinking alcohol have nothing to do with smoking. In this case, the negative side could say, "We consider the definition unreasonable because injecting, eating or drinking narcotics or stimulants have nothing to do with the motion that expressly mentions smoking. However, we do consider that smoking both legal tobacco and illegal drugs such as cocaine should be banned because they injure the health and are antisocial."

In the example above, the negative side has then accepted the issue promoted by the affirmative but has properly linked the definition and their case to the motion.

8.5.2 Argument

An argument is a connected series of statements intended to establish a definite proposition. Arguments are not assertions that have yet to be proven to be logically true. An argument concerns the logic and the evidence supporting a particular claim or conclusion. In other words, an argument must have supporting logic and evidence that can demonstrate its validity.

What makes a good argument?

- Relevance

A good argument must be relevant to the motion. The points made in support of an argument must also be linked to the motion.

- Clarity

A good argument should be clear enough to be understood.

- Organization

A good argument should be well structured.

- Logic

A good argument should be explained, illustrated and proved by the chain of reasoning.

- Effective use of evidence

A good argument should be supported by relevant evidence such as facts, examples, statistics, and references to expert opinion, etc.

How to structure an argument?

As a matter of fact, everyone has made an argument before. If you've ever persuaded your parents to buy you a new laptop, convinced your teacher to raise your grades, or participated in thesis oral examinations, you may have already known the basics of building an argument. In debate, argumentation is the foundation of every speech. Developing the skills necessary to make a persuasive, organized argument is the key to winning a debate.

Look at the following example.

At the dinner table, Jane says:

"Mother, may I be excused from the table"?

(1) "I need to go to the library tonight."

(2) "We are beginning a unit of study on quantum physics and I would like to get a head start by doing some background research."

(3) "This is a very important unit and the final assignment from the unit will be worth 50% of my grade for the marking period."

(4) "So you can see why I need to go to the library tonight."

In this example, the **claim** that Jane asserts is (1). She asserts that she needs to go to the library tonight. She offers an **explanation** in (2), where she details her original request. In (3), she offers a clear and justifiable **reason** for going to the library; finally, in (4), she **recaps** her initial **assertion**.

This is exactly what should be done to create an argument:

- The claim is STATED.

- The claim is EXPLAINED.
- The claim is supported by EVIDENCE and reasoning.
- A TIEBACK for the original claim is made.

Argument Structure

Statement—A short and comprehensible phrase that captures the essence of the argument. Explanation—A twofold logical explanation: why the statement is true; why the statement is important.

Evidence—Back up the claim /assertion using relevant evidence.

Tieback—Connect the statement back, showing why the statement has been proved.

- An example of SEET (motion: This house would install bike lanes in major cities.)

Statement: *Bike lanes are safer for cyclists.*

Explanation: *Both being on sidewalks and unprotected roads can be dangerous for cyclists. If pedestrians or cars fail to see cyclists, it can pose incredible safety issues. This makes cycling an inaccessible option for some people.*

Evidence: *In Beijing, the introduction of bike lanes has led to a 56% reduction in injuries or collisions overall to all street users including cyclists, pedestrians or even drivers.*

Tieback: *Bike lanes provide a safer environment for all kinds of traffic, so it is critical to add protected bike lanes on all major streets.*

How to argue?

One essential skill involved in debating is to construct a reasoned argument and especially to recognize a fallacious or fraudulent argument. Basically, an argument is a series of sentences coupled with words like "because" and "therefore". The more sentences we couple in this way, the more developed our argument is. This means we're constantly answering the question "why?"

Suppose the motion is: THW allow the death penalty. One of the arguments could be: it is an effective means to deter future criminals. However, this argument can be more or less fully developed, as shown in the following:

- **Less fully developed:**

    —Death penalty will deter criminals,

    —because criminals don't want to die.

- **More fully developed:**

    —Death penalty will deter criminals,

    —because criminals weigh the costs and benefits of doing a crime.

    —And whereas right now, the maximum cost of a serious crime is lifelong imprisonment.

—Whereas in our model the maximum cost would then be "death",

—and we can reasonably expect that criminals find "dying" a higher cost than"lifelong imprisonment".

—Because people in general value their life most highly,

—the death penalty will deter criminals.

As can be seen in the second argument, there are more possible "why?"s being answered. This can account for why people are more likely to be convinced by the fully developed arguments.

Functional Expressions Concerning Argument Agreement and Disagreement

1) How to Agree Strongly with an Opinion.	2) How to Half Agree with an Opinion.
(1) I couldn't agree more!	(1) Yes, perhaps, however ...
(2) That's absolutely true!	(2) Well, yes, but ...
(3) Absolutely!	(3) Yes, in a way, however ...
(4) I agree with your point.	(4) Hmm, possibly, but ...
(5) I'd go along with you there.	(5) Yes, I agree up to a point, however ...
(6) I'm with you on that.	(6) Well, you have a point there, but ...
(7) That's just what I was thinking.	(7) There's something there, I suppose, however...
(8) That's exactly what I think.	(8) I guess you could be right, but ...
(9) That's a good point.	(9) Yes, I suppose so, however ...
(10) That's just how I see it.	(10) That's worth thinking about, but ...
3) How to Disagree Politely with an Opinion.	**4) How to Disagree Strongly with an Opinion.**
(1) I am not so sure.	(1) I disagree.
(2) Do you think so?	(2) I disagree with your idea.
(3) Well, it depends.	(3) I'm afraid I don't agree.
(4) I'm not so certain.	(4) I'm afraid your idea does not hold water.
(5) Well, I don't know.	(5) I can't agree with you.
(6) Well, I'm not so sure about that.	(6) I couldn't accept that for a minute.
(7) Hmm, I'm not sure you're right.	(7) You can't actually mean that.
(8) I'm inclined to disagree with that.	(8) I wouldn't go along with you there.
(9) No, I don't think so.	(9) It's possible you are mistaken about that.

8.5.3　Logical Reasoning

1) Deductive reasoning

Deductive reasoning is a basic form of valid reasoning. Deductive reasoning, or deduction, starts with a general statement, or hypothesis, and examines the possibilities to reach a specific, logical conclusion.

Deductive reasoning usually follows several steps. First, there should be a premise, then a second premise, and finally an inference. A common form of deductive reasoning is syllogism, in which two statements, i.e., a major premise and a minor premise, reach a logical conclusion. For example, the premise "Every A is B" could be followed by another premise, "This C is A." Those statements would lead to the conclusion "This C is B." Syllogisms are considered as a good way to test deductive reasoning to make sure the argument is valid.

For example, "All men are mortal. Harold is a man. Therefore, Harold is mortal." For deductive reasoning to be sound, the hypothesis must be correct. It is assumed that the premises, "All men are mortal" and "Harold is a man" are both true. Therefore, the conclusion is logical and true. In deductive reasoning, if something is true of a class of things in general, it is also true for all members of that class.

2) Inductive reasoning

Inductive reasoning is the opposite of deductive reasoning, which makes broad generalizations from specific observations. Basically, there are data, and conclusions are drawn from the data.

An example of inductive logic is, "The coin I pulled from the bag is a penny. The second coin from the bag is a penny. A third coin from the bag is a penny. Therefore, all the coins in the bag are pennies."

Even if all of the premises are true in a statement, inductive reasoning allows for the conclusion to be false. Here's an example: "Harold is a grandfather. Harold is bald. Therefore, all grandfathers are bald." The conclusion does not follow logically from the statements and thus is false.

3) Abductive reasoning

Another form of scientific reasoning is abductive, which usually starts with an incomplete set of observations and proceeds to the most likely possible explanation for the group of observations. It is based on making and testing hypotheses using the best information available.

For example, Mike walks into their living room and finds torn-up papers all over the floor. Mike's dog has been alone in the room all day. Mike concludes that the dog tore up the papers because it is the most likely scenario. Of course, Mike's 6-year old niece who has stayed in the room for a while may have torn up the papers, but the dog theory is the more likely conclusion.

Abductive reasoning is useful for forming hypotheses to be tested. For example, abductive reasoning is often used by doctors who make a diagnosis based on test results and by jurors who make decisions based on the evidence presented to them.

8.5.4 Logical Fallacies

Logic is the chain of reasoning used to prove an argument. Fallacies are common errors in reasoning that will undermine the logic of an argument. Fallacies can be either illegitimate arguments or irrelevant points that lack evidence to support the claim. Understanding logical fallacies will not only be conducive to evaluating arguments before presenting them, but also facilitating assessment and refutation of the arguments presented by the other side during a debate. Here are commonly found fallacies in a debate.

1) Strawman fallacy (also known in the U.K. as Aunt Sally)

This fallacy occurs when a speaker over-simplifies or misrepresents the argument (i.e., setting up a "straw man") to make it easier to attack or refute. Instead of fully addressing the actual argument, speakers relying on this fallacy present a superficially similar but ultimately not equal version of the real stance.

Example: *John: I think we should hire someone to redesign our website.*

Lola: You're saying we should throw our money away on external resources instead of building up our in-house design team? That's going to hurt our company in the long run.

2) The Bandwagon fallacy

A significant population of people believing that a proposition is true doesn't automatically make it true. Popularity alone is not enough to validate an argument, although it is often used as a standalone justification of validity. Arguments in this style don't take into account whether or not the population validating the argument is actually qualified to do so, or if contrary evidence exists. Truth to be told, there are various bandwagon arguments in advertising (e.g., "three out of four people think X brand toothpaste cleans teeth best").

Example: *Sarah: I believe social media is damaging to relationships. We are deprived of opportunities for face-to-face interactions and very often, communication can be misunderstood through social media.*

Derek: Well, I don't think so. All of my friends have joined and talk to each other through this medium, so it cannot be that bad.

3) The appeal to authority fallacy

While appeals to authority are by no means always fallacious, they can quickly become dangerous when relying too heavily on the opinion of a single person, especially if that person is attempting to validate something outside of his/her expertise. The appeal to authority fallacy occurs when one misuses the testimonies of (alleged) authorities in an attempt to back up a certain claim or position.

Example: *Despite the fact that our Q4 numbers are much lower than usual, we should push forward using the same strategy because our CEO Barbara says this is the best approach.*

4) Ad hominem

Ad hominem means "against the man", and this type of fallacy is sometimes called name-calling or the personal attack fallacy. It occurs when someone attacks the person instead of attacking his or her argument.

Example: *Alex: I think that our government should increase the spending on public schools.*

Bob: You clearly don't even care about public education, since you sent your own kids to a private school.

5) The hasty generalization fallacy

This fallacy occurs when someone draws expansive conclusions based on inadequate or insufficient evidence. In other words, they jump to conclusions about the validity of a proposition with some but not enough evidence to back it up, and overlook potential counterarguments.

Example: *Two members of my team have become more engaged employees after taking public speaking classes. That proves we should have mandatory public speaking classes for the whole company to improve employee engagement.*

6) Circular argument

The fallacy of the circular argument, known as *petitio principii* ("begging the question"), occurs when the premises presume, openly or covertly, the very conclusion that is to be demonstrated.

Example: *Eighteen-year-olds have the right to vote because it's legal for them to vote. This argument is circular because it goes right back to the beginning: Eighteen-year-olds have the right to vote because it's legal. It's legal for them to vote because they have the right to vote. Therefore, the listener requires additional evidence to get out of the argument loop.*

7) Red herring

This is a diversionary tactic that avoids the key issues, often by avoiding opposing arguments rather than addressing them.

Example: *Reporter: It's been two years since your policies were implemented, and so far they have failed to reduce unemployment rates.*

Politician: I have been working hard ever since I came into office, and I'm happy to say that I met with many business leaders throughout the country, who all say that they are glad to see that our hard work is paying off.

8) Slippery slope

This type of fallacy argues that one action will lead to a series of other, increasingly unacceptable, events or consequences, without proving a causal connection between the first action and the consequent events.

Example: *If you break your diet and have one cookie tonight, you will just want to eat 10 cookies tomorrow, and before you know it, you will have gained back the 15 pounds you lost.*

8.5.5 Refutation and Rebuttal

In most cases, the word rebuttal can be used interchangeably with refutation, both of which include contradictory statements in an argument. However, strictly speaking, the distinction between the two is that a rebuttal must provide evidence, whereas a refutation merely relies on a contrary opinion. To be more specific, refutation involves any counterargument, while rebuttals rely on contradictory evidence to provide a means for a counterargument. A successful refutation may disprove evidence with reasoning, but rebuttals must present evidence.

Rebuttal presents a unique feature of debate which is different from more or less one-way communication of public speaking. Without rebuttals, a debate becomes merely a succession of speeches that do not necessarily bear any relation to each other. Rebuttal shows that a speaker has listened to each other, and understood why the two teams' opinions diverged. A good rebuttal is the sign of a good debater, as it shows the speed of analysis and the ability to swiftly put thoughts into words.

The key to a good rebuttal is to uncover how the opposing argument is irrelevant or contains logical fallacies. A good rebuttal should be well organized and easy to follow. It includes the following:

- a statement of the counterargument
- a statement of your position and why it differs from the counterargument
- evidence to support your position

How to rebut in a debate?

The argument the opposing team adopts is one that they believe will appeal to the audience and increase their chances of winning the debate. However, all arguments are inherently biased towards one side or the other, and every argument can be opposed. Speakers need to analyze each argument put forward by the opposing team and decide which approach to adopt to attack the argument.

1) Attacking assumptions

The key to this type of rebuttal is to attack an assumption supporting the argument. For example, suppose you are debating on the topic of video games and violence. Your position is that video games do not cause an increase in violent behavior, but the counterargument is that they do. You might make a rebuttal like this:

"While some people argue that video games lead to an increase in violence, my position is that no studies have proved a cause and effect relationship between the two. The opposing argument is based on a correlation between violence and video game use, but a correlation is not the same as cause and effect. There have been no studies to indicate that video games cause violent behavior."

2) Attacking relevance

This type of rebuttal involves attacking the relevance of the opponent's argument. For instance, if you are debating on the topic of whether homework promotes learning for students, the opposing argument might be that homework doesn't take that much of a student's time. You could make a rebuttal like this:

"It's true that homework doesn't take that much time, but that point has nothing to do with whether homework promotes learning. Free time is important, but it has no bearing on learning."

3) Attacking impact

A rebuttal can also attack the impact of the counterargument. Will it really impact the way that the opposing team claims? Is their logic correct in the way that they draw out the links from cause to consequence?

For example, in response to the argument that the death penalty should be abolished since taxpayers have to pay for the high cost of implementing the death penalty, you may rebut that argument this way:

"Have you ever thought about that taxpayers even have to pay for a higher cost to fight against crimes if the death penalty is abolished, for example, crime prevention measures and correctional services?"

4) Attacking irrelevant examples

Debaters should also listen out for whether the opposing team is backing up their argument with relevant examples. Particularly, if there are no examples being used to support an argument, this should certainly be pointed out as part of the rebuttal. Debaters can also challenge the speaker to come up with examples. The advantage of this challenge is that the credibility of a speaker who is unable to find examples to support an argument will be shattered and undermined.

Debaters should also attempt to find counter-examples, that is to say, examples which prove the reverse of the opposing team's arguments. If found, the speaker in the opposing team should then be challenged to explain which of the examples given are more typical. The benefit of doing this is to force the opposing team onto the defensive, making them spend more of their speech time in defending previous arguments, which, in turn, prevents them from spending time on developing further constructive arguments to support their case.

Integrating rebuttal into speeches

To use rebuttals, debaters need to develop the ability to follow arguments, detect flaws and address them. They also need to develop the skills to make their speeches flexible, and to be able to adapt them in order to use rebuttal efficiently and effectively. It is not always straightforward to integrate rebuttals into a speech, especially since rebuttals are often developed much later than the main content of a speech, usually when the structure of a speech has already been determined. However, if rebuttals can be integrated into speeches effectively, they can contribute to great persuasiveness in argumentation.

There are **two points in a speech** at which rebuttals may be most easily **inserted**:

(1) Directly after the introduction, and before the main arguments are developed. Speakers will often say after their introduction something like "*Now, before I move on to my first argument, I would like to respond to something that the opposing team has said …*". This allows them to cover the rebuttals, which may be unrelated to other constructive arguments that they wish to develop, and then to move into their speech with as little disruption to their prepared structure as possible.

(2) If the rebuttal is relevant to one of the areas that the speaker will cover, it may be used as part of the development of that argument. In these cases, a speaker will say, partway through their speech, something like "*… and now I would like to address area A. Before I give my constructive argument, I would just like to respond to something that the opposing team said on this topic …*". This makes the rebuttal more effective since the audience will see the direct contrast between the two teams' views on this particular point. However, it is also more difficult to structure a speech in this

way, since it makes more demands on the speaker. Nonetheless, either method is a good way of delivering rebuttals, without losing the overall structure of a speech.

> **FAQ: Can I bring up "new" arguments in rebuttals?**
>
> Debaters often want to know what they can and can't bring up in rebuttals. The answer is somewhat dependent on the specific round of a debate, but here are some general guidelines:
>
> • You are always allowed to directly answer your opponents' arguments.
>
> • You may extend arguments made earlier by presenting clarification and additional supporting evidence.
>
> • You should not bring up totally new main ideas in rebuttals.

8.6   Debating Speeches

This part introduces a framework with which debaters can model the development of their argument into effective speeches of appropriate lengths. It also discusses when they need to make adjustments to their speeches.

8.6.1   A General Structure of Debate Speeches

1) Constructive speeches

A well-structured speech will be the one in which the arguments flow from one to the next in the order that the speaker introduces them, so that the audience can follow the speaker's reasoning most easily. The structure should include the following:

• A beginning (Introduction)

Speakers should begin with a couple of sentences, informing the audience of what they intend to cover during the speech. This is usually done by saying something along the lines of "... *in support of my team, I shall be looking at areas A and B. To begin with area A ...*". In this way, the audience knows what to expect, and also understands more clearly why the speaker is using the material in question since they know the aim and structure of the overall speech.

• A body (Development)

The main body of the speech is the development of the arguments, as announced in the introduction. This is the largest part of the speech, usually taking up over 80% of its length. The key to structuring "the body" is **sign-posting**. Sign-posting essentially means telling the audience explicitly what is going on in terms of the structure of a speech. For example, when moving from discussion of one argument to another, a speaker should say something along the lines of "*... and that is why argument A is so crucial, and why it means that our team should win this debate. I would now like to move on to discuss argument B ...*". In this way, it is clear to the audience that the material now being discussed by the speaker pertains to the new argument. This prevents the audience from becoming confused, which happens easily if the material is complex. It is also a means of regaining the audience's attention, especially if some of them have lost the thread of the speech. Sign-posting will make a good point for them to start listening again.

- An end (Summary)

Finally, the speech should end with a summary and a conclusion, which usually constitutes no more than 10% of the speech. The speaker should remind the audience of the main points covered during the speech, the key conclusions drawn and the issues which the audience should remember. The conclusion of the speech as a whole is usually "*... and that is why you should vote for my team!*", so it is important that the summary leads up to this.

2) Reply or summation speeches

In a reply speech / summation speech, one team should not just summarize and reproduce all the materials, but should focus on the points that will make the audience believe that the team should win the debate: the clever points, the key rebuttals, the killer example, and so on. In other words, a summation speech delivers a biased summary of the debate and is designed to impress the audience.

No new material is allowed to be included in summation speeches, with the exception of new rebuttals. Summation speakers need to show the main arguments and principles used by both sides, and how they fit together. They need to remind the audience of the key points that their team has made. They also need to avoid focusing on the opposing team's minor weaknesses, since the audience will soon notice if key elements are being omitted.

Summation speakers must always ensure that the material in their speech favors their own team. If a strong argument for their team has been ignored or left unresponded by the opposing team, this should be highlighted as an example of how the opposing team simply has failed to address it. Equally, if the opposing team's argument has been well rebutted, the audience should again be reminded of this fact, so as to show how the opposing team has only been able to produce weak and wrong arguments to support their case.

8.6.2 Flexible Adjustment to Speeches in Debate

A debate is not a succession of prepared speeches. Speakers respond to each other in order to show the audience why they, rather than the opposing team, should win the debate. It is therefore important that, when speakers stand up to speak, they do not think *"this is the speech I have prepared, so it is the speech I will deliver"*, but rather *"What is my job now?"*. When they stand up, they should be ready for departing from what they have prepared.

If everything is going on according to the plan, speakers will be able to deliver the materials prepared ahead of time. But in most cases, speakers need to be able to adjust their speeches throughout the entire debate. In adjusting their speeches, debaters need to decide on the most appropriate point to slot in the new information and whether they should spend less time on their original arguments, or omit sections of their speeches altogether. If they have time to discuss with their teammates (perhaps passing notes to each other), they should do so, since their teammates need to deliver part of their omitted sections in their own speeches later on. In what follows, you will be introduced to several possible situations in which adaptations of the speech will occur.

- The teammate has made a mistake

If a teammate has made a mistake, the team should try to rectify it as soon as possible, before too much damage is done. If it is simply a case of forgetting to deliver one of the points they are supposed to, other members should try to include it in their speech instead. If it is a case where the teammate is confused and expresses something contradictory to the team's main case, then members in the team should try to clarify the situation for the audience. Subtlety, without fail, will be required to do this effectively. If the mistake is not put right, there is a strong possibility that the opposing team will spot it and use it for the attack.

- The Opposition has left a gap for attack

When the opposing team has made a mistake, the team needs to point this out to the audience before the opposing team can control the damage as described above. Time should be spent in explaining the mistake to the audience, showing how the opposing team is confused, and therefore should lose the debate. Due to the time devoted to identifying the opposing team's mistake, adjusting prepared speeches and structures will take place so as to adhere to the speech time limit.

It is also possible that the opposing team has just come up with a very strong argument, which will subject your team to great disadvantages, if it is not rebutted quickly. This rebuttal will take time to explain in detail to the audience, but it is crucial to do so to convince the audience not to believe that the opposing team should win. Again, the time that this rebuttal takes means there is less time for members of the team to cover their own arguments, and your team will also need to adjust speeches.

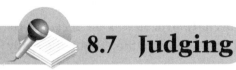

8.7 Judging

1) How to assess style?

Style addresses how content is presented, which includes assessing the effectiveness of body language, pace of speech, choice of vocabulary, eye contact, use of humor and empathy, as well as the overall confidence and presence of the speaker. Good style not only makes a speech clear, easy to follow, compelling, and persuasive, but also complements and enhances the effectiveness of content. It helps arguments and analysis get through to the audience, helps them understand what is said, and draws them into the speech.

Elements of the good style include

- Eye contact-the speaker is able to address and engage the audience, reading through notes rather than from them.

- Gestures–natural movements that enhance, rather than distract from what the speaker is saying.

- Stance–facing the audience with a calm and confident posture and limited movement (e.g., pacing) that could be distracting to the judge or audience.

- Speed–speaking at a pace that allows the judge and audience to listen and engage with what is being said, and using deliberate variation in speed to emphasize important parts of the speech and maintain interest.

- Voice modulation–varying volume and tone for emphasis, or to keep the speech interesting and effective use of pauses.

- Clarity of language–using clear language which can be easily understood to evoke emotions or compel the audience. It is not appropriate to consider the speaker's command of the English language, or their accent unless this presents a genuine barrier to understanding what is said.

2) How to assess content?

The content criterion concerns with the strength of the arguments, the quality of the analysis (i.e. the sufficiency of the logical linkage, the quality of the explanations) and the examples presented in support (whether they were relevant and compelling). The assessment should cover both constructive materials and rebuttals of the opponents' arguments. Moreover, the analysis accompanying the definition of the motion, the context presented for the debate, and the conclusions reached will all be taken into account. Good arguments are substantiated rather than asserted. Good conclusions are connected to the argument and the motion, and explained fully rather than simply stated. Good examples are relevant, drawn from credible contexts or sources, and general rather than personal or overly specific. Good rebuttal attacks the specific arguments made by the opposition rather than misrepresenting the argument, or attacking the argument partially or tangentially. Strong rebuttals logically explain the response, rather than simply asserting that the original argument is false.

Under no circumstances should a judge evaluate arguments on the basis of specific personal knowledge or expertise. The judge shouldn't assess the quality of arguments by referencing other possible arguments the team could have made, or rebuttals the judge could have made him/herself. The judge should evaluate arguments made during the debate, and should not fill in gaps or complete missing logical links on any team's behalf.

3) How to assess strategy?

The strategy captures the decision-making and techniques used to decide what content to spend time on, and how to fit it into the overarching structure/framework of the debate. Speakers with good strategies prioritize the arguments and examples in a way that reflects the order of importance. By contrast, speakers with poor strategies focus on irrelevant details, have poor time management, and contradict themselves or others in their team. The assessment of strategy includes the following:

- The interpretation of the motion and how this has been translated into a case (e.g., the effectiveness of the model, the grounds chosen to emphasize or to reasonably exclude, and the context presented, etc.).

- The visible prioritization of materials in the speech, the ordering of the points made, the time allocated to each argument, and the things the speaker chooses to emphasize being aligned to what is important to the debate.

- The structure of the speech, including a clear beginning, body and an ending, with signposts along the way to help the audience follow along.

- Consistency between arguments and with the rest of the team.

Strategy is the appropriate category used to reward speakers who demonstrate a sophisticated or insightful understanding of the "meta debate", i.e., the debate as a competition, rather than simply a contest of ideas.

Key Takeaways of This Chapter

★ An argument is a series of sentences, statements, propositions where some are the premises and one is the conclusion and where the premises are intended to give a reason for the conclusion. Arguments are the building blocks of debating.

★ Responding to arguments is the core element of debate and is broadly divided into two categories: refutation and rebuttal. Refutation is the process of answering an opponent's argument while rebuttal is the process of defending one's arguments against an opponent's attacks.

★ The two major types of reasoning, deductive and inductive, refer to the process by which someone creates a conclusion as well as how he/she believes the conclusion to be true. Deductive reasoning starts with a statement or hypothesis, followed by testing whether it is true through observations, whereas inductive reasoning starts with observations and moves back towards generalizations and theories.

★ Fallacies are common errors in reasoning that will undermine the logic of an argument. Fallacies can be either illegitimate arguments or irrelevant points and can be identified because they lack evidence to support the claim. The ability to discern a valid argument from a false one is an important skill in argumentation.

Part II

Exercises

I. Discuss the following questions.

1. What is the purpose of debate? What kind of benefit can the debaters reap from debating?
2. What are the three types of statements that are suitable for argumentation? Please give an example of each.
3. What makes a good argument and how could an argument be structured?
4. What is the difference between inductive and deductive reasoning?
5. How does refutation differ from rebuttal?
6. Could you list some possible strategies to rebut the opposition's case in the debate?

II. Identify the type of logical fallacies.

A. Strawman   B. Band Wagon   C. The Appeal to Authority
D. Ad hominem   E. Hasty Generalization   F. Circular Argument
G. Red Herring   H. Slippery Slope

1. Low carbon diets must be healthy. All my friends are trying them and losing tons of weight! ( )
2. You must obey the law because it's illegal to break the law. ( )
3. Albert Einstein, one of the smartest people ever, said that the best and healthiest breakfast is bacon and eggs, so it must be true. ( )
4. Joanna: "Why did you buy that new fishing rod? It exceeds our monthly budget that we both agreed upon." John: "Well, because it was on sale. I had to buy it now." ( )

5. Jane: "Bicycle infrastructure should be expanded because cycling is a sustainable mode of transportation." Tom: "We should not build bike lanes because cyclists run red lights and endanger pedestrians." (　)

6. She is for raising the minimum wage, but she is not smart enough to even run a business. (　)

7. If we allow the children to choose the movie this time, they are going to expect to be able to choose the school they go to or the doctors they visit. (　)

8. My dad has smoked 2 packs of cigarettes every day for 20 years, and he doesn't have any health problems. Smoking can't be dangerous! (　)

Ⅲ. Identify the type of logical reasoning.

A. Inductive　　　B. Deductive　　　C. Abductive

1. If you brush and floss your teeth daily then you will have fewer cavities. Marie brushes and flosses her teeth daily. Thus, she will have fewer cavities. (　)

2. It has been observed that earthquakes precede the eruption of volcanoes. Thus, earthquakes cause volcanoes to erupt. (　)

3. Every time you eat peanuts, you start to cough. You are allergic to peanuts. (　)

4. Billy likes playing tennis with Tommy. Billy will not play tennis today. Thus, Tommy will not play. (　)

5. All of the managers at my office have college degrees. Therefore, you must have a college degree to become a manager. (　)

6. The dog's food was in the bowl, but the food is now missing. The likely explanation for the dog food being missing is that the dog ate the food. (　)

7. The career counseling center at my college is offering free resume reviews to students. I am a student and I plan on having my resume reviewed, so I will not have to pay anything for this service. (　)

8. Mike walked down the street and noticed that the sidewalks were wet. He concluded that it was raining. (　)

Ⅳ. Choose one motion from the given ones and conduct a mini-debate according to the procedures listed. Student judges can use the rubrics suggested to evaluate their peer's performance.

Suggested Motions

1. Private educational institutions should be encouraged in China.
2. The benefits of the commercialization of sports outweigh the negative effects.
3. Tradition inevitably gives way to modernization.
4. Urbanization helps improve the quality of living.
5. Information technology dominates rather than facilitates people's lives.

6. The younger generation knows better than their parents.
7. China should abolish English as a compulsory subject in the postgraduate entrance examination.
8. Contestants who have undergone cosmetic surgery should be prohibited from competing in the beauty pageant.
9. All money currently spent on Confucius Institutes abroad should be spent instead on alleviating domestic poverty.
10. People should be legally required to get vaccines.
11. Social media use has improved human communication.
12. The development of artificial intelligence will help humanity.

The Mini-Debate Format
1. Three speakers speak for each side of the issue.
2. Teams may flip a coin to determine sides and the speaking order.
3. Speakers should take notes during opposing speakers' presentations for crossfire questions.

Mini-Debate Activities Sequence and Time Limits

- Team A

    Speaker 1 (1A)— 2-minute limit
- Team B

    Speaker 1(1B)—2-minute limit

    Timeout – 1 minute
- Crossfire

    Speaker 2 (A2) & Speaker 2 (B2)—3-minute limit

    Timeout – 1 minute
- Team A

    Speaker 3 (A3) summary—1-minute limit

    Speaker 3 (B3) summary—1-minute limit
- Grand Crossfire (all speakers)—3-minute limit

    Timeout – 1 minute
- Team B

    Last Shot from Speaker 3 (B3)—2-minute limit
- Team A

    Last Shot from Speaker 3 (A3)—2-minute limit

    Total Time Including Timeouts = 18 minutes

Speaker Instructions—Each speaker needs to outline the presentation so that it fits into the time limit. When the opposing team speaks, each will take notes for the crossfire period.

Crossfire Instructions—During the crossfire period, debaters are expected to keep questions and answers succinct. In the Grand Crossfire, all six students have the floor. The first question must be posed by the team which did not speak just prior to the Crossfire period.

Summary Speaker Instructions—Summary speakers will take notes of the most compelling reasons presented by themselves and their partners that are most likely to counter the arguments of their opponents and will rebuild audience connections by refocusing upon the central issue.

Last Shot Instructions—Last Shot speakers choose the one issue which matters the most and use the importance of this issue to frame the final parting shot.

Judging the Debate—Students in the class should be active in judging the debate to determine a winning side based on a rubric scoring system. The instructor can make copies of the rubric system for students to use and then work as the timekeeper.

For Evaluating a Mini-Debate: The following are examples of evaluative criteria that the instructor can use to build a rubric evaluation model for the mini-debate.

Use of Evidence

1. Did the team show connections between particular events or issues and large social, economic, and/or political concerns, trends or developments?

2. Did the team supply appropriate and sufficient evidence to support the arguments and apply that evidence clearly and logically?

3. Did the team adequately explain and/or analyze the evidence offered during the debate?

Analysis and Argumentation

1. Did the team present logical, reasonable, and convincing arguments?

2. Did the team clearly and effectively discuss, explain and evaluate the issues and arguments offered during the debate?

3. Did the team respond directly to opposing arguments, interpretations, and/or analyses, with clear explanations of the weakness of opposing arguments?

4. Did the team apply clear evaluative criteria to the arguments, interpretations, and/or analyses offered during the debate?

5. Did the team demonstrate an understanding of the social, political, and/or economic issues involved in the debate?

Crossfire

1. Did the debater provide relevant, focused and brief questions?

2. Did the debater respond effectively to questions?

3. Did the debater demonstrate respect for opponents by cooperating in a polite "give and take" without dominating the discussion?

Presentation

1. Did the debater communicate in a clear, organized, and understandable manner, presenting an easy listening path to follow?

2. Did the debater exemplify the highest standards of language usage, style and vocabulary, avoiding slang, poor grammar, and mispronunciation?

3. Did the speaker use effective body language (poised stage presence, appropriate gestures, facial expression, and eye contact)?

4. Did the speaker use effective oral presentation skills (volume, diction, rate of delivery) and understandable and persuasive delivery?

5. Was the debater respectful and courteous to opponents?

Here is an example of the student rubrics model to participate and determine the debate winner.

Levels of Performance for AFFIRMATIVE Team

Criteria	4	3	2	1	Grade:
1. Organization & Clarity: Main arguments and responses are outlined in a clear and orderly way.	Completely clear and orderly presentation	Mostly clear and orderly in all parts	Clear in some parts but not overall	Unclear and disorganized throughout	
2. Use of Argument: Reasons are given to support the resolution	Very strong and persuasive arguments given throughout	Many good arguments given, with only minor problems	Some decent arguments, but some significant problems	Few or no real arguments given, or all arguments given had significant problems	

(to be continued)

(continued)

Criteria	4	3	2	1	Grade:
3. Use of cross-examination and rebuttal: Identification of weakness in Negative team's arguments and ability to defend itself against attacks.	Excellent cross-exam and defense against Negative team's objections	Good cross-exam and rebuttals, with only minor slip-ups	Decent cross-exam and/or rebuttals, but with some significant problems	Poor cross-exam or rebuttals, failure to point out problems in Negative team's position or failure to defend itself against attacks.	
Presentation Style: Tone of voice, clarity of expression, precision of arguments all contribute to keeping audience's attention and persuading them of the team's case.	All style features were used convincingly	Most style features were used convincingly	Few style features were used convincingly	Very few style features were used, none of them convincingly	
Total					

(to be continued)

Levels of Performance for NEGATIVE Team

Criteria	4	3	2	1	Grade:
1. Organization & Clarity: Main arguments and responses are outlined in a clear and orderly way.	Completely clear and orderly presentation	Mostly clear and orderly in all parts	Clear in some parts but not overall	Unclear and disorganized throughout	
2. Use of Argument: Reasons are given to go against the resolution.	Very strong and persuasive arguments given throughout	Many good arguments given, with only minor problems	Some decent arguments, but some significant problems	Few or no real arguments given, or all arguments given had significant problems	
3. Use of cross-examination and rebuttal: Identification of weakness in Affirmative team's arguments and ability to defend itself against attacks.	Excellent cross-exam and defense against Affirmative team's objections	Good cross-exam and rebuttals, with only minor slip-ups	Decent cross-exam and/or rebuttals, but with some significant problems	Poor cross-exam or rebuttals, failure to point out problems in Affirmative team's position or failure to defend itself against attacks.	

(to be continued)

(continued)

Criteria	4	3	2	1	Grade:
Presentation Style: Tone of voice, clarity of expression, precision of arguments all contribute to keeping audience's attention and persuading them of the team's case.	All style features were used convincingly	Most style features were used convincingly	Few style features were used convincingly	Very few style features were used, none of them convincingly	
Total					

Ⅴ. An important Note on Debating Ethics.

Manipulation in debating involves the management of facts, ideas or points of view to play upon inherent insecurities or emotional appeals to one's own advantage. Debaters are expected to treat the audience with respect, and deliberately manipulating the audience by means of fear, guilt, duty, or a relationship is unethical. Similarly, deception involves the use of lies, partial truths, or the omission of relevant information to deceive the audience. No one likes to be lied to, or made to believe something that is not true. Deception can involve intentional bias, or the selection of information to support one's position while framing negatively any information that might challenge one's belief. Therefore, in debating, debaters are supposed NOT to:

- use false, fabricated, misrepresented, distorted or irrelevant evidence to support arguments or claims.
- intentionally use unsupported, misleading, or illogical reasoning.
- represent yourself as informed or an "expert" on a subject when you are not.
- use irrelevant appeals to divert attention from the issue at hand.
- ask your audience to link your idea or proposal to emotion-laden values, motives, or goals to which it is actually not related.
- deceive your audience by concealing your real purpose, by concealing self-interest, by concealing the group you represent, or by concealing your position as an advocate of a viewpoint.
- distort, hide, or misrepresent the number, scope, intensity, or undesirable features of consequences or effects.
- use "emotional appeals" that lack a supporting basis of evidence or reasoning.
- oversimplify complex, gradation-laden situations into simplistic, two-valued, either-or, polar views or choices.
- pretend certainty where tentativeness and degrees of probability would be more accurate. advocate something which you do not believe in.

Chapter 9

British Parliamentary Debate

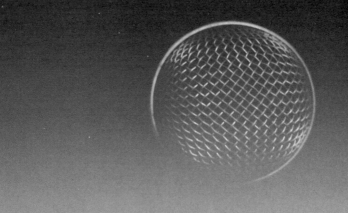

Part I

Introduction to British Parliamentary Debate

1. Debaters are supposed to critically evaluate and summarize arguments from various schools of thought and thoroughly examine one argument; most importantly, they should develop their own unique argument characterized by sharp wit and logical rigor. (论也者，弥纶群言，而研一理者也 …… 并师心独见，锋颖精密，盖人伦之英也。)

   —*The Literary Mind and the Carving of Dragons* (《文心雕龙》)

2. Dialogue is the essence of parliamentary politics.

   —*Sharad Pawar*

9.1 Some Basics of British Parliamentary Debating

British Parliamentary (BP) style debate derives from debates in the British Parliament. It was first adopted by UK universities and has become very popular in debating competitions around the world.

Speeches are usually between five and seven minutes in duration. The debate consists of four teams of two speakers, sometimes called factions, with two teams on either side of the case. Two teams, called the "First Proposition" and the "Second Proposition" teams, are charged with the responsibility of supporting the proposition while two other teams, "First Opposition" and "Second Opposition", are charged with opposing it. Two speakers represent each of the four teams and each speaker gives a speech of seven minutes. The following chart describes the basic format and time limits of the BP debate. As seen from the chart, each speaker is given a unique title.

British Parliamentary Debate Format

Speaker	Time
Prime Minister 1st speaker for 1st proposition	7 minutes
Leader of Opposition 1st speaker for 1st opposition	7 minutes
Deputy Prime Minister 2nd speaker for 1st proposition	7 minutes
Deputy Leader of Opposition 2nd speaker for 1st opposition	7 minutes
Member of Government 1st speaker for 2nd proposition	7 minutes
Member of Opposition 1st speaker for 2nd opposition	7 minutes
Government Whip 2nd speaker for 2nd proposition	7 minutes
Opposition Whip 2nd speaker for 2nd opposition	7 minutes

As shown, the first four speeches are delivered by the First Proposition and the First Opposition teams, and the last four speeches are delivered by the Second Proposition and Second Opposition teams. Therefore, the First Proposition (also named Opening Government, OG) and First Opposition (also named Opening Opposition, OO) teams are generally responsible for the first half of the debate and the Second Proposition (also named Closing Government, CG) and Second Opposition (also named Closing Opposition, CO) teams have the responsibility for the second half.

9.1.1 Speech Timing

Each speech will be 7 minutes. Points of Information are allowed after the first minute and before the last minute of all speeches. Timing of the speech starts when the speaker begins speaking; all materials including acknowledgments, introductions, etc. will be timed. A timekeeper will provide a series of signals during each speech as follows:

Timing	Signal
1:00	Single ring of a bell (POIs allowed)
6:00	Single ring of a bell (POIs no longer allowed)
7:00	Double ring of a bell (conclusion of speaking time)
7:15	Continuous ringing (conclusion of grace period)

Once the double ring has sounded, speakers have a 15-second "grace period", during which they should conclude their remarks. The grace period is not a time for new matters to be introduced, and any new matter offered in the grace period may be discounted by adjudicators. Speakers continuing after this "grace period" will be penalized by the adjudication panel.

9.1.2　Roles of Speakers

Each speaker has a role and each speech should have a purpose. The descriptions of speaker roles and speech purposes listed below are suggestive and are not intended to be exhaustive or exclusive. Debaters will be judged on the overall strength of each team's arguments, not simply on whether or not they have fulfilled the roles and responsibilities listed in the table below.

All speakers, except the final speakers for the Proposition and Opposition (Proposition and Opposition Whips), should introduce new ideas into the debate. All debaters, except the opening speaker (Prime Minister), should engage in refutation.

Speaker Responsibilities for the British Parliamentary Debate

Speaker	Speaker Responsibilities
Prime Minister (PM)	• Define the motion. This might include defining specific terms in the motion, advocating specific policy change(s), and/or articulating the roles of relevant stakeholders. • Provide a complete case. Establish that a problem exists, and provide reasons why your team's advocacy resolves it. If necessary, signpost the new materials your partner will add.

(to be continued)

(continued)

Speaker	Speaker Responsibilities
Leader of Opposition (LO)	• Refute the PM's case. Be specific. Criticize the case you've just heard. • Oppose when necessary. Why is the motion itself problematic? State your team's position and provide reasoning to support it. • Construct your case. Provide one or more arguments against the Prime Minister's interpretation of the motion.
Deputy Prime Minister (DPM)	• Rebuild the PM's case. Defend your team's case by answering the LO's refutation. Reiterate the key elements of your team's position. • Refute the LO's case. Be specific. Criticize what you've just heard. Compare it to your team's position. • Follow through on promises. If your partner declared that you would present new materials in support of your team's position, do so. At the very least, add depth to the original case by providing additional details, examples, or explanations.
Deputy Leader of Opposition (DLO)	• Rebuild. Defend LO's case from the DPM's refutation. Reiterate the key elements of your team's position. • Refute. Address new, relevant materials presented by the DPM. Illustrate any important tension(s) between the PM & DPM speeches. Highlight LO's refutation that was ignored or insufficiently covered by the DPM. • Add depth. Add something to your team's case by providing additional examples, explanation, or analysis to support a previous claim. You can present a new argument.
Member of Government (MG)	• Defend the general direction and case of the 1st Proposition • Continue refutation of 1st Opposition team • Offer an "extension". Add something new either by choosing to present an entirely new argument, or opting to develop an important argument that the 1st Proposition has underdeveloped. • Explain how your team's position fits into the debate. Avoid contradicting 1st Proposition case. Explain why what you're adding is important in relation to the 1st Proposition case.

(continued)

Speaker	Speaker Responsibilities
Member of Opposition (MO)	• Defend the general direction taken by the 1st Opposition. • Continue general refutation of 1st Proposition case • Offer an "extension". Add something new by choosing to present a new argument or to further develop the 1st Opposition argument. • Explain how your team's position fits into the debate. Illustrate why your position is important in relation to the 1st Opposition case.
Government Whip (GW)	• Summarize the entire debate from the point of view of the Proposition, defending the general viewpoint of both Proposition teams with a special eye toward the case of the 2nd Proposition. • Sell the "extension". Demonstrate how your team's material relates to other important content in the debate. Articulate why your position defeats the most important arguments presented by the Opposition. • Refute. Challenge the contribution made by the Member of Opposition. Engage in holistic refutation of the Opposition. • Avoid making new arguments. You may, however, add details or examples in support of previous claims.
Opposition Whip (OW)	• Summarize the entire debate from the point of view of the Opposition, defending the general viewpoint of both opposition teams with a special eye toward the case of the 2nd Opposition. • Sell your team's contribution. Explain how your team's position relates to other important arguments in the debate. Articulate why your position defeats the most important arguments presented by the Proposition. • Avoid making new arguments. You may, however, add details or examples in support of previous claims.

1) Prime Minister

The primary role of the first Proposition team is to establish the foundation for a meaningful debate on the motion. The Prime Minister has two basic responsibilities: to define and interpret the motion in a reasonable fashion and to develop the case for the Proposition. The definition or interpretation are particularly important because it sets the stage for the entire debate. If the Prime Minister's interpretation is a poor one, it will result in a poor debate.

In order to properly define and interpret a motion, the Prime Minister is expected to:

- define any ambiguous terms in the motion.

- show how these definitions are reasonable ones.

- outline a model that will be used by all teams in advancing the debate.

The second responsibility of the Prime Minister is to construct a case for the Proposition. Simply put, a "case" consists of one or more arguments supporting the Prime Minister's interpretation of the motion. In many cases, the Prime Minister does not need to present all of the arguments for the first Proposition team, and can leave some less important arguments to be presented by the Deputy Prime Minister.

Note:

Typically, the first speaker presents the case and the first two arguments, beginning with the most important one because it will be debated most. For example, concerning the motion of **banning smoking in public places**, two main arguments could be related to health and possibly, environment.

On health, one could argue that passive smokers need to be protected. Studies have proved that smoking passively can be just as dangerous as smoking actively. Spreading cigarette fumes in virtually every openly accessible area could affect thousands, if not millions, of people in society, especially children. This can result in high death rates, high health costs and, in the age of aging societies, can be seen as a threat to the social cohesion of a nation when the younger people die early. On top of that, the waste being disposed of can be seen in streets, public transport and parks, etc., therefore making it an environmental issue as well.

Then, the second speaker on the team will elaborate on the social implications a bit more (possibly, the third argument).

---

2) Leader of the opposition

The Leader of Opposition has three primary responsibilities: to accept the definition and interpretation of the motion, to refute part or all of the Prime Minister's case, and to present one or more arguments in support of the Opposition's case.

First, the Leader of Opposition should explicitly accept the definition and interpretation of the motion as presented by the Prime Minister. In extraordinary cases, when the definition is completely unreasonable to preclude meaningful debate, the Leader of Opposition has the right to challenge and reject the definition by pointing out why the definition is problematic.

Second, the Leader of Opposition should refute the Prime Minister's arguments for the motion. Due to the time limit, the Leader of Opposition should respond to the most important arguments presented by the Prime Minister.

Finally, the Leader of Opposition should present one or more arguments directed against the Prime Minister's interpretation of the motion. These arguments should be different from those arguments offered in refutation and more importantly, they should consist of the most persuasive ones that could convince the audience to reject the Proposition.

The following shows an example of possible responses to the PM's speech.

There are numerous examples of people who have been smokers during their whole life have lived quite long. So there may be a health hazard, but it's absolutely not going to end this way for everybody. Besides, there are a lot more pollutants in the air, for example, from cars, from the haze especially in urban areas which are even more dangerous to our health. Should we not rather consider a ban on cars from public places as well? Surely, this can't be the case. In addition, to smoke or not to smoke is a decision that every person should be allowed to make themselves in liberal democracies. Banning smoking in public places could therefore be seen as an infringement of the individual right of choice.

Note: The time used for rebuttal and constructive arguments should ideally be around 35% and 65% respectively. After rebuttals, the Leader of Opposition should present the substantive parts of constructive arguments, which sometimes aren't aimed at deconstructing what the Proposition has stated, but defending the status quo. For example, a possible Opposition defense could draw the picture that there have been enough anti-smoking campaigns in the past, such as a ban on advertising smoking in all public spaces. However, The number of people who smoke does not decline significantly.

In Germany, for instance, it takes ID that proves your legal age to buy cigarettes and the bar is quite high enough to get your hands on cigarettes. This implies more protection for non-smokers. But why there are still many smokers? In the long run, more efforts should be put into anti-smoking awareness rather than banning smoking publicly.

---

3) Deputy Prime Minister

The Deputy Prime Minister has two primary obligations: to defend the case presented by the Prime Minister by refuting any independent arguments presented by the Leader of Opposition, and to add one or more arguments to the case presented by the Prime Minister.

First, the Deputy Prime Minister defends the case presented by the Prime Minister by engaging in any refutation presented against the case by the Opposition side. Like the Leader of Opposition, the Deputy should not try to refute all arguments, just the most important ones. Thus, at the end of the Deputy's speech, the audience should be able to see that the case originally presented by the Prime Minister still stands as strongly as it did when initially presented.

Second, the Deputy Prime Minister should add one or two arguments to the case presented by the Prime Minister. The reasons for adding new arguments in this speech are two-fold. First, the Prime Minister may not have adequate time to develop all of the arguments that the first Proposition team wishes to present. Second, presenting these additional arguments gives the judges and audience an opportunity to evaluate the performance of the Deputy Prime Minister with respect to the ability to construct arguments.

4) Deputy Leader of Opposition

The duties of the Deputy Leader of Opposition are similar to those of the Deputy Prime Minister. The Deputy Leader should defend the arguments offered by the Leader of Opposition by refutation and add one or more new arguments to those being offered by the first Opposition team.

First, the Deputy Leader should defend the arguments presented by the Leader of Opposition to ensure that these arguments still stand firm. To achieve this goal, the Deputy leader needs to consider each argument one by one, engage any refutation offered by the Deputy Prime Minister, and therefore rebuild each argument.

Second, the Deputy Leader presents one or more arguments against the Proposition. These arguments can be similar to those arguments raised by the Leader of Opposition, yet they should be new ones to give the judges and audience the opportunity to assess the Deputy Leader's argument construction skills.

5) Member of Government

The Member of Government initiates the second half of the debate. The Member of Government is expected to defend the general direction taken by the first Proposition team but needs to offer a new perspective from the second Proposition team. The obligations of the Member of Government include defending the general perspective of the first Proposition team, continuing to refute arguments made by the first Opposition team, and developing one or more new arguments that are different from but consistent with the case offered by the first Proposition team.

The first responsibility of the Member of the Government is to defend the general direction of the debate started by the first Proposition team. To this end, the Member of Government should demonstrate a sense of loyalty to the other debaters defending the proposition. This part of the Member's speech is important but should not be time-consuming. One or two minutes devoted to this aspect of the speech will probably be sufficient.

Second, the Member of Government should continue refuting arguments made by the first Opposition team. The Member of Government should not use the same refutation as provided by debaters of the first Proposition team, but introduce new points of refutation unique to the second Government team. In particular, the refutation should focus on the arguments presented by the Deputy Leader of the Proposition.

Finally, the Member of Government should develop one or more arguments that are different from but consistent with the arguments offered by the opening government. These new arguments sometimes are referred to as an "extension". The extension is one of the most important elements of the Member of Government's case as it provides an opportunity to distinguish the second Proposition team from the first Proposition while simultaneously remaining consistent with their overall approach.

6) Member of Opposition

The Member of Opposition begins the second half of the debate for the Opposition side. Like the second Proposition team, the goal of the second Opposition team is to remain consistent with the first Opposition team while presenting a unique perspective of their own. To accomplish this goal, the Member of Opposition needs to fulfill the following obligations, such as defending the general direction taken by the first Opposition team, continuing the refutation of the case presented by the first Proposition, particularly those introduced by the Member of Government, and presenting one or more new arguments that are consistent with, yet different from, those presented by the first Opposition team.

First, the Member of Opposition should defend the general perspective taken by the first Opposition team. This does not need to be a time-consuming enterprise, but the Member of Opposition should make clear that the second Opposition team is loyal to the arguments of the first Opposition team.

Second, the Member of Opposition should continue the refutation of the case presented by the first Proposition team. Again, this continued refutation should be brief and involve new points of refutation not yet considered by members of the first Opposition team. More attention should be given to more specific refutation of arguments introduced by the Member of Government because these are completely new ones supporting the Proposition side and have not yet been joined by the Opposition side.

Finally, the Member of Opposition should present an extension, i.e., an argument consistent with, yet different from what has been presented by the first Opposition team. Like the Government's extension, this is an important responsibility of the Member of Opposition because it allows the second Opposition team to show its loyalty to the first Opposition team while clearly differentiating themselves from the first Opposition.

7) Government Whip

The whip speakers for both teams have the responsibility to close the debate for their respective sides. The Government Whip should accomplish three goals: to refute the extension offered by the Member of Opposition, defend the extension offered by the Member of Government, and summarize the debate from the perspective of the Proposition side.

The first responsibility of the Government Whip is to refute the extension offered by the Member of Opposition. This extension has yet to be discussed by the Proposition team and doing so is an important responsibility of the Government Whip.

Second, the Government Whip should defend the extension offered by the Member of Government. The Member of Government's extension is a vital part of the second Government's case and defending this extension is deemed as an important responsibility of the Government Whip.

The final, and perhaps the most important responsibility of the Government Whip is to summarize the debate from the perspective of the Proposition side. The summary may be accomplished in a number of ways. One of the most effective ways is to identify the most crucial issues in the debate and discuss how each side has dealt with each. The summary should, of course, be made from their side's perspective while appearing to be fair-minded. In other words, the summary should be fair to the first Proposition team but should focus on the arguments pursued by the second Proposition team.

8) Opposition Whip

The responsibilities of the Opposition Whip are almost identical to those of the Government Whip except they are accomplished from the perspective of the Opposition side. Again, the Opposition Whip should refute the extension offered by the Member of Government, defend the extension offered by the Member of Opposition, and summarize the debate from the perspective of the Opposition side.

The details of this speech are exactly like those of the previous speeches except that they focus on the Opposition side of the debate rather than the Proposition side. Once again, the primary goal of this speech is to summarize the debate from the perspective of the Opposition side, particularly from the point of view of the second Opposition team. This summary should fairly support the Opposition side of the debate while focusing on the accomplishments of the second Opposition team.

9.1.3 Parliamentary Points of Information

1) What are Points of Information?

A point of information (POI) is a question, comment or statement raised while a speaker of the opposing team is speaking. Points of information (POIs) enable debaters to keep involved throughout the whole debate. Teams that offer very few points of information are likely to be penalized heavily for failing to engage in the debate. Before and after the speech, debaters can't just sit quietly and enjoy the other speeches. They must keep the adjudicators aware of their presence, ideas and arguments. In addition, POIs can be used as a weapon to undermine and even destroy an argument being made by the speaker. Actually, POIs are the most important and interesting parts of the British Parliamentary debate because they introduce an element of spontaneity to the debate and give each debater the chance to demonstrate critical thinking skills.

2) Purposes of Points of Information
- **To ask for clarification**

Especially when the Prime Minister presents a vague or unclear case statement in the constructive speech, a POI can be used to pin the Government team down on the specifics of their case and save the round from degenerating into a long definitional argument.

- **To point out a contradiction in the opposing team's argument**

If a speaker blatantly contradicts what his/her partner previously has stated, a POI can be used to point out this contradiction and hurt the other team's credibility.

- **To respond to an argument made by the opposing team**

Just as in a constructive speech, a speaker may use a POI to directly challenge an argument made by the speaker holding the floor. Particularly, if the argument made relies primarily on emotional or unsubstantiated assertion, a 15-second POI may be enough to greatly damage it. Be careful, however, if the speaker can immediately fire back with a valid counter-response, the original argument may seem stronger than ever.

- **To point out a fact missed or misstated by the other team**

Sometimes, a speaker will, either intentionally or unintentionally, buttress his/her arguments with faulty or irrelevant factual claims. POIs give the opposing team an opportunity to impeach these statements. While the parliamentary debate is not primarily concerned with empirical disputes, pointing out an obvious factual inaccuracy will definitely weaken the opponents' case.

- **To preview an upcoming speech**

A well-placed question or statement can set the stage for a major point which debaters plan to bring up in a subsequent speech. In addition, hitting a previously unanswered point or raising a new line of analysis with a POI makes it possible to reiterate and expand upon that argument or response in rebuttal without being called on a new point.

- **To inject some humor into the round**

A short, witty and to-the-point interjection can often make a point better than several minutes of dry prose. POIs offer the perfect way to interject humor into the debate and simultaneously catch the opponent off guard.

Debaters may offer a POI (either verbally or by rising) at any time after the first minute, and before the last minute of any speech. The first and last minute of each speech are "protected" against interruption. The debater holding the floor may accept or refuse POIs. If accepted, the debater making the request has 15 seconds to present the POI. During the POI period, the speaking time of the floor debater continues.

Only a debater defending the opposite side of the Proposition as the speaker can request a POI. In other words, the debaters for the Proposition can request a POI of members of the Opposition teams and vice versa. To request a point of information, a debater rises and politely says something like "point of information please", or "on that point".

The debater giving the speech has the authority to accept or to refuse the request for a POI. Debaters can indicate the acceptance of a POI by saying "Accepted", "Yes, please", or "Go ahead". The person offering the POI is not allowed to follow up with additional questions.

In general, debaters are expected to accept a minimum of two points during their speech. Accepting more than two points is not advisable because the constructive speech may be disrupted. To decline a POI, the speaker can verbally resort to expressions such as "No, thank you", or "Not at this time, thank you". Alternatively, debaters may simply use a hand gesture to indicate the person making the request to sit down. How a debater may decline a POI is determined by his/her personal preference, but waving an opponent down may be less disruptive to the flow of the arguments.

3) Dealing with points of Information
(1) Deciding when to take a POI

Debaters are expected to plan on when to accept POIs during the speech. Before giving the arguments, determine when to address POIs and only accept them during these periods. The best time to accept POIs is during the parts of the speech where you are most confident and knowledgeable about what you are stating.

- Taking POIs at the beginning of the argument will allow you to focus on the substance of your ideas for the rest of the time without worries of being interrupted. However, taking POIs early can delay getting into the substance of your ideas and may create problems if you don't manage your time well for the rest of your speech.

- Waiting until the end of your speech to accept POIs can be an advantage because they will come during the strongest time in your argument, giving you a position to answer them. However, delaying acceptance of any POI until the end may discourage your opponents from asking them, leaving you with no POIs to address.

- Spreading POIs out between the first and last part of your argument will demonstrate to the judges that you are comfortable addressing POIs at any point in your argument. This is probably the best strategy to adopt.

Moreover, when a POI is raised, remember that you are still the one in control. Do not let the opponent derail your argument with a POI. In addition, you can decline a POI if you believe disruption will undermine the effectiveness of your argument. When you are in the middle of a strong and passionate section of your argument, consider taking a POI when you finish your arguments. Moreover, do not accept a POI during a particularly weak section of your argument, which could be easily attacked by your opponents.

(2) Responding to a POI

How you respond to the POI should be dependent on the strategy your opponent used in posing it during the debate. But the following tips can help you better cope with POIs.

- Keep your response within the scope of your original argument.

If the POI pushes the premise of your argument to its logical extent, remind your audience that the proposed scenario is beyond the scope of your argument.

- Respond to the POI concisely.

You have a set amount of time for delivering your argument during a debate. As a result, you need to avoid giving a lengthy response to a POI so that you can return to your prepared argument as soon as possible.

- Transition from the POI to your argument smoothly.

Remind the audience and the judges how the POI connects back to your argument at hand. Use transitional phrases like, "This connects back to what I have said before", or "I'm going to return to this idea in a moment". Transitioning back to your ideas places the emphasis on your own argument as you move forward in your ideas.

- Remain confident even if you don't know how to respond to a POI.

You will be likely to face a time when you are unable to respond to a POI because you do not know the answer to the question or cannot come up with an adequate rebuttal. When possible, reiterate the positive aspects of your argument. Alternatively, you can point out the shortcomings of the question. Don't appear flustered by stalling with phrases like "Um" and "Uh, well, maybe." Even a faulty POI can look strong if you become nervous and agitated while trying to respond.

- Address the audience and judges.

When you are asked a POI, remember that you are still speaking to the audience. Don't turn your attention to the opponent asking the POI, for you are not having a private side-conversation with the opponent but getting your message across to the general audience. Keep your body posture and voice level consistent with delivering the main body of your argument.

4) Structure of a speech

A team's argument should be logically ordered in a sequence that flows naturally from one point to another. Each individual speech should reflect the team's overall case (a thematic approach is preferable to a collection of independent arguments). Speeches should be clearly structured, easy to follow and respond to the dynamics of the debate. A well-structured speech will have:

- an interesting opening that captures the attention of the audience
- a clear statement of the purpose and a general direction of the speech
- a logical sequence of ideas that shows a clear development of the speaker's argument
- a proportional allocation of time to the speech as a whole, and to each major point
- a conclusion or summary of the major points made in the speech

The following is a rough outline of how to structure your speech. You may use it as a guideline and, ideally, develop a style and structure which you are most comfortable with.

1st Minute (0:00-1:00)	<ul><li>Define your speech, i.e. state what you will address and how.</li><li>Ideally state your argument in a single, short sentence.</li><li>Define your team approach, i.e., what your partner will say (or has said).</li></ul>
2nd Minute (1:00-2:00)	<ul><li>Don't take any POI until you have developed your speech a bit.</li><li>Layout your argument.</li><li>Usually propose/oppose on three points (e.g. political, economic, social, etc).</li><li>Begin your first point.</li></ul>
3rd-6th Minute (3:00-6:00)	<ul><li>Accept 2 to 3 POIs. Outline, for example, political aspects and deal with them.</li><li>Then take a POI on that. Do the same for the other aspects (i.e. economic & social).</li><li>Use these four minutes to make all your points.</li><li>Refer back to the single, short, core sentence one or two times.</li></ul>

(to be continued)

(continued)

7th Minute **(6:00-7:00):**	• Once the sixth-minute bell has gone, you can't be offered POIs.
	• Finish the point you are on as quickly as possible.
	• Don't introduce any new points or arguments.
	• Sum up. Reiterate your main points and arguments (and those of your partner if you are the second team speaker).
	• If possible, restate the single, core sentence as concluding remarks.

5) Case extensions

The second half of the debate is where BP differs from other debates. The Closing Government and Opposition teams have to produce a "Case Extension": a new point that is consistent with the opening team's case, but provides a different perspective on the issue. In other words, member speakers should bring in a new substantive contribution to the debate in the form of new constructive material/arguments, a reframing of the debate, or rebuttals. What's important is that the "extension" has to be distinct from the arguments that have already been made in the opening half. Of course, this doesn't mean that member speakers can not use the framework the opening team has set up. Actually, member speakers can deepen the analysis of some arguments or provide a lengthy example to validate the most important argument proposed by the opening team. What matters is that extension speakers need to show why their ideas are not just derivatives of those being heard of, but are the most important ones in the debate.

Suppose we are debating on the motion *THW abolish the death penalty*. The first affirmative team argues that the death penalty is inhumane, and does not deter crime. The second affirmative team could, for example, run the following case extension by adding a new argument:

The death penalty should be abolished due to the possibility that innocent people may get convicted.

If the first team covers everything in the debate, the second team should take a small part of the first team's case that wasn't covered in enough depth, and make that become their case extension. Some other ways for developing extension speeches are presented in the following.

How to develop extension speeches?

(1) Stakeholder analysis

The tried-and-tested formula for extensions, when you're totally unsure of what new arguments to add, is to think about who may be affected by a motion. For instance, if you can prove that a motion has a significant impact on a marginalized group, you can often win the debate on that basis. One of the reasons this kind of extension is attractive to newer debaters is because there's often an implicit assumption on the part of judges that if someone proves an impact on a vulnerable group, this will leave very positive memories on them.

What does a stakeholder extension look like? Suppose you're in a round on the motion *THW allow the use of performance-enhancing drugs in sport*. The opening team has probably talked a lot about the personal effects this will have on the youngest sport fans. Then the closing team may further argue and emphasize that *"Especially considering marginalized groups or bullied kids who often see sports icons as personal heroes and idols, they will learn from the youngest age that talent is only marginal, what matters the most is your willingness to use certain substances"*.

In this case, picking a particular group and talking about them can yield arguments that you might not immediately think of when first reading the motion. Crucially, though, you need to prove why that group is important. If you substantiate these links, you're well on the way to showing that your arguments are the most important ones in the debate.

(2) Impact extensions

It's quite common for an opening team to have left some of their claims unimpacted, or at least to have failed to impact them to the fullest extent. It's totally legitimate to take their arguments and impact them much harder than they did. Judges vary in how they look upon this: some won't think that you can come above your opening team if your impacts are reliant on their analytical framework, but others are a lot more open-minded. The key is to show what has been left out so far, and why it's so important to talk about the effects you're going to analyze. As with all impacting, it's absolutely crucial to maintain plausibility: gradate your impacts, moving from the most likely (and probably least harmful) to the harder-to-reach outcomes, showing how each leads to the next. You are expected to frame your case in such a way that it looks as though what you're saying doesn't simply follow implicitly from your opening's case, but requires in-depth analysis to reach.

How does this play out in the context of a debate? Suppose you're CO on the motion *This House would ban zoos*. OO has talked a lot about the value of zoos as an educational resource, as well as the way that they can be helpful in keeping endangered species alive and in conditions where they're able to reproduce. In extension, you might then talk about the economic benefits of zoos in terms of allowing people to have a direct link with the natural world which gives them some emotional investment in the creatures that are at risk, making them more amenable to donating money to conservation organizations. This could then be impacted into a case that talks about the ways in which this money can be used to carry out the mission of conservation, and why without that money (which would be lost when zoos were banned), we would be less capable of caring for the planet as a whole. This is related to, but distinct from, the material covered in the opening team, and would constitute an extension.

(3) Changing scope

This is quite a specific and common strategy in developing extension speeches. Opening teams will often examine the first few arguments that come to mind when a motion is announced. This means that they probably focus on regions, districts or countries they're familiar with, or the immediate consequences of a motion. One way to extend effectively is to consider changing the scope of the debate. For example, you could move the debate to developing nations if you're talking about patents on pharmaceuticals. You could also talk about what happens when children become adults if the debate revolves around instilling particular norms in kids. When you intend to use this type of extension, it's critical to justify your choice here. If you're reaching for the long-term consequences, you need to be aware that things in the future are harder to predict accurately. Therefore, you need to either prove that the things you have mentioned are definitely going to occur, or that there are a number of plausible options, all of which fall on your side. If you want to talk about different places, give one or two lines of analysis as to why those places are more important than the setting of the debate thus far.

(4) Rebuttal extensions

Rebuttal can be your extension as well! It's entirely legitimate to run a case which is purely destructive, and it's possible to win with it. However, this is recommended only in instances when you have absolutely nothing new in terms of constructive material and want to take a respectable second to your opening team.

The way to run this kind of extension is to frame your rebuttals as substantive materials. However, you need to ensure what you're trying to rebut hasn't been rebutted, or at least make it look as though it's still in contention. This might involve pointing out one particular link which hasn't been knocked down, which allows an argument to go through. Then, you need to use your rebuttals to build up an alternative view of the issue, counter to what has been given by the other team. You could underscore that not only the benefits claimed by the opponent can not be obtained, but a more likely scenario that something harmful could happen instead.

9.2   Research & Evidence

It is essential that debaters provide support for the arguments they make. The quality of the support for arguments is a key to successful debating. One way to support the arguments is to use logical reasoning and the other way is to provide evidence to claims. To achieve this, we should develop the basic skills to gather, organize, and use evidence in the debate.

Let's begin with the assumption that what we personally know is quite limited. Generally speaking, very few students are experts on the topics they will debate on. Therefore, debaters need to use outside sources of information to enhance the credibility and quality of support for their arguments. Hence, in preparation for a debate, improving research skills becomes critical.

9.2.1   Research Process

Step 1. Formulate research questions

Before you begin any research, you should identify the questions that need to be addressed. It is important to identify research questions rather than topics. A question gives you a specific goal, whereas a topic is too open-ended. A good question is one that meets the following criteria:

- The wording of the question is clear and specific

- The question can be answered

- The answer to the question is meaningful (i.e. the question leads to something important)

If you are new to a topic, adjust your questions accordingly. You should begin with building general topic knowledge before trying to answer specific questions. For example, suppose you are learning about China's economy, you may ask "What is the current status of China's economy?" As your topic knowledge grows, your questions should be more in-depth such as "Currently, what specific programs can be utilized to encourage foreign direct investment in China?"

Step 2. Select research sources

There are a variety of ways to find answers to your questions. Debaters who try various sources usually find more success and end up with deeper research. Some good sources for researching include:

- Article databases. The school library probably has several databases which are easily searchable. You may also have access to more powerful databases like Lexis/Nexis[1].

- General Internet searches. If you don't know of a specific site that will be helpful, you may try a general Internet Search. Google/Bing is a good place to start for English resources.
- Specific Internet Sites. You may know of specific sites on the Internet that have excellent resources on the topic.
- Printed materials in the library (most periodicals and newspapers can be found online).
- Books (advantage: depth; disadvantage: time-consuming)
- Personal interviews (including e-mail requests for information; online surveys)

Step 3. Develop a system for recording your results

Make sure you have the ability to take something away from your research. Always have a notebook to jot down notes (good websites, important names, guides for further research, etc.). Furthermore, make sure you are getting full source citations. If you are printing or copying articles, it is a good idea to staple them together and write the full source citation on the top right away. This will avoid confusion later.

9.2.2 Making evidence cards

Once you have gathered and read the information necessary to answer your questions, it is time to transform collected materials into evidence cards—a format that can be easily used during a debate. When you present evidence in a debate, you actually present three different pieces of information: a tag, a citation, and the body of the evidence. Each part is very important to effectively use the evidence in the debate.

Step 1: Mark useful passages

As you read your articles, you should mark passages that you believe will make good evidence quotes. The best way to mark passages is by putting brackets around the sentences that will be cut out and placed on index cards or paper. As you bracket the quotes you intend to use, you may also want to make notes in the margin about what the main idea of the quote is.

Step 2: Cut & paste

At one time, debate evidence was written out by hand or manually typed on

---

1   LexisNexis refers to a database which contains legal documents and archives of periodicals. Some examples of publications classified under periodicals include newspapers, magazines, and journals.

cards. Today, you find it most efficient to cut and paste from copies or computer printouts. Some debaters even copy text directly from electronic sources into word processing programs. Regardless of the method, the idea remains the same, that is, to transfer information from an article to a self-contained card or brief that can be filed. In a way, the article is "harvested" when the useful parts are identified, picked, and stored and the useless parts are recycled. Here are some guidelines for bracketing:

- Cut in context. Make sure you do not alter the meaning of the article by omitting any important information.
- Always cut full sentences. Even if you do not intend to read it, have full sentences on your final product.
- Ensure a piece of evidence has a proper length. A good evidence card usually contains 3-7 sentences. Very short sentences lack credibility and reasoning whereas quite long sentences are not useful because they are too time-consuming and probably bore the judge and audiences.

Step 3: Source citation & tag

The excerpt alone is not complete without a source citation and tag. For printed materials, a full source citation consists of:

- Author
- Author's qualifications
- Publication (name of the periodical, book, or report)
- Date of publication
- Page number(s)

For electronic sources (like Internet sites), the full citation consists of:

- Author
- Author's qualifications
- Publication
- Date of publication
- Webpage link

A tag is like a headline for the excerpt. It should summarize the main idea of the passage using powerful language and a minimum of words (ideally five or less). The tag should not exaggerate the quality of the information it represents. The tag serves two main purposes. First, it allows debaters to know the contents of a particular piece of evidence at a glance. Second, the tag is often written during a debate in a competitor's notes. It represents the content of the evidence and therefore needs to be accurate and concise.

Step 4: Organize the evidence

Much of a debate is spontaneous. As one side makes an argument, the other side responds quickly with counter-arguments which require evidence. Typically, evidence is sorted two ways. First, the debater decides whether it is affirmative, negative, or both. Of course, some evidence may be useful for both sides depending on the specific argument. If possible, the debater should label the evidence *aff.* for affirmative and *neg.* for negative. Secondly, the evidence is sorted by the topic. These files will be alphabetized or otherwise grouped. When a debater needs evidence on a topic, he or she can quickly go to the appropriate file and pull out what has been prepared. The following table is an Evidence Card checklist that you can use to evaluate your work. Does your evidence measure up to the following criteria?

Evidence Cards Checklist

What makes an excerpt a good piece of evidence?
_____Relevance: The excerpt supports an argument that you will make.
_____Authoritative: It is from an expert, cites a credible study, or gives strong reasoning or data to support the argument. It should also be free from possible bias.
_____Presentability: The excerpt should be short enough to be readable in a debate. Because the evidence is read verbatim during the debate, an ideal passage communicates the idea with a minimum of words (usually 3 to 5 sentences).
_____In Context: An excerpt should never alter the meaning the author intends. Additionally, statements the author disagrees with should not be represented as the author's view.

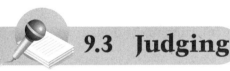

9.3 Judging

9.3.1 Judging Style

Style, essentially, is about the delivery of content and strategy. Most importantly, the speaker should be audible and clear while keeping eye contact with the audience, and judges and shouldn't make any hectic, distracting moves. Additionally, the speaker should adhere to courtesy towards the other team.

Style is the most subjective category, and it should be assessed free from any prejudice towards a debater's character, gender, or cultural background. What judges are generally looking for is a debater who isn't side-tracked by POIs and can attract the attention of the audience by his/her sheer quality of presenting him/herself as an orator with effective rebuttals and quick wit.

9.3.2 Judging Content

Content primarily assesses the quality of what has been stated in the debate. Any motion can have various arguments to speak for or against it, but what matters is whether the arguments chosen are logical, necessary for achieving the team's aims and linked to the overall framework or case (or model). In the example of *THBT smoking in public places should be banned*, the environmental issue may have come across as a bit weak, since littering through smoking may not be such a vital contribution to the case as health to society is. Therefore, choosing "health" as a core argument, along with social implications can be considered logical and purposeful.

The most important argument should be mentioned first, as this will be expected to be most debated over from both sides. If chosen arguments miss the core of the matter or fail to reach the team's aims, especially in connection with a case improbable of reaching a broad appreciation, the judge should show this by marking the debater down in content, despite his charming performance.

Content also includes weighing the balance between rebuttal and clash. In other words, if the second speaker from the Opposition only refutes and rebuts, without giving his/her speech in any substantive matter, this obviously shows weaknesses in delivering content as well.

9.3.3 Judging Strategy

The strategy mostly deals with timing as well as prioritizing and linking the issues correctly. An Opposition speaker rebutting the most important arguments poorly will be marked down in content, but in terms of strategy, the debater has depicted the correct areas of contention that need to be addressed.

All arguments, reasons for these arguments and examples chosen must be coherently linked and follow the logical structure of putting the most important arguments first. There is an expected amount of both substantive matter and rebuttal, as well as satisfactory use and response to POIs.

Debaters will be marked down in strategy if they go excessively over or stay below allowed speaking time. In addition, they will also lose points if the speech organization is not easily understandable and lack of effective signposts indicating where the speaker is in the debate (i.e., I will now get to my second point", "...which brings me to the next argument of..." etc.). In other words, a debater should present a concise speech, with an introduction, the main part and a nice wrap-up, mostly done through summarizing what has been said. It is a weak strategy if the debater keeps going back and forth between the same points, or uses them repetitively. It is a good strategy to deal with different points in a successive fashion.

It is also imperative that speakers keep in line with the case of their side. If they contradict their own case or arguments brought up by other members of their team, this shows a huge lack of consistency and strategy.

In a word, A judge should ask himself/herself the following questions when marking on the debaters' overall performance: ·

- Did the speaker have a convincing and persuasive appearance?
- Did the debater make appropriate use of the palm cards or sheets (did they present the argument or read out the argument?)
- Did I like to listen to him/her?
- Was I able to follow?
- Did the speaker make it easy to follow (with sign-posting, clear voice, gestures and facial expressions, adequate speed and effective use of vocabulary)?
- Did the speaker deal with POIs in a polite but persuasive manner?

Key Takeaways of This Chapter

★ Definitions are the foundations of BP debates. Definitions provide the framework in which the debate takes place by establishing what the debate is supposed to be about, and thus restricting the playing field, because different arguments are permissible under different definitions.

★ The first proposition team speaker (the Prime Minister) has a particular job to do: He/She defines the debate and sets out what the "line" of the proposition in the debate will be. The first opposition speaker sets out the opposition line to the proposal.

★ Speakers in the second position will have (should have) been allotted points by the first speaker. These points must be considered: it is a serious teamwork flaw if a point to come is promised by one member of the team but not delivered by the other; in addition, speakers need to rebut the materials provided by the preceding speaker(s) on the other side. A fault common to speeches made in the second position is giving too much time to rebuttal and not enough time to substantive materials.

★ Speakers in the third position are supposed to show what their team has to offer in terms of extensions. Importantly, the second half of the table is not a new debate. The second teams in BP debates must not contradict the materials set out by the first teams on their sides (neither the principle, nor the policy, nor the examples, nor anything else).

★ Last speakers are expected to offer a summation of the debate. Ostensibly, they look back and tell us what happened in the debate.

★ Points of information are extremely important; along with discussing the matter raised by other speakers, they are the prime method of showing involvement throughout a debate and are one of the most obvious distinctions between debating and public speaking.

★ Beginning a speech with a quick introduction and then giving an outline of the speech's structure (and sticking with it) can help develop an involvement on the part of listeners, contribute to an understanding of where the speaker is heading and what they are trying to achieve. The delineation of one idea or theme from another is helpful in both understanding and following a speaker and engaging with his/her argument.

★ Debating is a team activity. Plenty of individuals speak very well and still lose. Thus, two debaters on the same team should ensure that each understands the points the other will give. They should fully exchange information and talk to each other before the debate, and write notes to each other during the debate as things change, noting new lines of argument and agreeing responses.

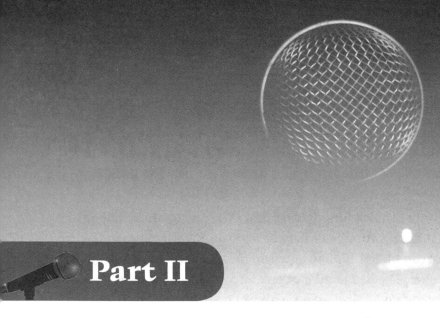

Part II

Exercises

I. Discuss the following questions.

1. How could you define and interpret a motion in the BP debate?
2. What kinds of responsibilities should each speaker in the BP debate fulfil?
3. Could you name some possible methods that can be used to extend cases in the BP debate?
4. How can you structure your constructive speeches?
5. What are the techniques and strategies that you can use in rebuttals?
6. How can you deal with POIs effectively in the BP debate?

II. Decide whether the following statements are true or false. Write T/F in the brackets.

1. ( ) BP debate has eight people: two teams of four people.
2. ( ) The debate starts with the 1st speaker of the 1st Gov (Prime Minister). The opposition leader will then rebut the government and present new arguments.
3. ( ) A POI is a short question or comment presented by a debater on the other side.
4. ( ) The Opening Government team can define the topic in a way they like and the Opposition side should accept the definition to ensure the debate continues.
5. ( ) The 2nd Affirmative and Negative teams have to produce a "Case Extension": they each must produce a new positive case that is consistent with the 1st team's case, but provides a different perspective on the issue.
6. ( ) Points of Information can be delivered at any time throughout the debate.

A speaker is suggested to accept many points of information to show the involvement in the debate.

7.　( ) If you are stumped by a POI, you can restate your caseline, provide a token refutation, or say you'll cover it later.

8.　( ) Extension speakers and deputies are supposed to devote more than half their time rebutting since this could undermine the strength of arguments proposed by the opponent.

9.　( ) When preparing for the debate, you must anticipate the opposition's arguments and prepare against them.

10.　( ) In order to accurately follow the development of the arguments in debate for refutation and rebuttal, you are suggested to take effective notes.

Ⅲ. Let's debate. Conduct a debate in your class using the BP style.

Suggested motions:

1.　THW have a Men's day.
2　THW legalize euthanasia.
3.　TH believes that doctors should never lie to patients, even for their own good.
4.　THW criminalize academic dishonesty.
5.　THW establish inheritance tax on the rich intended to prevent wealth transference between generations.
6.　THW allow prisoners to donate organs in exchange for lessened prison sentences.
7.　THW ban all cosmetic surgeries.
8.　THW ban war simulation games.
9.　THW support global maximum wealth limits for individuals.
10.　THBT we should suffer now to protect the ecological inheritance of the next generation.
11.　THBT further research into the development of Artificial Intelligence would result in more harm than good.
12.　THW allow the use of performance-enhancing drugs in sport.
13.　TH regrets the rise of social media as a primary source of news distribution.
14.　THB that governments should prioritize the economic improvement of minority communities over the preservation of their culture.
15.　THW implement filial responsibility laws.

Chapter 10

Public Speaking and Debating Competitions

Part I

Introduciton to Public Speaking and Debating Competitions

1. Those who argue will distinguish the right from the wrong, examine what brings order out of chaos, understand the similarities and differences, and know the truth.（夫辩者，将以明是非之分，审治乱之纪，明同异之处，察明实之理。）

—*Mo Zi*

2. We improve ourselves by victories over ourselves. There must be contests, and we must win.

— *Edward Gibbon*

After learning the previous chapters on public speaking and debating, you have stepped on the way to being a qualified speaker and debater. This chapter is designed to introduce some major events regarding speaking and debating competitions across China.

10.1 Public Speaking Competitions in China

10.1.1 "FLTRP·ETIC Cup" English Public Speaking Contests

The "FLTRP Cup" English Public Speaking Contest (abbreviated as "FLTRP Cup" hereinafter) now named the "FLTRP·ETIC Cup" English Public Speaking Contest (English Test for International Communication (ETIC) is one of the most prestigious national English speaking contests in China and is sponsored by the Foreign Language Teaching and Research Press in Beijing. First launched in 2002, it has aroused extensive attention both at home and abroad and has gradually developed into an English public speaking event of the highest level and with the largest number of participants in China.

Originally, the contest was co-sponsored with CCTV under the title of the "CCTV Cup" English Speaking Contest from 2002 to 2009. Since 2010, it has been renamed as the "FLTRP Cup", with the support of the National Advisory Committee on the Teaching English Language to Majors and the Advisory Board for College Foreign Language Teaching, both under China's Ministry of Education.

For those college students who are willing and ready to express themselves and improve their ability to communicate in English, the contest is one of the best choices. In the first audition, every participant needs to deliver a three-minute prepared speech in English on the given topic of that year. In addition to the offline contest at the school level, thousands of contestants could choose to participate in the online contest, which was initiated in 2014 and parallel to the offline contest.

1) Procedure (online contest)

The preliminary: The online contest judging panel organized by the Organizing Committee will assess all submitted videos and select 300 videos for the next round of the online contest. The shortlist of the 300 contestants will be announced on the official website.

The semi-final: The online contest judging panel organized by the Organizing Committee will assess the 300 videos and select 150. The shortlist of the 150 contestants will be announced on the official website.

The final: The 150 contestants will be given their impromptu speech topic on the official website at the designated time (The specific time will be notified by the Organizing Committee). They will be required to upload their speech video within 30 minutes. The online contest judging panel organized by the Organizing Committee will assess and score all submitted videos and the top 90 contestants ranked by scores will go to the National Final.

Announcement of the online contest results: The Organizing Committee will announce the results of the online contest for public notification for two days on the official website. Any contestants found violating the contest requirements will be disqualified.

2) Procedure (offline contest)

Contestants for the National Final are selected either from provincial contests or online voting, and invited from overseas and from Hong Kong, Macao, and Taiwan. They come to Beijing for the final and will draw lots to determine the order of participation in each phase of the National Final. The order cannot be changed after drawing lots. The form of the final has undergone minor changes over the years varying from prepared speech, impromptu speech, extended speech, question and answer, quizzes, and debate.

The contest consists of four phases as follows:

Phase 1

1. Prepared speech: Each contestant is required to deliver a three-minute prepared speech on the topic released by the Organizing Committee.

2. Response to questions: The speech is immediately followed by questions raised by the judges. A total of two questions will be asked about the speech and the contestant has one minute to respond to each question.

Scoring:

1. The scores for Phase 1 will be calculated by using a trimmed mean (the highest and lowest scores will be discarded and the remaining scores will be averaged).

2. The first five contestants in each group will be scored together through discussion by the judging panel; their scores will then be announced; the scores of other contestants will be announced immediately after the Response to Questions session.

Scoring Criteria (100 points)

Prepared Speech (60%)		Response to Questions (40%)	
Content	30%	Content	20%
Language	20%	Language	10%
Delivery	10%	Delivery	10%

Phase 2

The qualified contestants advancing to Phase 2 will be divided into groups by drawing lots. The order of participation in each group will be determined by drawing lots. The scores for Phase 1 will not be counted in Phase 2.

1. Impromptu speech: The contestants will receive a topic for their speech according to their order of participation and will have 20 minutes for preparation. They then deliver a three-minute speech. All topics will be kept confidential before use.

2. Response to questions: The impromptu speech is immediately followed by questions raised by the judges. two questions about the speech will be asked by the judges and the contestant has one minute to respond to each question.

3. Quizzes: Each contestant will answer four general knowledge questions and will have only five seconds to respond to each question. The total point is 1 (0.25 points for each question), which will be included in the final score for Phase 2. The questions will be varied, including common knowledge, knowledge of the language, history, culture, and current affairs. The questions will be kept confidential before use.

Scoring:

1. The scores for Phase 2 will be calculated by using a trimmed mean (the highest and lowest scores will be discarded and the remaining scores will be averaged).

2. The first five contestants in each group will be scored together through discussion by the judging panel and their scores will then be announced; the scores of other contestants will be announced immediately after the Response to Questions session.

Scoring Criteria (101 points)

Impromptu Speech (60%)		Response to Questions (40%)		Quizzes
Content	30%	Content	20%	1 point
Language	20%	Language	10%	(0.25 points per item)

Phase 3

The contestants in Phase 3 will be divided into groups. In each group, the contestants will use the same speech topic and the order of speeches will be determined by drawing lots. The scores for Phase 2 will not be counted in Phase 3.

1. Assigned speech: The speech topics will be kept confidential and the contestants will choose a topic one day before the contest by drawing lots. The contestants will each deliver a two-minute speech on their assigned topic according to the order determined by drawing lots.

2. Response to question: After all contestants of each group finish their speeches, the judges will ask the contestants questions according to the order in which the speeches were given. Each contestant will be asked one question and will have one minute to respond to the question.

3. Extension speech: The contestants of each group will each make a one-minute extension speech and these speeches will be given in reverse order.

4. Group quizzes: The contestants in each group will compete against each other to answer a group of questions (5 questions). The contestants will receive 0.2 points for each correct answer and 0.1 points will be deducted for each incorrect answer.

The contestant with the highest score from each group will go on to Phase 4 of the contest. All members of the Organizing Committee will be asked to vote and choose one contestant out of the remaining ones to compete in Phase 4.

Scoring:

The scores for Phase 3 will be calculated by using a trimmed mean (the highest and lowest scores will be discarded and the remaining scores will be averaged).

Scoring Criteria (101 points)

Items	Assigned Speech(60%)	Response to Question(20%)	Extension Speech(20%)	Group Quizzes
Content	30%	10%	10%	1 point
Language	20%	5%	5%	(0.25 points
Delivery	10%	5%	5%	per item)

Phase 4

The contestants in the final phase will compete for the championship, the runner-up and second runner-up places. The scores for Phase 3 will not be counted in Phase 4. The contest procedure will be announced by the Organizing Committee.

3) Contestants' awards

There are minor changes in awards each year, and an example of the year 2020 is given here for your reference.

Grand Prize

The top 9 contestants advancing to Phase 4 of the National Final include one champion, two runners-up, and six second runners-up.

- Champion

The Champion will receive a trophy, a certificate, and the opportunity to attend an exchange program at George Mason University in July 2021.

- Runner-up

The Runners-up will each receive a certificate, and the opportunity to attend an exchange program at George Mason University in July 2021.

- Second Runner-up

The Second Runners-up will each receive a certificate and the opportunity of training and competing at the Asian Debate Institute in August 2021.

The time arrangements of the exchange programs are subject to the final announcement by the Organizing Committee, and the current time arrangements are for reference only.

First Prize

This prize goes to the top 15 contestants advancing to Phase 3 of the National Final but failing to reach Phase 4. First Prize winners will each receive a certificate and an opportunity to go abroad or to Hong Kong and Macao on an exchange visit.

Second Prize

This prize goes to the 64 contestants advancing to Phase 2 of the National Final but failing to reach Phase 3. Second Prize winners will each receive a certificate and an award.

Third Prize

This prize goes to the contestants advancing to Phase 1 of the National Final but failing to reach Phase 2. Third Prize winners will each receive a certificate and an award.

Special Awards

These awards will be granted to the individuals for their special accomplishments. The winners will each receive a certificate and an award.

Unipus Scholarship

Winners of the National Final will each receive a 1,000 RMB gift card for the online courses on Ucourse website.

4) Speaking topics

Each year, the topic of the prepared speech would be announced by the organizing committee in advance.

Year	Topic
2010	_____ is my top concern
2011	A word that has changed the world
2012	What we cannot afford to lose
2013	When Socrates meets Confucius
2014	Change the unchangeable
2015	Make a three-minute speech based on the video from *Chuang Tzu*. Please give your speech a title.
2016	Communication is wonderful
2017	China, a global view
2018	The stone, _____
2019	My big story in 2049
2020	Challenge to all

In fact, topics in The "FLTRP·ETIC Cup" English Public Speaking Contest change with time, and many topics are closely related to current social situations and concerns. You may go to the official website for more related information.

10.1.2 The Three Minute Thesis Competition (3MT)

Originally created by the University of Queensland in 2008 for Ph.D. candidates, the Three Minute Thesis Competition or 3MT, is now an annual competition held in over 200 universities worldwide. With just three minutes to give a compelling presentation on their thesis topic and its significance to an intelligent audience with no background in the research area, the 3MT competition encourages research candidates to consolidate their ideas and crystallize their research discoveries. This exercise develops presentation, research and academic communication skills and supports the development of research students' capacity to explain their work effectively.

Since 2019, The Academic English Speaking Contest has been included in The "FLTRP·ETIC Cup" English Public Speaking Contest, but the topic is set ahead as a kind of prepared speech. It is of great significance to improve Chinese students' critical thinking ability, logical expression, accurate thinking and full demonstration.

1) Rules for presenters

- A single PowerPoint slide is permitted and there must be no slide transitions or other animated elements.

- No additional electronic media, no sound and/or video files are permitted.
- No additional props, including costumes, instruments either musical or laboratory, or other items are permitted.
- Presentations are to be spoken word, so no poems, raps or songs.
- Presentations are to commence from the stage.
- Presentations are considered to have commenced when a presenter starts their presentation through either movement or speech.
- Presentations are limited to three minutes maximum. Competitors exceeding three minutes will be disqualified.
- The decision of the adjudicating panel is final.

2) Judging criteria

At every level of the competition, each competitor will be assessed on the two judging criteria listed below. Please note that each criterion is equally weighted.

(1) Comprehension and content

- Did the presentation provide an understanding of the background and significance to the research question being addressed, while explaining terminology and avoiding jargon?
- Did the presentation clearly describe the impact and/or results of the research, including conclusions and outcomes?
- Did the presentation follow a clear and logical sequence?
- Was the thesis topic, research significance, results/impact and outcomes communicated in language appropriate to a non-specialist audience?
- Did the presenter spend adequate time on each element of their presentation or did they elaborate for too long on one aspect or was the presentation rushed?

(2) Engagement and communication

- Did the oration make the audience want to know more?
- Was the presenter careful not to trivialize or generalize their research?
- Did the presenter convey enthusiasm for their research?
- Did the presenter capture and maintain their audience's attention?
- Did the speaker have sufficient stage presence, eye contact and vocal range; maintain a steady pace, and have a confident stance?
- Did the PowerPoint slide enhance the presentation—was it clear, legible, and concise?

3) Procedure

The preliminary contest

- A 300-word abstract for the presentation should be submitted to uchallenge@unipus.cn. No delayed abstracts will be accepted.
- The abstract should not include any information that identifies the presenter, e.g. the person's name, affiliated institutions, location, etc.
- The abstract will be reviewed for (1) relevance to the topic; (2) compliance with general guidelines; (3) academic skills and literacy expressed.
- The judging panel will review and select 20 speakers for the Final Contest and the results of the review will be announced on the official website.

The final contest

- All contestants should give a three-minute presentation on the released topic. Each presentation will be followed by two questions.
- PPT slides and/or other visual aids (e.g. Prezi, video, infographic) can be used. All visual aids need to be in English.

4) Scoring Criteria

Academic Speech (100%)	
Content	50%
Language	30%
Delivery	20%

5) Topics

The Topic for the Academic English Speaking Contest (2019)

World heritage buildings record the development of human civilization. They preserve the past, mirror what we live with today, and are a legacy we pass on to future generations. Despite their historical and cultural value, some buildings have suffered devastating damage in recent years. To address various problems concerning the protection of these precious world heritage buildings, solutions from different disciplines are called for.

Suppose you were to give a presentation at an academic forum, proposing solutions for the protection of world heritage buildings from the perspective of your discipline. You can choose your subtopic and decide the title of your speech. You may choose a specific building or talk in general about preservation.

> The Topic for the Academic English Speaking Contest (2020)
>
> Food wastage is a growing global crisis that is affecting the health of the entire planet and its population. According to the United Nations Food and Agriculture Organization, it is estimated that over 1 billion tons of food is wasted globally every year. Food waste occurs throughout every phase in the food system, including production, storage, processing, distribution, retail, and consumption.
>
> To reduce food wastage, society requires a systematic methodology to categorize different types of wastage, analyze all possible causes and adopt management procedures. Citizens also need to be educated about the dangers of a lack of food security, and how to plan meals and tackle food wastage at home.
>
> Prepare a presentation for an academic forum, proposing solutions to reduce food wastage from the perspective of your discipline. Choose a specific subtopic and decide a title for your speech.

6) Tips for preparing a successful academic speech

Before preparing for an academic speaking contest, you should make one key point clear, that is, you are addressing an intelligent but non-specialist audience on the ideas you are researching, the new knowledge you are hoping to find and the benefits and significance of that knowledge. So the tips to make it successful include:

Tip 1: Make a big picture.

This is the first step in your speech, which means that you should tell the audience what you will talk about and how you will structure it. The main purpose of this step is to establish a context, so to help the audience get the general idea of your research.

Problem: It may be difficult to ignore details in your research, but keep your goal in mind.

Tip 2: Focus on your slide layout.

In an academic speaking contest, if there is more text in your slide, the audience will not listen but to read, so only absolutely necessary words will appear on your slide. But with too few words, you may lose some audience who can't understand your visual explanations.

Problem: It's not easy to decide what words or how much should be posted on the slide, so practice and try more times to find the best solution.

Tip 3: Choose appropriate words and phrases.

There may be some words to be kept being used in your speech, which are the ones audience may understand, and also some words to change in your speaking process, which refer to the words the audience may not understand. The purpose of doing so is to avoid losing an audience who cannot catch up with you.

Problem: It's difficult to know how much you need to explain. Just use some general terms to establish the big picture and while in detail, try to replace the specific terms with easier ones or explain to them if necessary. But don't explain too much, because you only have three minutes; on the contrary, don't avoid explaining some technical terms, or you will lose some of your audience.

10.1.3 "21st Century Cup" National English Speaking Competition

The "21st Century Cup" National English Speaking Competition is an English-speaking competition that has been held annually for two decades and has helped forge a good atmosphere for language study and public speaking on campuses throughout China. With the slogan of "let the world hear you", "the 21st Century Cup" National English Speaking Competition adheres to the principle of public welfare and voluntary participation, aiming to develop quality education and promote the international communication ability of young Chinese students.

Hosted by China Daily since 1996, "the 21st Century Cup" National English Speaking Competition has been acting as an indicator for the quality of English teaching in China. The competition has been the only official selection competition in China for the International Public Speaking Competition (IPSC) held in London, UK in May every year. The winner will represent China to show the style and features of young Chinese students on the international stage.

The competition is divided into two parts: domestic and international. The domestic events are divided into youth group, university group and senior high school group. International events are held for young students aged 16-22.

1) Procedure
- Domestic events

Registration and the regional preliminary competition, campus trials: September to November

Regional semi-finals: November to December

National semifinals / Finals: March to April of the following year

International: May of the following year

- International events

Stage one: Online preliminary contest / campus preliminary contest

All works submitted and uploaded will be scored. Countries will be ranked based on the top individual score of each country's contestants.

By the end of the online contest, all the countries with at least one contestant registered will be ranked by the highest score by a contestant from this country. The top 50 countries will each have two spots in the online final, with those two contestants being the highest scorers in their country. The organizing committee will inform all contestants who have reached the finals.

Some contestants recommended by the competition cooperation units can also take part in the semifinal/final, but all together no more than three competitors from one country can advance to the online final.

Stage two: Online finals

At the online final, each contestant will deliver a prepared speech, an impromptu speech and answer two questions from question masters, one based on their prepared speech and one on their impromptu speech.

Contestants ranked in the top 30 in the online final will advance to the global semi-finals/finals. No more than two contestants from one country can advance. All contestants in the online final will receive certificates.

Stage three: Global semifinals/finals

30 contestants who have advanced through the online finals and some invited contestants will compete in the global semifinals/finals in March or April of the following Next year.

2) Assessment

The assessment is generally divided into three parts: prepared speech, impromptu speech and on-site Q & A.

The evaluation criteria are as follows: prepared speech accounts for 30%, impromptu speech accounts for 40%, and on-site Q & A accounts for 30%. In each part of the score, the content accounts for 40%, which requires close to the theme, clear structure, reasonable argumentation, rigorous logic, vivid and creative content;

language expression accounts for 40%, requiring proper use of words, accurate pronunciation, standard intonation, clear enunciation, proper pause, fluent expression and strong appeal; comprehensive impression accounts for 20%, which requires a generous manner, proper behavior, strong expression, and flexible and effective use of eyes, expressions and body language to communicate with the judges and audience.

The "Evaluation committee" and "Organization committee" are respectively responsible for the evaluation and organization of the activities.

During the past 20 years, millions of students have participated in the competition and it has become a leading brand in the recognition of students and English teaching experts in China.

Topics for prepared speech

Year	Topic
2010	The power of sports in personal development: lessons about life that we get from sports champion
2011	Youth and faith: does belief make a difference to our life?
2012	Cultural clashes vs. coexistence between China and the West: my personal perspective
2013	The road not taken in life
2014	What we talk about when we talk about happiness
2015	The balance of Yin and Yang—a youth perspective
2016	Man and technology: "the Brave New World"
2017	Belt and Road: China and the world
2018	Reform and opening-up: a personal perspective
2019	A glimpse into the future
2020	No person is an island

Topics for the impromptu speech

1. The film 2012 is based on an old Mayan legend about the world ending in 2012. If that tale were true, what would you do with your remaining time?
2. It's been over 30 years since Shenzhen was set up as a special economic zone. What is the key to Shenzhen's success as a special economic zone: preferential policies, constant innovation, abundant resources, or something else?
3. Many of Japan's elderly live alone and have no one to talk with. So, they have invented robots that can answer simple questions or joke with people to help the people deal with loneliness in old age. Can a robot make older people happy and how should society look after its senior citizens?

(to be continued)

(continued)

4. A CCTV report on cheating on the CET-4 and CET-6 exams once found that many students used a tiny speaker to get the answers over a radio frequency and they thought cheating was OK because they weren't hurting anyone. Some people say students are getting more practical in a very bad way. What is your opinion?

5. The global advertising business is worth billions and billions of dollars today but many people think that the vast amount of advertising is harmful and could cause people to want too much, to want things they can't afford. Do you think that advertising does more harm than good?

6. We have Superman, Spiderman, Batman. They're only part of an imaginary world but they get so much attention, especially among children. Are they truly superheroes or are they just idols who mislead kids?

7. There is age discrimination in the workplaces when it comes to deciding about hiring, promotions and firing. In China, it can be very difficult for even highly qualified professionals to find a new position after the age of 50. Should age discrimination be made illegal?

8. If you have any experience in working with a team, you might agree that a good leader is vital to successful teamwork. So, what kind of person is best suited for a leadership role?

9. The age of information technology has taken a lot of people by surprise. While it's already a way of life for some, plenty of others know very little about it and they may never learn. That means that eventually, we'll have a polarized society and it could lead to serious social problems. Do you think this is likely to happen?

10. Recently, some college grads have chosen to be village officials, and, after a period of time, they find that their major is useless there and it is hard for them to enter the local community. If you faced such a problem, what do you think you would do?

11. Some students think that history is boring and useless. If that's so, how should history be taught to make it more exciting and interesting?

12. The pace of life is accelerating at a surprisingly high rate these days, and people feel much more mental pressure. How do we protect our mental health under these conditions?

13. Zero is a women's clothing size in the US (80cm chest, 60cm waist and 86cm hips). There's been a debate over whether zero-sized models should be banned from fashion shows because they represent a "culture of thinness" that influences young women. What's the truth about zero-size models?

14. Men fall in love with a girl immediately just because she looks gorgeous, which is sometimes accused of being shallow. But is it okay if someone falls in love at first sight?

15. The Chinese need more than affluence, they need a feeling of real security and a greater sense of equality. But just what is equality and how do we get it?

16. The saying "Clothes make the man" reflects the importance of appearance, but now, that idea has grown. Some think it's okay to use plastic surgery to tamper with physical form for a better appearance. Others think that natural beauty's the best. Which is true?

3) How to prepare for a public speaking competition

Public speaking competitions challenge people to perform both prepared and unprepared speeches on certain topics. Many competitions are judged on how organized your speeches are, how well you engage with the audience, and how you present yourself. If you enter a public speaking competition with hopes to win, make sure you prepare all of your materials and stay confident and you'll be sure to nail it!

4) Tips for prepared speech

Tip 1. Write a prepared speech and practice.

Look at the guidelines for the competition to figure out the topic and how long to make your speech. How much information you include depends on if you need to give a three-minute or five-minute speech.

Start your speech with a surprising fact, personal anecdote, or rhetorical question to get your audience interested in your topic. Following the hook, state the purpose of your speech, why it's important, and the main points you'll be talking about. Think about the arguments and points you want to discuss on your subject and organize them in a way that flows naturally. Aim to have 2-3 main talking points in your speech that are well-researched so your audience knows you're an expert on the subject. At the end, start by reemphasizing why the topic you're speaking about is important so it sticks with the audience. Summarize the main points of your speech before your last statement. When you're finished, try to ask a question or pose a challenge to the audience to keep them interested and engaged.

Practice your speech multiple times before the competition. Try reading your speech out loud in front of a mirror to watch yourself as you deliver it. If you can, ask friends or family members to sit down and listen to your speech and ask for feedback. Make adjustments to your speech's content based on the feedback you receive. It's fine to reference notecards while you're presenting, but don't rely on other visuals, such as slideshows or graphs.

Tip 2. Engage your audience.

While you are speaking, maintain eye contact with the audience to form a connection. You are suggested to smile often. Smiling not only helps hide any nervousness while you give your speech, but it also makes your voice sound happier. If you smile while you present, the audience will see you as a friendly, approachable, and confident presenter. Speak clearly and loud enough for everyone to hear. Speaking in a clear voice helps portray that you are confident and makes it easier for your audience to understand you, and please change the speed you're talking to add emphasis to points. Use good posture and body language while presenting. Stand up straight and keep your shoulders relaxed so you look more confident. Avoid slouching or crossing your arms while you're talking since it will look like you aren't interested in what you're speaking about. Move around while you're presenting rather than staying in one place so you seem more engaging and confident.

5) Tips for impromptu speech

Tip 1. Brainstorm your prompt and use a simple structure to organize your points.

Many impromptu speeches during competitions give you a few minutes to prepare the material. Think about the prompt you've been given and write down the main points you want to address on notecards. Make sure to keep all your points succinct and related to the prompt. Stick to a 3-4 point structure to address the issue. Even though the structures are simple, you can adapt them to many prompts and situations.

Tip 2. Give a direct response to the prompt.

Since impromptu speeches tend to run for a shorter time than prepared speeches, keep your information short and to the point. Judges for the competition will look first and foremost to see if you've addressed the prompt you're given. Make sure to discuss the point of your speech right away in the beginning so your audience knows what you'll be talking about.

Tip 3. Elaborate your response with arguments.

Expand on the main point of your speech in 1-2 talking points. Make sure they are directly related to your topic and explain the argument you're making.

Tip 4. Conclude your speech with a question for your audience to think about.

Leave a lasting impression with your audience by reiterating your point, and asking a rhetorical question. This can make your speech more cohesive and it engages the audience so they're more likely to remember your speech.

6) Handling question-and-answer session

Question and answer sessions are the best way to reinforce your key messages from a speech or presentation. Hearing different voices can be a good way to get the attention of the audience, but the purpose is to allow members of the audience to obtain both clarification and confirmation of your key messages. It therefore reduces the chance that any members of the audience will leave your presentation with any misunderstandings about the concepts delivered.

The question and answer sessions can be seen as a series of impromptu speeches by the presenter that follow a prepared speech. This, potentially, makes it harder than the actual presentation. Even though you won't know precisely what the listeners will ask, many questions can be predicted. You can imagine that you're an audience member and ask yourself the following questions when anticipating the possible questions from the audience:

What do I expect to learn from listening to this talk?

What are some of the things I can take away from this presentation?

How can I apply this material to my own situation?

What do some of the technical terms mean?

In what follows, some suggestions are proposed to help you with the Q&A period. Done well, this period can be an interactive and lively part of the presentation.

(1) Listen carefully to the question and repeat it aloud.

Look at the person asking the question, and repeat it, especially if there is a large audience and when you need a moment to think. By repeating the question, you also ensure you understood what the person asked. However, do not continue looking at the person once you start to answer the question. Remember that you are still in a public speaking situation and that the whole audience should hear your answer, not just the person who asked the question. When you finish your answer, look back at the person and his/her facial expression will tell if you answered the question satisfactorily.

(2) Respond concisely.

When you reply to a question, direct your answer to both the questioner and other members of the audience. Try to keep your responses as focused as possible, leaving space for other questions. To avoid going into too much detail, check back with the questioner to see if you have answered their query.

(3) Refer to the speech you have delivered.

Whenever possible, tie your answer to a point in your speech. Look upon these questions as a way to reinforce and clarify your speech.

(4) Give a conclusion after the question and answer.

Consider having your conclusion after the question and answer period. This technique allows you to control the end of your time in front of the audience. Be prepared with some appropriate closing remarks. End with a summary statement that wraps up the essential message you want them to remember, with which you can end in a positive and upbeat way.

10.2   English Debating Contests in China

"FLTRP Cup" National English Debating Competition

"FLTRP Cup" National English Debating Competition was founded in 1997 and held once a year. It is the largest and highest level spoken English contest in China. The "FLTRP Cup" National College Students' English Debating Competition is hosted by the School Department of the Central Committee of the Communist Youth League, the China Federation of Students, Beijing Foreign Studies University (admissions office), Foreign Language Teaching and Research Press and China Education Television. After more than ten years of brand accumulation and unremitting efforts, the authority, scale and brand influence of the "FLTRP Cup" English Debating Competition have been recognized by the majority of English teachers and college students in China, and enjoy a high reputation in colleges and universities. Over the past decade, more than 1000 colleges and universities have carefully trained and selected excellent talents to participate in the competition.

With the rapid expansion of the reputation of the competition, an increasing number of universities are eager to participate in the "FLTRP Cup". The system of regional preliminaries was born. Each year, there are 6-8 competition areas in the whole country, each of which can accommodate 12 teams to sign up. As a result, the number of participants has increased significantly, which greatly meets the needs of college English learners and encourages their enthusiasm.

At the same time, the Ministry of Foreign Affairs, the Ministry of Education and cultural celebrities also began to pay attention to and attend the finals of the FLTRP Cup. The first competition in 1997 was hosted by Lady Appleyard, the wife of the British Minister to China then. In the 12th "FLTRP Cup" National English Debating Competition, William Ehrman, British Ambassador to China, attended the final and delivered a speech; Mr. Zhang Jianmin, Director of the Translation Office of the Ministry of Foreign Affairs, and Ms. Yang Lan, President of Sunshine Media Group, all have shown up in different competitions.

In 2005, "the FLTRP Cup" National English Debating Competition boldly took the first step towards the international competition system and transformed into the general model of the American Collegiate debate contest, namely American Parliamentary style (AP). After four years of continuous promotion and training, "FLTRP Cop" has finally made the majority of English learners familiar with the competition system. Since 2010, British Parliamentary style (BP) has been introduced in the contest, and the first, second and third place teams sponsored by "FLTRP Cup" have repeatedly won awards in international and continental debates on behalf of China.

1) Topics

The debating competition highlights the essence of the "parliamentary system" and closely conforms to the current events and policies of contemporary college students. The depth and breadth of the debate also keep pace with the times. In summary, there are mainly more than 10 fields to which the topics are related.

Category	Example
Society	THBT charities should not use adverts which depict their targets in pain.
Education	THW abolish educational track systems in schools.
Economy	THW welcomes the advent of a global trade war.
Politics	THW prefers a world with free immigration and no borders.
Laws	THBT the state should pay reparation to victims who suffer from recidivism of robbers, burglars and thieves.
Medicine	THW ban all non-medically essential cosmetic surgeries.
Technology	THW plug into this experience machine.
Religion	THW, as the Catholic Church, regrets Pope Francis' progressive economic message.
Environment	THW criminalize climate change denialism.
Morality	Assuming the technology exists, THW program adherence of the criminal law into citizens' minds.

Most topics in "the FLTRP Cup" National English Debating Competition are revolving around two major categories according to the theme: Value motions and Policy motions. The two are different and interlinked. Some relevant background materials can be obtained from mainstream websites at home and abroad, such as China Daily, CNN, BBC, UN, etc., or from professional debate websites such as www.idebate.org, www.joyofdebate.org, www.combat.org, etc.

2) Mastering debate etiquette

(1) Remain calm, rational, and reasonable at all times.

Debates often get heated in competitions, especially when people disagree on positions they are very passionate about. Shouting or insulting your debate partner makes you look unfriendly, out of control, and incapable of coming up with quality arguments.

- Remember that you are not here to attack your opponent. You may feel like they are failing to understand your position, but keep trying to convince them instead of losing your cool.

- Getting upset may be taken as a sign of weakness and cause your opponent to conclude they have you on the ropes. It can make your opponent feel more confident in their position.

(2) Use effective speech and grammar when speaking.

You don't need to talk like a university professor to be effective and convincing. Instead, focus on organizing your thoughts into complete, flowing sentences. Stay away from big or confusing words in an attempt to sound more intelligent. Avoid words the audience may not understand and explain your points as needed. One of the most important parts of debating is being able to speak clearly and confidently.

- For instance, during a debate about school uniforms, don't go overboard explaining specific school policies or technical details that will be confusing. Keep it simple and understandable.

- If you're debating in front of an audience or a judge, look to them for signals. If they look confused or are shaking their heads at a point you made, then change your tactics.

(3) Practice patience during the debate.

As long as both you and your opponent debate in a respectful manner, be willing to spend time explaining your position. Changing someone's mind is not easy. People don't enjoy feeling like they are mistaken or losing an argument. They may also be very passionate about what they believe, so don't expect to convince anyone right off the bat.

- Be aware that many debate topics don't have easy answers. School uniforms, for instance, are controversial.

- Your goal is to be as convincing as possible, even if you don't personally agree with the position you may be forced to take.

(4) Stay humble and prepared to lose a debate.

A skilled debater understands that sometimes the other person's arguments are stronger. If you find yourself unable to refute points, be honest and reasonable about it. Congratulate your opponent and move on. If you happen to win a debate, don't try to rub it in.

- Take both wins and losses as an educational experience that makes you better equipped for the next debate.
- If you lose a debate, it doesn't mean you're obliged to change your opinion. You might use it as an opportunity to figure out new ways to respond to criticisms of your beliefs.

Part II

Exercises

I. Choose the correct answer.

1. What does "FLTRP" mean in "FLTRP Cup"?

   A. Federal Language Testing & Training Press.

   B. Foreign Language Teaching and Research Press.

   C. Foreign Language Teaching & Training Press.

   D. None of above.

2. Originally, "FLTRP Cup" English Speaking Contest was co-sponsored with CCTV under the title _____ .

   A. "FLTRP Cup" & CCTV   B. "FLCCTV Cup"

   C. "CCTV Cup"   D. "CCTV Press Cup"

3. Since _____ , the competition has been renamed as the "FLTRP Cup".

   A. 2010   B. 2005   C. 1997   D. 2015

4. What are the assessing criteria in speaking contests?

   A. Justice, fairness and adherence to agreed-upon criteria.

   B. Tolerance, fairness.

   C. Respectfulness, justice.

   D. Justice, fairness.

5. Contestants for the National Final are selected from _____ .

   A. provincial contests

   B. online voting

   C. the contestants invited from overseas and from Hong Kong, Macao, and Taiwan.

   D. all above

6. The slogan of "the 21st Century Cup" National English Speaking Competition is

    _____.

    A. "Let the world hear you"   B. "Nothing is impossible"

    C. "Less is more"   D. "Let's talk"

7. The assessment of "the 21st Century Cup" National English Speaking
    Competition is generally divided into _____.

    A. 3 parts: prepared speech, impromptu speech and on-site Q & A

    B. 2 parts: domestic and international

    C. 3 parts: pronunciation, gesture and delivery

    D. 2 parts: coherence and conciseness

8. Which of the following are appropriate responses if embarrassing silence occurs
    in Q & A session?

    A. Wait and Wait and Wait till someone offers a question.

    B. Say directly "A question that people often ask me is...", then proceed with
       one of the questions you've prepared in advance and spend time answering it.

    C. Sing a song for the audience.

    D. Go to a specific point you made in your presentation; ask your audience:
       What do you think of the idea that...?

9. "The FLTRP Cup" National English Debating Competition was founded in 1997
    and held _____.

    A. once a year   B. twice a year

    C. every other year   D. twice in 3 years

10. Since its adoption by the _____, the BP format has spread around the world
    and is now the most widely practiced format of debating.

    A. China Open   B. FLTRP   C. WUDC   D. IDEA

Ⅱ. **Decide whether the following statements are true or false. Write T/F in
    the brackets.**

1. ( ) All college students in China can participate in "the FLTRP Cup" English
    Public Speaking Contest.

2. ( ) After the online test, not every participant can participate in the offline test.

3. ( ) The preliminary will decide who will be the winner in the contest.

4. ( ) There is no requirement for Judging Panel for the Online Contest.

5. ( ) The final contest is not just limited to the prepared speech.

6. ( ) The contestant's response to adjudicators' questions are not counted in the
    final score.

7. ( ) Topics for prepared speech in English speaking contests are mainly about
    Chinese culture.

8. (　) To prepare a prepared speech, you should write it out word by word and practice a lot.

9. (　) You should think extremely clearly and cautiously about your ideas to avoid mistakes before you speak in a debating competition, or you'd better keep silent.

10. (　) Not everyone needs to be the group leader, but everyone does have an important role in debating.

参考文献

1. Anderson, C. (2016). *TED talks: The official TED guide to public speaking*. London: Headline Publishing Group.

2. Brydon, S., & Scott, M. (2008). *The art and science of public speaking*. New York: Mcgraw-Hill Higher Education.

3. George, M. W. (2008). *The elements of library research: What every student needs to know*. Princeton: Princeton University Press.

4. Gibson, C. (2008). 英语演讲实训指南. 北京：外语教学与研究出版社.

5. Hamilton, G. (2010). *Public speaking for college and career*. New York: McGraw-Hill Higher Education.

6. Lucas, S. E. (2010). *The art of public speaking*. 北京：外语教学与研究出版社.

7. O'Hair, D., Stewart, R., & Rubenstein, H. (2007). *A speaker's guidebook: Text and reference* (3rd ed.). Boston: Bedford/St. Martins.

8. Pirie, M. (2006). *How to win every argument: The use and abuse of logic*. London: Continuum.

9. Sprague, J., Stuart, D., & Bodary, D. (2010). *The speaker's handbook* (9th ed.). Boston: Wadsworth Cengage.

10. Trapp, R., Barnes, E., Chen, X., Franke, M., Green, T., He, J., Kimokeo-Goes, U., Miller, J., Spring, K., & Yang, G. (2016). *Building global relations through debate*. 北京：外语教学与研究出版社.

11. Weissman, J. (2009). *Presenting to win: The art of telling your story*. Bergen: Pearson Education.

附录　课堂演讲评价表

Peer evaluation Form

Name: _____   Student ID: _____

Grade: _____   Date: _____

	Criteria			
	4	3	2	1
Introduction and closure	delivers open and closing remarks that capture the attention of the audience and set the mood	displays clear introductory or closing remarks	clearly uses either an introductory or closing remark, but not both	does not display clear introductory or closing remarks
Eye contact	holds attention of entire audience with the use of direct eye contact	consistent use of direct eye contact with audience	occasional eye contact with audience.	no eye contact, reads notes the entire time
Poise	relaxed, confident with smiles	little or no tension	mild tension	tension and nervousness is obvious
Visual aids (e.g. ppt, slides, posters)	enhances presentation and keeps interest	thoughts explained clearly, but not engaging	adds nothing to presentation	poor, distracts audience and is hard to read
Professionalism of Presentation	well organized and holds audience interest	thoughts explained clearly, though not engaging	Thoughts don't flow, not clear, not engaging	Audience has difficulty hearing, confusing

(to be continued)

(continued)

	Criteria			
Questions and Answers	Answer all the questions confidently, precisely and appropriately	Answer most of the questions confidently, precisely and appropriately	Answer some of the questions confidently and appropriately	Answer inaccurately and inappropriately
Time frame	Presentation falls within required time frame		Presentation is more than maximum time	Presentation is less than minimum time

Confidence (2 points)_____

Other comments: _____

_____

_____

Assessor Group: _____ Group Leader: _____

Assessor Group members: _____

Speech Self-Assessment Form

Name: _____ Student ID: _____ Date: _____

Overall performance (□ very good/ □ good/ □ average/ □ poor)

Directions:

put ✓ beside the things that you think you are doing well

put × beside the skills you'd like to improve

_____ Clear idea of how to plan a presentation

_____ Develop professional engaging slides

_____ Managing nervousness beforehand

_____ Building rapport with the audience

_____ Dynamic opening of presentation that captures audience attention

_____ Well-paced presentation (e.g. pace of speech, amount of information)

_____ Well-modulated voice

_____ Practice presentation beforehand

_____ Present with spontaneity rather than read or memorized

_____ Mastering use of technology during presentation

_____ Dealing with Questions

Other areas you would you like to improve?

_____

_____